SCIENCE ENCYCLOPAEDIA

Om KIDZ | Om Books International

Reprinted in 2019

Corporate & Editorial Office
A-12, Sector 64, Noida 201 301,
Uttar Pradesh, India,
Phone: +91 120 477 4100
Email: editorial@ombooks.com,
Website: www.ombooksinternational.com

Sales Office
107, Ansari Road, Darya Ganj,
New Delhi 110 002, India
Phone: +91 11 4000 9000
Email: sales@ombooks.com
Website: www.ombooks.com

© Om Books International 2016

ISBN: 978-93-84625-98-6

Printed in India

10 9 8 7 6 5 4 3 2

SCIENCE
ENCYCLOPAEDIA

Om
KIDZ
An imprint of Om Books International

CONTENTS

Energy

Laws

Metals and Non-Metals

Machines

Gravity

Electricity

Light and its Sources

Particle Physics

Cells

Evolution

Ecology

Scientists

STUDYING
SCIENCE

Science is the systematic study of the structure and behaviour of the physical and natural world. It is a way of discovering what the universe is made of and how it works. Over the centuries, various scientists from around the world have contributed to the available body of knowledge through their discoveries, inventions and theories. The advances made in the various branches of science help to develop new technologies, treat diseases and solve other problems.

Broad Branches of Science

The branches of science are broadly divided into four categories: chemical, physical, life and mathematical. These four categories constitute the fundamental sciences, which form the basis of interdisciplinary and applied sciences, such as engineering and medicine.

Studying chemicals and their reactions.

Chemical science

Chemical science, also known as chemistry, is defined as the study of matter and its interactions with other matter and energy. Everything involves chemistry as all matter is made up of atoms. Even the human body is made up of various chemical elements and its different activities involve chemical processes.

Central science

Chemistry acts like a crossroad for other branches of science as many of its branches have common features with other sciences, like physics. So, it is considered as the "central science". Scientists who study chemistry are called chemists.

Physical science

Physical science, also known as physics, is one of the major branches of science that explains the measure of different physical quantities like speed, distance, energy, motion, etc., which play a vital role in daily human life.

All about the math

Physical science relies heavily on mathematics. Models and theories in physics are articulated using mathematical equations. Although physics uses mathematics to explain the material world, mathematics generally deals with abstract concepts. These two fields significantly overlap each other in an area known as mathematical physics.

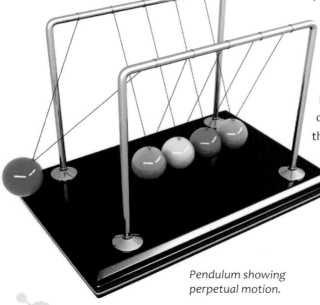

Pendulum showing perpetual motion.

Mathematical science

The combined study of mathematics and science is called mathematical science. Statistics, for example, is mathematical in nature, but is evolved through scientific observation. Other fields that are sometimes considered as mathematical sciences include computer science, computational science, population genetics, operations research, cryptology, econometrics, theoretical physics and actuarial science. Innovations in technology could not have been possible without mathematical science.

The spectrum of mathematical science.

Life science

Life science is the study of living organisms. It describes the characteristics, classification and behaviour of organisms, how species came into existence and the interactions that they have with each other and the environment. It has many sub-branches that focus on a specific type of life form, for example, zoology is the study of animals, botany is the study of plants, etc.

Life science plays an important role in the agriculture, medicine and food science industries. Thus, it helps to improve the standard of human life. Life science is very closely related to chemical science.

Exploring different life forms.

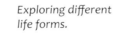

These fields also fall under the science category!

1. **Linguistics** is the scientific study of language. A person who studies languages is called a linguist. Linguists study every aspect of human language, ranging from translating cuneiform tablets to tracking tweets to attempting to isolate and analyse the faces that children make when they are lying.

2. **Criminology** is the scientific study of crime. It involves studying the causes of crimes, responses by law enforcement agencies and crime prevention methods. It is a sub-group of sociology, which is the scientific study of social behaviour. Many fields of study are used in the field of criminology, which include biology, statistics, psychology, psychiatry, economics and anthropology. A person studying such a field is called a criminologist.

3. **Planetary geology**, also known as **astrogeology**, involves the study of the geology of celestial bodies, such as planets and their moons, asteroids, comets and meteorites. It mainly deals with determining the internal structure of terrestrial planets and also examines planetary volcanism. The structures of giant planets and their moons are also studied along with minor bodies of the solar system, such as asteroids, the Kuiper Belt and comets.

History of Science

Before science was recognised as a distinct field and various discoveries were made, people attributed various scientific phenomena to magic! It took a while to understand the reasoning behind these occurrences. Different civilisations around the world devised their own theories and made significant contributions to the field of science. Let us look at some of their achievements.

During the reign of Nebuchadnezzar, priests calculated the paths of planets and plotted the orbits of the Sun and the moon.

Babylonian science

Babylonians used a numeral system with 60 as its base. This allowed them to divide circles into 360 degrees. They were remarkably talented in astronomy, where magic, mysticism, astrology and divination were the main drivers. They believed that the movement of celestial bodies predicted terrestrial events. They kept complete lists of eclipses and by 700 BCE, it was known that solar eclipses only occurred during new moons and lunar eclipses during full moons.

Egyptian science

Despite their belief in superstitions, Egyptian priests encouraged the development of many scientific disciplines, especially astronomy and mathematics. The Rhind Mathematical Papyrus is an ancient mathematical treatise, dating back to around 1650 BCE. It explains how to calculate the area of a field, the capacity of a barn and it also deals with algebraic equations of the first degree. The Egyptians were also the first to calculate the value of "pi" as 22/7 (3.14).

The construction of the pyramids and other monuments would have been impossible without significant mathematical knowledge.

Indian science

The Vedas, a body of texts composed between 1500 and 1000 BCE in India, explained some aspects of astronomical science. They divided the year into 12 lunar months, sometimes adding another month to adjust with the solar year. Many ceremonies and sacrificial rites in ancient India were regulated by the position of the moon the Sun and other astronomical events.

Development of geometry

The fundamentals of geometry can be traced back to the rigid religious rules followed for the construction of sacrifice altars in India. One of Ancient India's greatest achievements however, was the study of arithmetic. This included the development of numbers and decimals, still in use, today, across the world. Even the 'Arabic numbers' were first observed on rock edicts from the Mauryan period of Emperor Ashoka, over 1000 years before they appeared in Arabic literature.

Greek science

Unlike other parts of the world where science was strongly connected with religion, Greek scientific thought had a stronger connection with philosophy. The Greek scientific spirit had a more secular approach and was able to replace the notion of supernatural explanation with the concept of a universe that is governed by the laws of nature. According to Greek tradition, credit goes to Thales of Miletus, who lived somewhere in 600 BCE, for proposing that natural laws best explain the world.

Influence of Egyptian math

The influence of Egyptian mathematics was first seen in Greece, back in the 26th Dynasty (c. 685–525 BCE), when Egyptian ports began trading with the Greeks. Babylonian astronomy came with the conquest of Mesopotamia and Asia Minor by Alexander.

The Sun is one of the many gods that Indians worship. This is why a lot of occasions and events are planned based on its position in the solar system.

Chinese science

In ancient China, government officials were concerned with areas of scientific progress. Astronomy and mathematics interested the court astronomers who understood the importance of the calendar and the happenings in the sky. From the time of Confucius, Chinese astronomers were known to have successfully recorded eclipses. The need to measure land led to the development of geometry. Ancient Indians gave us the knowledge of Algebra. The Ancient Chinese have also been credited with the discovery of the compass, gunpowder and wood and paper printing. However, the period between the Han dynasty and the fall of the Manchu dynasty (1912 CE) saw negligible progress in the industrial development of China.

FUN FACT

Every time an eclipse occurred, the Vikings assumed that the Sun and the moon were being chased by two wolves, Skoll and Hati. When either of the wolves successfully caught their prey, it would result in an eclipse.

Paper was one of China's many inventions.

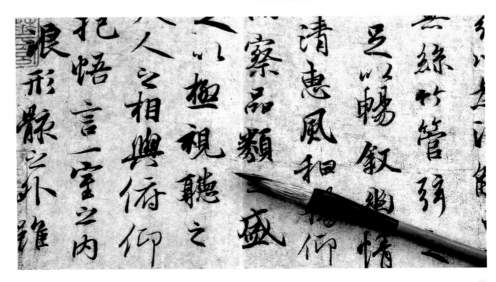

Science Today

Science has come a long way in the last 150 years. Gregor Mendel began investigating the sphere of plant genetics in the 1800s. Around 150 years later, modern plant genetics laboratories employed the latest DNA sequencing techniques. J.J. Thomson discovered a new particle of matter—the electron—at the turn of the century using vacuum tubes, magnets and simple wiring. Today, 100 years later, scientists searching for particles like the Higgs boson are using a supercollider—a 27-km-long machine and generating data analysed by the most powerful supercomputer. Let us explore the pathbreaking progress that science has made in the last few decades.

The human embryonic cell.

Human embryonic stem cells

Human embryonic stem cells can alter themselves into any tissue in the body. In 1998, scientists isolated the first human embryonic stem cells, which raised hopes for new cell-based therapies. However, as human embryos are destroyed during the process of cell extraction, the process raised ethical concerns. In 2007, two teams of researchers used genetic modification to transform ordinary skin cells into cells that appear to function like embryonic stem cells. The use of these reprogrammed cells, known as induced pluripotent stem (IPS) cells, might resolve the ethical concerns.

Contribution of life science

The era of modern science is majorly marked by research in the field of life science, which has significantly contributed to improving human life, in the areas of food, health and other areas of industry. The advances in life sciences have especially helped in the development of effective methods of diagnosis, treatment and prevention of several diseases.

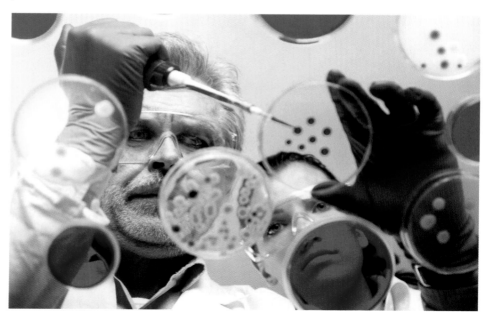

Advances in technology have led to several pathbreaking discoveries.

Century of science

The rapid progress in science and technology during the late nineteenth and early twentieth centuries gave birth to the electrical and chemical industry, and led to the invention of automobiles and aeroplanes. All these developments and inventions resulted in economic advancement. Therefore, the twentieth century is called the "century of science".

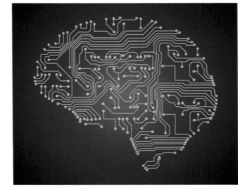

Human brain as an engineering processing machine signifying artificial intelligence.

Artificial intelligence

Artificial intelligence (AI) is based on the thought that the process of human thinking can be mechanised. During the 1940s and 50s, scientists from different disciplines started thinking about the possibility of creating an artificial brain. AI research began in 1956; one of its goals was to make computers communicate in languages like English. During the late 70s, despite difficulties like financial setbacks and a negative public perception of AI, new ideas were explored in logic programming, commonsense reasoning and other similar areas.

Nanotechnology

Nanotechnology involves working with any substance on the atomic or molecular scale. National Nanotechnology Initiative defines it as, "the understanding and control of matter at dimensions between approximately one and 100 nanometres". At the nano (10^{-9} mm) level, the material properties change drastically, which can be used to develop many products and processes. Nanotechnology can create many new materials and devices in the fields of medicine, electronics, biomaterials, energy producing materials, etc.

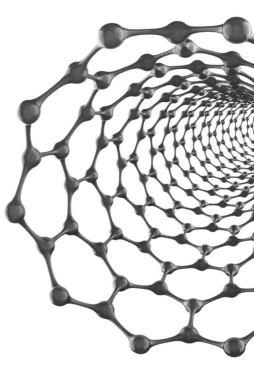

Nanotechnology is the study and application of very small things and can be used across all other science fields.

Neural network

Neural network refers to a computer modelled system that closely resembles the human brain and nervous system. During the 1940s, McCulloch and Pitts developed the first working neural model. Artificial neural networks are processing devices whose function is similar to that of the human neuronal system. They are widely used in biomedical research. They also have applications in the fields of diagnostics, robotics, business and medicine, where pattern recognition is required. In some specific areas, neural models achieve human-like performance over the more traditional AI techniques.

Neural networks are generally presented as systems of interconnected neurons.

Importance of Science

Today, we are living in a world that is governed by science. The present era is that of science and technology. Science emerged as a result of our curiosity. It is just a means of searching for answers for the many questions that we have.

Life of ease

Science has made a significant difference to humankind. Today, we are living a comfortable life with many convenient technologies because of advancements made in the various fields of science. From the time we wake up to the time we go to bed, we come across many scientific inventions that have changed the way we live.

Body of knowledge

Science is a system of knowledge that is concerned with the physical world. It involves the pursuit of knowledge, covering general truths or operations of the fundamental laws of nature. However, it is far from a perfect instrument of knowledge. Formulation of hypothesis and use of various scientific formulas and methods are the major ways to add to the body of knowledge. Science also deals with reasoning, which is used to arrive at conclusions.

Philosophy of science

"Philosophy of science" is the branch of philosophy that deals with the study of science. It is primarily the motivation behind various approaches of science. A general philosophy of science aims to describe and understand how science works within a wide range of sciences. Even a basic understanding would enhance the knowledge of scientists working in that area.

Important inventions and changes

Electricity is one of the greatest inventions of science. Because of electricity, we no longer have dark days. Electricity has made it possible to stay cool during the hot summers and stay warm during the cold winters.

Further, advances in healthcare have improved the quality of human life. They have also helped decrease the mortality rate to a great extent and thus increase the longevity of human life.

Other inventions

Today, science has made the impossible possible. It has made survival easier than it was 100 years ago. Advancements made in the fields of science and technology have enabled us to be in touch with our near and dear ones. We have reached the moon and Mars due to these advances. Television, telephone, air conditioner, mobile, refrigerator and the internet are some of the inventions that we use in our everyday lives. Today, satellite systems are so advanced that they can warn us about upcoming natural calamities.

A modern racing wheelchair.

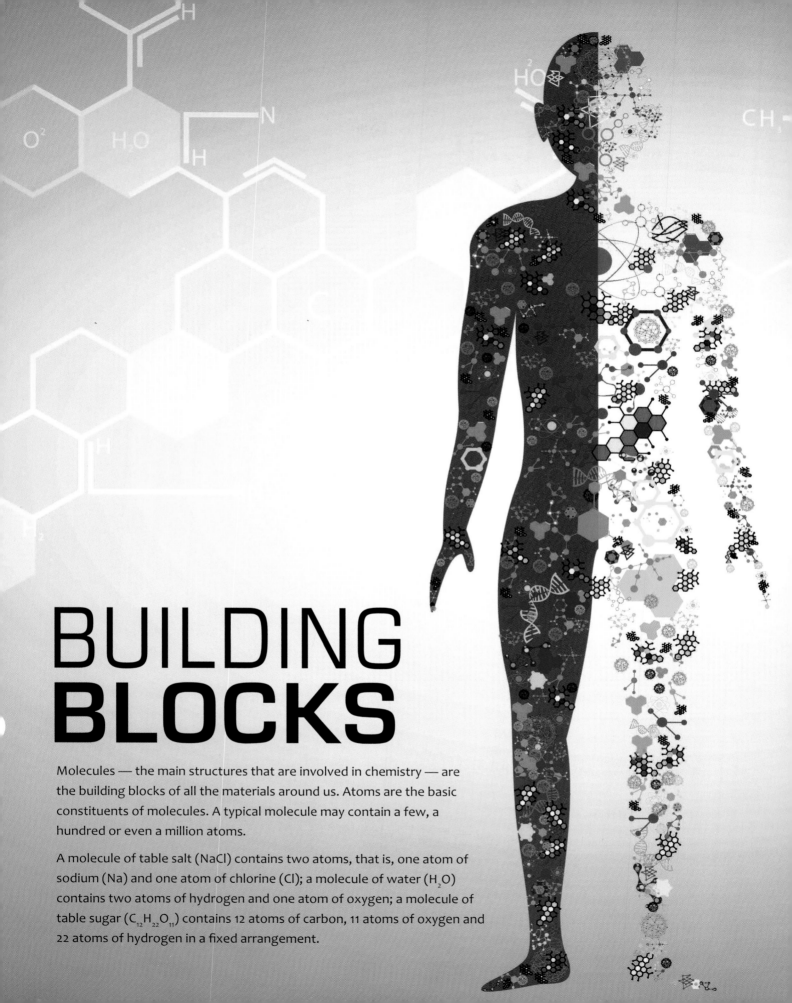

BUILDING BLOCKS

Molecules — the main structures that are involved in chemistry — are the building blocks of all the materials around us. Atoms are the basic constituents of molecules. A typical molecule may contain a few, a hundred or even a million atoms.

A molecule of table salt (NaCl) contains two atoms, that is, one atom of sodium (Na) and one atom of chlorine (Cl); a molecule of water (H_2O) contains two atoms of hydrogen and one atom of oxygen; a molecule of table sugar ($C_{12}H_{22}O_{11}$) contains 12 atoms of carbon, 11 atoms of oxygen and 22 atoms of hydrogen in a fixed arrangement.

Atoms

Atoms are considered to be the basic constituent of any element or material. Therefore, knowledge of the structure of an atom is very crucial for understanding the properties of elements. An atom comprises a nucleus that is made up of protons and neutrons and surrounded by electrons. But how many electrons, protons and neutrons are present in an atom?

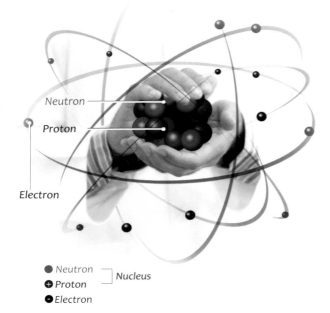

Structure of atom with respect to the position of electrons, neutrons and protons.

Neutron

Proton

Electron

● Neutron ⎤ *Nucleus*
⊕ Proton ⎦
● Electron

Construction of an atom

Atoms are composed of two regions: the nucleus and the electron cloud. The nucleus is the centre of the atom and it contains the major mass of the atom. The region around the nucleus where electrons are found occupies most of the space in the atom and is termed as an electron cloud. Protons and neutrons are found in the nucleus. The number of protons in the atom is the atomic number. The protons and neutrons are collectively called "nucleons" (protons + neutrons = nucleons). Protons have a positive charge (+1), electrons have a negative charge (–1), while neutrons are neutral (having no charge). Atomic mass is the total number of protons and neutrons in the nucleus. Atomic number is the number of protons in the nucleus of an atom, which is characteristic of a chemical element and determines its place in the periodic table.

Magic numbers in physics

Neutron to proton (n/p) ratio is defined as the ratio of the number of neutrons to the number of protons. The stability of the nucleus depends upon various factors including the n/p ratio. If the ratio is less than 1:1 or greater than 1.5:1, then the nucleus is considered to be highly unstable. To find the n/p ratio, find the number of neutrons by subtracting the number of protons from the atomic mass and divide by the number of electrons (which is the same as the atomic mass). The ratio generally increases with an increase in atomic number due to an increase in the repulsive force between the electrons and protons. Maria Goeppert-Mayer and other physicists proposed the concept of magic numbers, which give us the arrangement of nucleons inside an atomic nucleus. Magic numbers also determine the structural stability of an atom. The most recognised magic numbers are 2, 8, 20, 28, 50, 82 and 126.

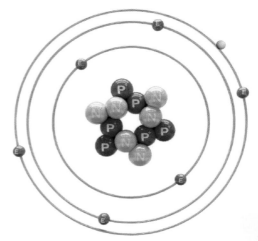

A schematic representation of an atom. Neutral atoms possess equal number of electrons and protons; however, they may possess varying numbers of neutrons.

Molecules

A molecule is a neutral component that is composed of two or more atoms of different elements that form a chemical bond. If we think of atoms as letters, then molecules are the words that the letters form. Thus, atoms are the building blocks of a molecule. A molecule can have a few or a hundred or more atoms.

Molecule of
sodium chloride.

NaCl
- Na
- Cl

Elements like oxygen are unstable in their atomic state and so they react with another atom of their own to create an oxygen molecule (O_2). However, when reacting with hydrogen to create water, one atom of oxygen (O) reacts with two atoms of hydrogen (H_2) to form a water molecule (H_2O).

Dissimilarities from ions

Ions are atoms or molecules with a net electric charge due to the loss or gain of electrons. Molecules differ from ions as they don't have an electric charge. A molecule may have different complexes of atoms connected by covalent bonds (bonds formed by sharing electron pairs).

Crystals of molecules

Different molecules combine to form different substances, such as the components of the atmosphere. The minerals that comprise earth's core are composed of molecules of different elements. Usually, molecules of various elements form ionic bonds, thus combining to form compounds of various crystalline salts. When two molecules that differ in structure and electronic configuration form a compound, it results in a three-dimensional crystal, such as diamond.

Scientist conducting
research on molecules.

Haphazard arrangement of molecules

In substances such as glass, the molecules may be held together in a manner that cannot be defined with regularity. However, every separate unit can be considered a crystal. Such bonds are covalent, which are not as strong as ionic or electrovalent bonds (bonds formed by transfer of electrons). Glass is composed of a combination of similar molecules.

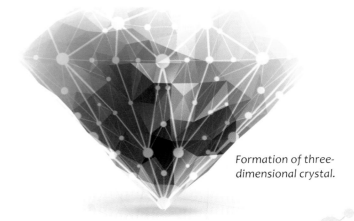

Formation of three-
dimensional crystal.

Electrons

Atoms are composed of three subatomic particles called electrons, protons and neutrons. Among them, electrons are the smallest and are found in shells or orbits that surround an atom's nucleus. The motion of electrons in the electron cloud is similar to the motion of the planets around the Sun.

Information about electrons

Symbol: e⁻ or β⁻

Discovered by: J. J. Thomson (1897)

Mass: 9.109×10^{-31} kg

Electric charge: -1.602×10^{-19} coulomb (C)

Here in 1897 at the old Cavendish Laboratory J.J.THOMSON discovered the electron subsequently recognised as the first fundamental particle of physics and the basis of chemical bonding electronics and computing

Plaque commemorating J. J. Thomson's discovery of the electron outside the old Cavendish Laboratory in Cambridge, UK

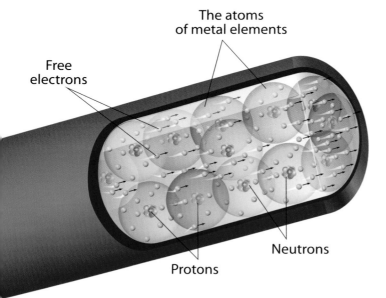

Electric current is the flow of electrons. In electric circuits, this charge is carried by moving electrons in a wire. A conductive metal contains free electrons, originating in conduction electrons.

Free electrons

The atoms of metal elements

Neutrons

Protons

A beam of electrons deflected in a circle by a magnetic field.

Mass and location of electrons

Electrons possess minuscule mass, such that they exhibit properties of both particles and waves. It is impossible to learn the precise locations of electrons within a molecule. Despite such a limitation, there are regions around an atom where electrons have a high probability of being found. These regions are atomic orbits.

Charge of a body depends on the electron

When a body does not have the sufficient number of electrons that are required to balance the positive charge of the nuclei, then that body will not remain neutral. Instead, it will have an electric charge. The body is termed as negatively charged if it has more than the required number of electrons to balance it. Similarly, the body is termed as positively charged if it has less than the number of electrons that are required to balance the positive charge of the nucleus. Independent electrons that are not bound to an atom's nucleus and move in a vacuum are known as free electrons.

Elements

An element is a pure substance that consists of only one type of atom and is distinguished by its atomic number. Each element in the periodic table has been classified as per its atomic number. Thus, before exploring an element, we should know what is meant by an atomic number.

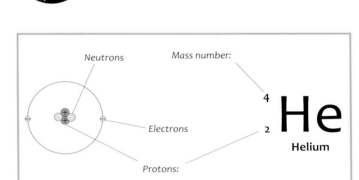

Atomic number

The atomic number of an element is defined as the total number of protons present within the nucleus of an atom of that element. It is conventionally denoted by the symbol Z. Therefore, atomic number (Z) is equal to the number of protons in the atom. For example, one atom of carbon contains six protons; thus, the atomic number of carbon is six. Every element has a unique atomic number. The modern periodic table has been arranged by placing the elements according to their atomic numbers because no two elements share the same atomic number. Elements are broadly divided into three groups: metals, metalloids and non-metals.

Russian chemist Dmitri Mendeleev created a periodic table of the elements that ordered them numerically by atomic weight.

Mass number

Mass number is defined as the total number of protons and neutrons present within the nucleus of an atom. The mass number of an atom is conventionally denoted by the symbol A. Therefore, mass number (A) = number of protons + number of neutrons.

Atomic and mass number depiction.

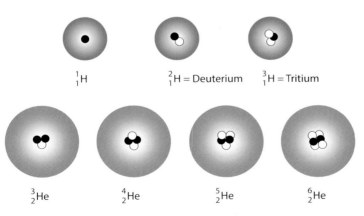

^1_1H ^2_1H = Deuterium ^3_1H = Tritium

^3_2He ^4_2He ^5_2He ^6_2He

Isotopes of hydrogen and helium.

Isotopes

We have heard a lot about C-13, C-14 isotopes as well as the isotopes of uranium. What are isotopes? Are they different from elements? Isotopes are the variants of an element, as they have the same atomic number (Z) but have different atomic masses because they possess a different number of neutrons in their nuclei. Neutral atoms possess an equal number of electrons and protons; however, they may possess a varying number of neutrons. The atoms of a given element that possess a different number of neutrons are the isotopes of that particular element. They occupy the same place in the periodic table and exhibit typically similar chemical behaviour.

Chemical Bonds

A chemical reaction refers to the making and breaking of chemical bonds. In order to understand a chemical reaction, we must understand what bonds are. The strength of a bond denotes the difficulty to break a bond. The length of a bond indicates the structural information and the positions of the atomic nuclei. "Bond dipoles" reveal the electron distribution around the two bonded atoms. From bond dipoles, we can derive electronegativity data that is useful for calculating the bond dipoles of bonds that may have never been made before.

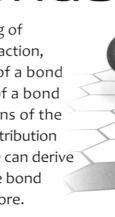

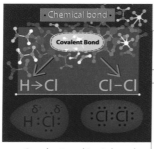

Covalent and ionic bonds.

Types of bonds

There are two fundamental types of bonds: covalent and ionic. In a covalent bond, an equal sharing of the electrons between the nuclei of atoms occurs. Covalent bonds are formed between atoms of approximately equal electronegativity (tendency to attract electrons). As each atom has a near equal pull for the electrons in the bond, the electrons are not completely transferred from one atom to another.

Forming of anion and cation

When the difference in electronegativity between two atoms in a bond is large, the more electronegative atom can strip an electron off of the less electronegative atom to form a negatively charged anion and a positively charged cation. The two ions are held together in an ionic bond because the oppositely charged ions attract each other, as described by Coulomb's Law.

Charles-Augustin de Coulomb

Hydrogen bonds (1) between molecules of water.

1

Bonding of atoms

In nature, some elements such as helium (He), neon (Ne) and argon (Ar) never bind to other atoms. Such elements are called noble gases. How are noble gases different from other elements? The answer lies in their closed shell electron configurations. Because the valence shell of a noble gas is completely full, it cannot accept another electron into the shell. The nucleus pulls the electron when it is positively charged. Therefore, the loss of an electron from a noble gas is critical. This is why noble gases are unreactive as they have filled valence shells.

Structure of xenon tetraflouride, one of the first noble gas compounds to be discovered.

MATTER

Matter is any material that has inertia and occupies physical space. According to modern physics, it consists of various types of particles, each having its own mass and size.

Matter can exist in several states, which are also referred to as phases. The three states are solid, liquid and gas. When different kinds of matter come together, substances that may not resemble any of the original ingredients are formed. For example, hydrogen (a gaseous element) and oxygen (another gaseous element) combine to form water (a liquid element). This process is called a chemical reaction. A chemical reaction involves interactions between the electrons of the atoms, but does not affect the nuclei of the atoms. In some situations, atomic reactions convert matter into energy. This is known as a nuclear reaction.

Definition of Matter

Matter is anything that occupies space and has mass. Matter is composed of atoms. Atoms are made up of subatomic particles called electrons, neutrons and protons. Neutrons and protons are the heaviest subatomic particles. They are clumped together in the centre of the atom and collectively form the nucleus.

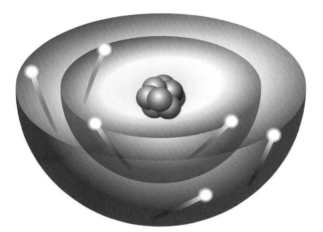

Inside of an atom.

What constitutes an atom?

Electrons, protons and neutrons together form atoms. There are more than 100 different types of atoms, each of which constitute a unique chemical element. Atoms combine to form a molecule. Atoms and/or molecules combine to form a compound.

Atoms are empty

The nucleus is surrounded by a cloud of electrons that are lighter than protons and electrons. More than 99 per cent of an atom is empty. Furthermore, atoms are composed of point particles that have no effective size or volume. These particles are called quarks and leptons. In an informal sense, matter refers to all physical objects. In a formal sense, matter could be defined as anything that has mass and volume.

Wolfgang Pauli, the scientist who proposed the Pauli Exclusion Principle.

For example, a pen is considered as matter because it has mass and occupies space. The simple observation that "matter occupies space" was made several decades ago, however its explanation is more recent. The explanation is believed to be the result of Pauli's Exclusion Principle.

Phases of Matter and Phase Diagram

Phases of matter refer to the regions where the physical properties of a material are essentially uniform. These physical properties primarily include state, density, mobility, refraction index and magnetisation among others. In the classical sense, matter basically has three phases: solid, liquid and gas. These phases are also referred to as states of matter. Besides solid, liquid and gas, there are other states such as plasma and more theoretical states such as the Bose–Einstein condensates and fermionic condensates. When considering the more fundamental particles, we get more states or phases like the quark–gluon plasma.

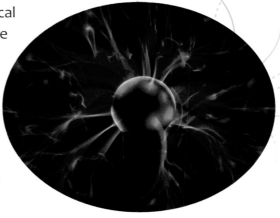

Plasma is one of the four fundamental states of matter, the others being solid, liquid and gas. Plasma has properties unlike those of the other states.

Inspection of water triple point cell.

Pressure and temperature

The state or phase of matter depends mainly upon pressure and temperature. Water is solid below 0° C under normal atmospheric pressure, but if the pressure is adequately low, it can melt below 0° C. In addition, water can be made to boil at a temperature higher than 100° C if the super incumbent pressure is adequately high. The phase diagram for a particular kind of matter is made by analysing its states under different pressure and temperature values. At a certain temperature and pressure, a certain kind of matter can exist in all three states. That point in the phase diagram is called triple point. For water, it is 0.01° C in the temperature axis and 6.1173 millibars in the pressure axis.

Effect of pressure

It is important to note that at a pressure other than the atmospheric pressure, the phase stability region would also change. Therefore, it is possible to keep water in the liquid state even at a temperature higher than 100° C by maintaining the pressure.

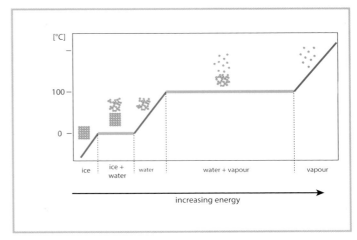

Phase stability of water at different temperatures.

States of Matter

Solid, liquid and gas are the three states of matter. We find materials in these states of matter every day. The existence of matter in a particular phase depends on the kind of temperature and pressure it is exposed to. Temperature is simply the measure of how hot or cold a substance is.

Molecular changes

All molecules of matter have a vibrating motion. When their temperature is raised or heat is supplied, the molecules get more energy and vibrate more vigorously. Once the molecules overcome intermolecular attraction, also called van der Waals force, as well as the pressure they are exposed to, they start to separate from one another, thus resulting in a phase change.

Geckos can stick to walls and ceilings because of van der Waals forces.

States of matter

Solids

The atoms and molecules of a solid are tightly packed together in a regular arrangement. The particles in a solid continue moving, but their movement results in a minor vibration. Therefore, they have a definite shape; for example, a round ball and a square book. Solids have a definite volume and a fixed shape.

Liquids

The molecules of a liquid are very close to each other and can also slip over each other to change their position. Liquids have a definite volume but they do not have a definite shape. Liquids can be pushed through a tube, but they cannot be compacted to fit into a limited space. They can move and take the shape of the vessel that they are in. Viscosity determines how easily liquids flow. Liquids that have high viscosity (such as honey) do not flow freely.

Gases

The molecules of a gas are not close to each other, and can move easily and quickly. Therefore, gases can expand to fill a vessel. Gases have a low density. They do not have a fixed shape or volume and thus they can be condensed, reducing the space between their particles. Most gases are invisible. Steam rising from a hot bowl of soup is only visible once it begins condensing and forms a vapour of water droplets.

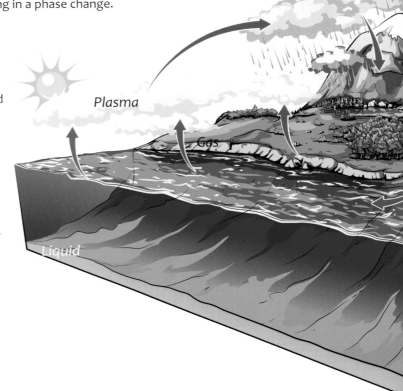

Plasma

There is a fourth state of matter called plasma. It is found throughout the universe but seldom on Earth. It is caused when radiation or very high temperatures pull electrons away from atoms. It exists in a gas-like state. This creates a gaseous cloud of positive ions and negative electrons. It is a good conductor of heat and electricity, and is found around the Sun. In natural light, it appears in the sky in the form of an aurora.

Transformation of matter

When matter melts

When matter melts, it changes its state from solid to liquid. This phenomenon occurs when the temperature is increased, causing the particles in a solid to vibrate rapidly. The temperature at which this occurs is called the melting point of the solid. Tungsten, a metal, has the highest melting point among metals, which is 3420° C.

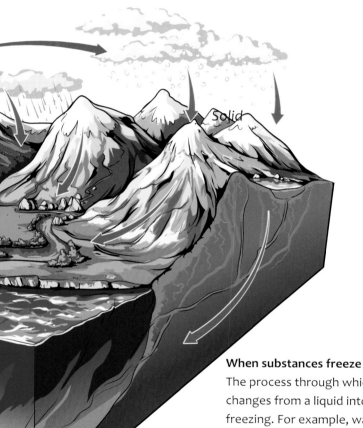

Solid

Illustration showing the states and transformation of matter.

When substances freeze

The process through which a substance changes from a liquid into a solid is called freezing. For example, water solidifies to form ice through the process of freezing. Different liquids have different freezing points, that is, the point below which they will transform into a solid. Water has a freezing point of around 0° C whereas mercury freezes at –38° C.

FUN FACT

There is a stark difference between the predicted rotations of the galaxy about its centre and the observed values. This difference is said to be the effect of dark matter.

Evaporation

Evaporation is the process in which a liquid changes into a gas. Evaporation occurs when molecules in the liquid's surface have sufficient energy to move away from each other and thus form a gas. For example, water on the road evaporates as water vapour into the atmosphere. In addition, liquids evaporate rapidly when heated. This is seen when water is kept to boil.

Condensation

Condensation is the process by which a gas on cooling turns back into a liquid. When gas molecules lose heat and energy they slow down. They move closer and form a liquid. An example of condensation is when water droplets form on the outside of a glass of cold water.

Dark matter

The rest of the universe consists of dark matter and dark energy. Dark matter is studied more in astrophysics and cosmology than in physical science. Dark matter cannot be perceived; neither does it give out any sort of electromagnetic radiation nor does it reflect any back. However, like all matter, its presence affects the gravitational fields and hence, its effects can be seen as those of gravitational forces on visible objects. An example would be the rotation of the Milky Way itself.

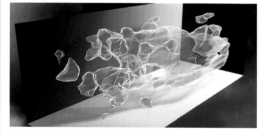

3D map of the large-scale distribution of dark matter, reconstructed from measurements of weak gravitational lensing with the Hubble Space Telescope.

Properties of Matter

All substances have a varied array of different characteristics called properties. The property of a substance denotes its features or qualities, right from its appearance to its chemical or physical attributes. Scientists and engineers use the information on the properties of various substances to choose an appropriate material for particular applications in industries and in research.

A diamond has a hardness rating of 10 on the Mohs scale of mineral hardness.

Hardness

This property determines how easy or difficult it is to shape or scratch a substance. A common method to measure the relative hardness of a substance is to use the Mohs scale. Ten minerals ranging from the hardest to the softest have been ranked on the scale. A substance's ability to resist getting scratched by another substance determines its hardness on the Mohs scale.

Conduction of electricity

Materials that are good electric conductors enable an electric current to pass through them with ease. Metals are good conductors of electricity. Copper is used to make electrical wires. Materials such as plastic, ceramics and glass are poor conductors of electricity. They are used as insulators that prevent electricity flow to places where it is not required.

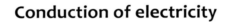

Copper wires (good conductor of electricity) covered by plastic (bad conductor of electricity).

Solubility

Solubility refers to the ability of a substance to dissolve in water. Some materials can dissolve in water or any other liquid to form a mixture. Water is often referred to as the universal solvent as most substances can dissolve in it.

Flexibility and elasticity

Flexibility refers to the ability of some materials to twist or bend, whereas elasticity refers to the ability of a material to absorb force as well as twist or stretch in different directions before returning to its original position. Interestingly, some materials have a limit to their elasticity. If they are stretched beyond their normal tolerance, they will not return to their original shape and size.

Mass and density

Density refers to the weight of a substance in relation to its size. To find the density of a material, divide its mass by its volume. Dense materials such as brass and lead are used for weights, whereas materials with low density (such as wood) float on water. Air-filled foam pellets have extremely low density and, therefore, are used to protect electronic goods and other fragile materials.

A graduated cylinder containing various coloured liquids with different densities.

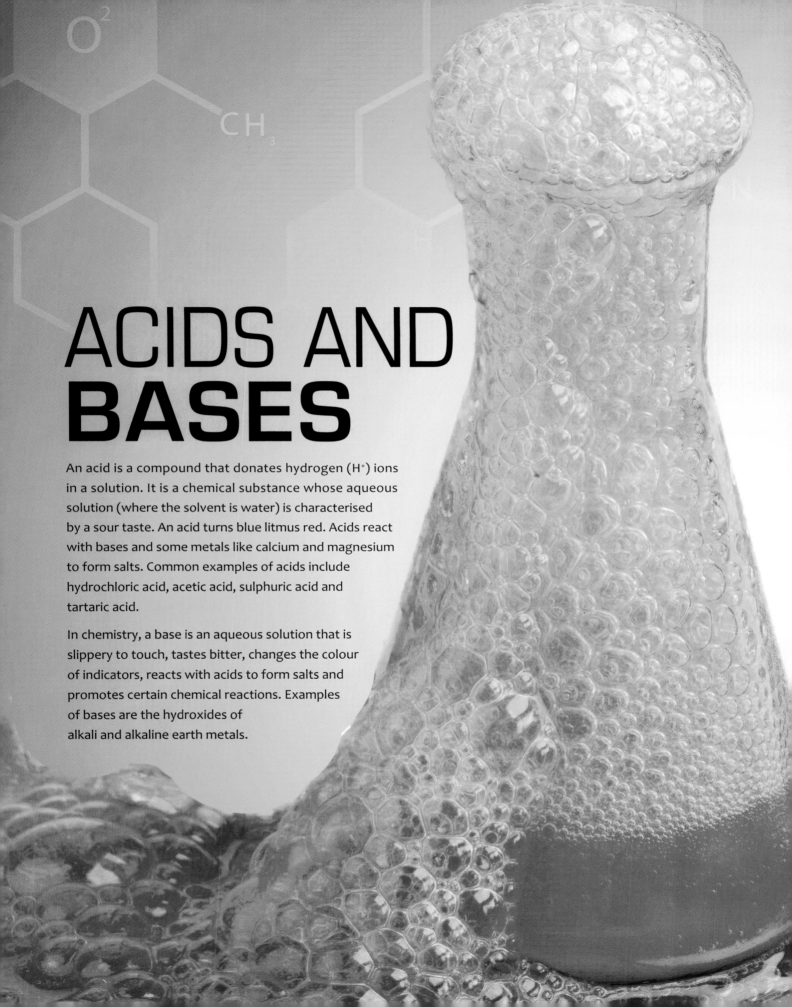

ACIDS AND
BASES

An acid is a compound that donates hydrogen (H^+) ions in a solution. It is a chemical substance whose aqueous solution (where the solvent is water) is characterised by a sour taste. An acid turns blue litmus red. Acids react with bases and some metals like calcium and magnesium to form salts. Common examples of acids include hydrochloric acid, acetic acid, sulphuric acid and tartaric acid.

In chemistry, a base is an aqueous solution that is slippery to touch, tastes bitter, changes the colour of indicators, reacts with acids to form salts and promotes certain chemical reactions. Examples of bases are the hydroxides of alkali and alkaline earth metals.

Acids and Bases: Fundamentals

The term acid is derived from the Latin term *acidus*, which means sour. Swedish scientist Svante Arrhenius defined an acid as "a chemical substance which, when dissolved in water, gives an hydrogen (H^+) ion and combines with the water molecule to form the hydronium ion (H_3O^+)". Acids are also characterised by their ability to react with bases and neutralise them.

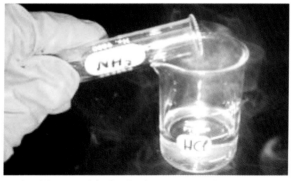

Hydrochloric acid (in beaker) reacting with ammonia fumes to produce ammonium chloride (white smoke).

Determining an acid

Any chemical substance whose aqueous solution tastes sour is either an acid or contains a certain amount of acid. However, the standard test for acidity is conducted using the litmus test, during which an acid can turn blue litmus paper red. An acid can also be defined as a substance that donates H^+ ions and when an acid is dissolved in water, the balance between the H^+ ions and hydroxide (OH^-) ions shifts. As, an acid donates H^+ ions, water has more H^+ ions than OH^- ions and the solution is called acidic. The pH value (scale used to measure acidity/alkalinity of a substance) of acids is less than seven. Examples of acids are sulphuric acid, nitric acid, hydrochloric acid and oxalic acid.

What is a base?

A base is a substance that can accept protons or H^+ ions. Its properties are opposite to that of an acid. It turns red litmus paper blue. Not all bases dissolve in water and those that do are known as alkalis. Bases usually taste bitter. According to Arrhenius, they give OH^- ions in an aqueous solution. Bases react with acids and neutralise each other to form a salt and water. This is called an acid–base reaction.

Accepting ions

A base can also be defined as a substance that accepts H^+ ions. Thus, when an acid is dissolved in water, the balance between the H^+ ions and OH^+ ions shifts in the opposite direction. As bases soak H^+ ions, water has fewer H^+ ions than OH^- ions and the solution is called alkaline. The pH value of alkaline solutions is greater than seven. Examples of bases are baking soda, milk of magnesia and ammonia solution.

pH indicators and tube with pH values.

Lewis Acids and Lewis Bases

Apart from Arrhenius, other scientists have also given definitions of acids and bases, as there are many other chemicals that exhibit certain acidic and basic properties even though they may strictly not give an H^+ ion or OH^- radical.

Classification of Lewis acid and base

GN Lewis proposed a definition, which focussed on electron transfer rather than proton transfer. A Lewis acid reacts with a Lewis base to form a Lewis adduct. A Lewis acid is a chemical species that accepts an electron pair and a Lewis base is a chemical that donates an electron pair to form the adduct. Trimethylborane (Me_3B) is a Lewis acid and ammonia (NH_3) is a Lewis base. Their adduct is represented as $Me_3B{:}NH_3$. The ":" means that a chemical bond is formed between the two chemical compounds. The adduct has a bond that is something between a covalent and an ionic bond.

1. *THF molecule*   **2.** *BH_3 molecule*   **3.** *Lewis adduct between BH_3 and THF*

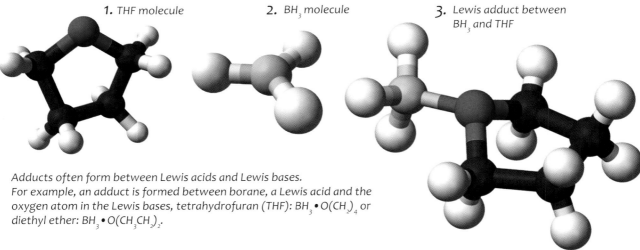

Adducts often form between Lewis acids and Lewis bases.
For example, an adduct is formed between borane, a Lewis acid and the oxygen atom in the Lewis bases, tetrahydrofuran (THF): $BH_3 \bullet O(CH_2)_4$ or diethyl ether: $BH_3 \bullet O(CH_3CH_2)_2$.

Structure

Lewis acids usually have a triangular planar molecular structure. Examples are boron trifluoride (BF_3), aluminium chloride ($AlCl_3$) or even more complex compounds, such as $Et_3Al_2Cl_2$. As seen from this example, Lewis acids are also chemicals with metal cations.

Boron trifluoride in 3D. It is a useful Lewis acid and a versatile building block for other boron compounds.

The Lewis base has a highly occupied molecular orbital. These include amines of the formula $NH_3–xRx$ (where R is an alkyl or aryl), phosphines of the formula $PR_3–xAx$ (where R is an alkyl, A is an aryl) and compounds of S, Se, O and Te having oxidation state 2.

Neutralisation and Titration

A chemical reaction in which an acid and a base reacts quantitatively so that no excess acid or base is left is called a neutralisation reaction. After such a reaction reaches its equivalence point (when equal quantities of acid and base mix together), the number of H^+ ions in the solution is equal to the number of OH^- ions in the solution. Therefore, nothing besides salt and water remains.

A salt is an ionic compound that results from the neutralisation reaction of an acid and a base.

How does it work?

A simple example would be:

$HCl + NaOH = NaCl + H_2O$

In this reaction, hydrochloric acid (HCl) and sodium hydroxide (NaOH) are taken in equal amounts, that is, the number of H^+ ions that HCl will give rise to in the aqueous solution is equal to the number of OH^- ions that NaOH will give rise to in the solution.

Concentration of acid

Titration is employed to find out the equivalence point. Titration is a method in which we can analyse the concentration of an analyte (substance whose properties are being analysed) in a solution or, in this case, the concentration of an acid in water. Take a certain amount of acidic solution in a conical flask along with a small litmus paper or phenolphthalein. The solution will be red or pink in colour. Now, add a base from a burette drop by drop until the solution becomes colourless, that is, until it becomes neutral or reaches its equivalence point. After finding out how much of a basic solution with a known concentration and molarity (measure of concentration of a solution) is required to neutralise an acidic solution of known molarity but unknown concentration, we can find out the concentration of the acid.

Analysis of soil samples by titration.

Titration

Titration is the process of chemical analysis where the quantity of a constituent of a sample is determined by adding an exactly known quantity of another substance to the measured sample with which the desired constituent reacts in a definite and known proportion. This process is conducted by gradually adding a standard solution (a solution of known concentration) of a titrant using a burette. The addition of this standard solution is stopped when the equivalence point is reached.

The pH and pOH Scales

Acidity or alkalinity are measured using a logarithmic scale known as the pH scale. Soren Peder Lauritz Sorensen proposed the concept of pH in 1909. A strong acidic solution may have a million times more H^+ ions than a strong basic solution. A strong basic solution may have a million times more OH^- ions than a strong acidic solution. To deal with such large numbers, scientists take the help of a logarithmic scale, known as the pH scale, which is basically pH = –log $[H^+]$, where $[H^+]$ is the concentration.

Standard scale for acids

The pH scale is a standardised scale that is used to measure the acidity or basicity of an aqueous solution. The scale ranges from 0 to 14. A solution with pH that is below seven is acidic, while a solution with pH that is above seven is basic. Therefore, the pH of a neutral solution should, by theory, be seven. Pure water has a pH that is very close to seven, but not exactly seven. It is important to note that the pH of an acid cannot be zero in practice.

Chart showing the variation of colour of universal indicator paper with pH.

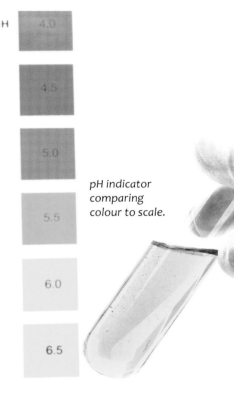

pH indicator comparing colour to scale.

Standard scale for bases

The pOH scale is similar to the pH scale. It measures the concentration of OH^- ions. It is a scale used to show the concentration of OH^- ions in a solution. This scale is based on the molarity of hydroxide ions in a solution with the formula pOH = –log $[OH^-]$.

Bases cannot have a pH of 14 or greater in practice. It is actually the negative logarithm of activity of the hydronium (H_3O^+) ion. pOH is approximately equal to 14 – pH.

pH meter to measure the acidity-alkalinity of liquids.

Reading the pH scale

The pH of a solution is measured using a pH meter, which gives pH readings of the difference in electromotive force (voltage) between suitable electrodes placed in the solution to be tested. Basically, a pH meter constitutes a voltmeter attached to a pH-responsive electrode and a reference electrode.

Important Acids

Acids that ionise (convert into ions by losing electrons) completely in a solution are called strong acids. An acid that leaves very little ionisation is a weak acid. Strong acids reduce the pH for a given molarity of a solution. Let us look at some common and important acids. Food items like lemon, raw mango, orange and curd taste sour as they contain acids.

Hydrochloric acid (HCl)

Hydrochloric acid is a strong acid. It ionises almost completely in water. It is colourless in appearance but has a very strong, irritating odour. It exists in the liquid form. It is formed by dissolving hydrogen chloride (a colourless gas) in water. As soon as the gas comes in contact with water, it sinks and mixes well with it.

FUN FACT

Dilute hydrochloric acid actually exists in our stomach and aids in the digestion of food. It has a pH between 1 and 2.

Hydrochloric acid is packaged and marketed in small containers for use in laboratories.

Citric acid ($H_3C_6H_5O_7$)

The most common sources of citric acid are fruits, such as tomatoes and lemons. Citric acid belongs to the carboxylic acid family. It is a colourless acid that forms a crystalline organic compound. It is present in almost all plants and even in the tissues and fluids of certain animals. It breaks down fats, carbohydrates and proteins into water and carbon dioxide. Citric acid was first removed from lemon juice by a chemist named Carl Wilhelm Scheele in 1784, using a fungus named *Aspergillus niger*. Citric acid aids in the production of sugar and molasses. It is also used to add flavour to various aerated drinks and sweets. It is also used in solutions that aid in the cleaning of metals, as well as to stabilise certain food items.

Lemons, oranges, limes and other citrus fruits possess high concentrations of citric acid.

Acetic acid ($HC_2H_3O_2$)

Acetic acid is a weak acid. It ionises very weakly with water. Acetic acid is also called ethanoic acid and it belongs to the carboxylic acid group. Vinegar is produced after a dilute solution of acetic acid is fermented and oxidised by natural carbohydrates. Acetate is a salt or ester of acetic acid. Metal acetates are prepared in industries in order to be used in printing presses.

Vinegar (produced from acetic acid) has a pH of 4.

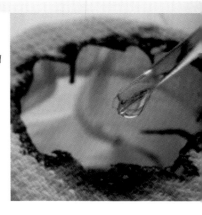

Drops of concentrated sulphuric acid rapidly dehydrate a piece of cotton towel.

Sulphuric acid (H_2SO_4)

Sulphuric acid is a strong acid. It completely ionises in water. Sulphuric acid is used extensively in chemical industries. It is also known as hydrogen sulphate or "oil of vitriol". It is a colourless acid that has an oily texture. Like nitric acid, sulphuric acid is a corrosive liquid. It is an important acid, as well as an important chemical for industries and is prepared as a result of its reaction with water and sulphur trioxide.

Sulphuric acid is used to prepare pigments, various drugs, fertilisers, detergents, inorganic acids and salts, explosives and dyes. Sulphuric acid is used in petroleum refineries. It is also used to store batteries.

Nitric acid (HNO_3)

Nitric acid is a strong acid that almost completely ionises in water. It is a highly corrosive liquid and colourless in appearance. As an acid, it can burn the human skin upon contact and is highly toxic to human beings. In water, nitric acid decomposes into nitrogen dioxide and oxygen, thus forming a yellowish brown solution with water. It is used in industries as one of the ingredients for fertilisers and explosives. Nitric acid reacts with ammonia to form ammonium nitrate, which is used to make fertilisers. It mixes with glycerol and toluene to form explosives like nitroglycerin and trinitrotoluene. Nitric acid is also used in the preparation of dyes and plastics.

Fuming nitric acid contaminated with yellow nitrogen dioxide.

Carbonic acid (H_2CO_3)

Carbonic acid is a weak acid. It barely ionises in water. It is created by the reaction of carbon dioxide with water. When carbon dioxide dissolves in water, it forms carbonic acid. Carbonic acid sometimes appears in rain when carbon dioxide dissolves in rain water. When this carbonic acid gives up one hydrogen ion, it forms a bicarbonate ion. It is mainly used in aerated drinks and can be found in blood and champagne. Carbonic acid keeps the pH level of our body stable. Hence, people are advised to consume lemons and tomatoes.

The tiny bubbles on the surface are proof that carbonic acid is present in champagne.

Important Bases

A strong base is a base that completely ionises in a solution. For example, sodium hydroxide is a strong base. On the other hand, a base that does not ionise completely or ionises very little in a solution is called a weak base. Sodium bicarbonate is a weak base. A strong base has a strong pH with the morality of a solution. Caustic soda and baking soda are slippery to the touch and have a bitter taste as they are bases.

Sodium bicarbonate comes in very fine and soft particles.

Sodium bicarbonate (NaHCO3)

Sodium bicarbonate is a weak base. It is also called "baking soda". You might have seen it being used in cakes. It ionises very little in water. The reaction for baking soda or sodium bicarbonate is:

$$NaHCO_3 + H_2O = H_2CO_3 + OH- + Na+$$

How do cakes "rise"?

When sodium bicarbonate comes in contact with an acid, the reaction gives out carbon dioxide. The reaction is indicated as:

$$NaHCO_3 + H+ = Na+ + H_2O + CO_2 \text{ (carbon dioxide)}$$

The above reaction takes place while baking a cake or cupcake. This is because baking powder has portions of sodium bicarbonate and cream of tartar, which is a weak acid. These do not react with each other unless they have been mixed with water, which is added at the time of cooking or baking.

Cakes tend to rise because sodium bicarbonate releases carbon dioxide in the mixture.

Gluten and puff pastries

Have you heard of food items with gluten in them? Gluten is another ingredient that allows foam to form in the mixture. The mixture for biscuits is beaten vigorously and mixed with gluten in order to create a foam.

Puff pastes are used to create pastries. The pastry mixtures are expanded by the use of steam or water vapour.

Puff pastries are named so due to their "puffiness", which they get due to baking soda.

Sodium bicarbonate as a medicine

Sodium bicarbonate is not only used to cook and bake, but also used as a medicine for minor problems. Sodium bicarbonate is prescribed as a medicine for heartburn, acid indigestion and for the reduction of the acidic content in blood or urine. Sodium bicarbonate might come in the form of tablets or powders, which need to be taken orally. Usually, when used as an antacid, sodium bicarbonate needs to be taken at least within two hours after a meal. This medicine is also used to increase the amount of sodium in one's body.

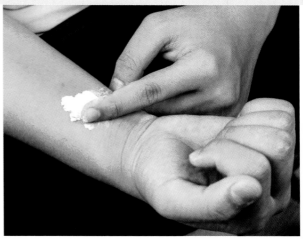
Sodium bicarbonate is used to relieve itching from rashes.

Sodium bicarbonate as a leavening agent

Many baked goods have a porous surface, which is created by the release of the gases present within. While these gases are released, the baked goods expand more than the original container and rise. The substance that causes all of this is called the "leavening agent".

During this process, the person producing the baked goods is required to continuously and vigorously mix the ingredients that need to expand or rise. This is in order to allow air bubbles and foam to be produced within the mixture. Egg whites are widely used in baked goods as they enable strong foams to form within the mixture.

Egg whites used in baked goods enable strong foams to form within the mixture.

Side-effects of sodium bicarbonate

Sodium bicarbonate, when taken in excess or small dosages, might cause gas and stomach cramps. Some might begin to feel more thirsty than usual. However, this is a minor side-effect.

Sodium hydroxide (NaOH)

Sodium hydroxide is considered to be a strong base. It is also called "caustic soda". Sodium hydroxide exists in solid state as an odourless crystalline substance. It tends to absorb the moisture present in the air. When this solid is dissolved in water, it releases heat, which is then used as a means to ignite flammable materials. Sodium hydroxide is corrosive in nature and is mainly used as a solid or as a solution with only 50 per cent of sodium hydroxide.

It is used in the manufacture of rayon, paper, dye and petroleum products. Sodium hydroxide is used to process cotton and other natural fabrics. It is also used to clean, bleach and launder other metal substances. Sodium hydroxide is used to clean commercial ovens and drains. Sodium hydroxide is corrosive to animal and plant tissue. However, it is used in most industries as an industrial alkali.

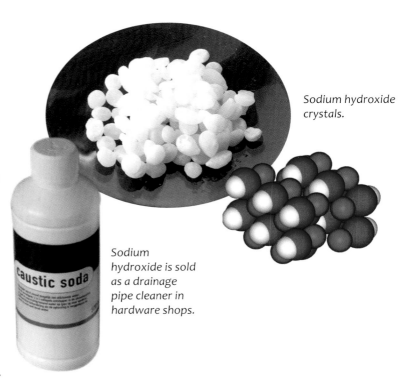
Sodium hydroxide crystals.

Sodium hydroxide is sold as a drainage pipe cleaner in hardware shops.

Acid-base Reactions

An acid and base react with each other when they are brought together. Their reaction causes a neutralisation of properties to take place in both the acid and the base, so that a salt is formed. This reaction produces water as the H+ cation of the acid mixes with the OH– anion of the base. It forms a compound called "salt". Different acids and bases react with each other to form different salts.

Salts formed from acid-base reactions

The reaction of acids and bases form other salts such as sodium bisulphate, potassium dichromate and calcium chloride. While all acid and base reactions form "salts", they are not all edible.

Calcium chloride

Calcium chloride is mainly used to remove the dampness in a room. It is marketed in the form of pellets. When used, it tends to absorb the moisture and water in the air. It reacts with this water and dissolves in it to leave behind a solution.

Sample of calcium chloride.

Sodium chloride (NaCl)

Common salt or table salt is the common name of sodium chloride. We use this salt in cooking. It is formed by the reaction of hydrochloric acid with the base, sodium hydroxide. This reaction is written as:

HCl + NaOH = H2O + NaCl
(acid) (base) (water) (salt)

Sodium chloride is also found in a mineral called "halite" and hence is also called "rock salt". Particles of this salt exist in cubic crystals, which form a cubic lattice pattern. The bonds between the sodium and chloride atoms of this salt are one of the most basic and common examples of ionic bonding.

Crystal salt

Sodium bisulphate (NaHSO4)

Sodium bisulphate, along with potassium dichromate (K2Cr2O7), is used as a bleach for photographic lenses and cameras. It reacts very badly with the skin so while handling this salt, people make sure to wear gloves and other bodily protection. It is also used as poison as it reacts very strongly when consumed.

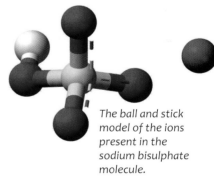

The ball and stick model of the ions present in the sodium bisulphate molecule.

FUN FACT

When people accidentally swallow acidic liquids like bleach, they are made to drink baking powder solution so that it reacts with the acid, creating salt and water, causing them to throw up.

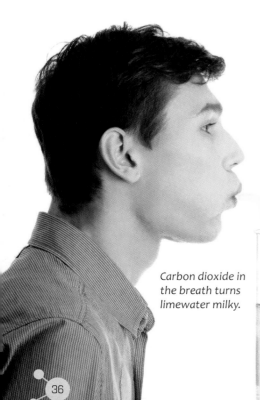

Carbon dioxide in the breath turns limewater milky.

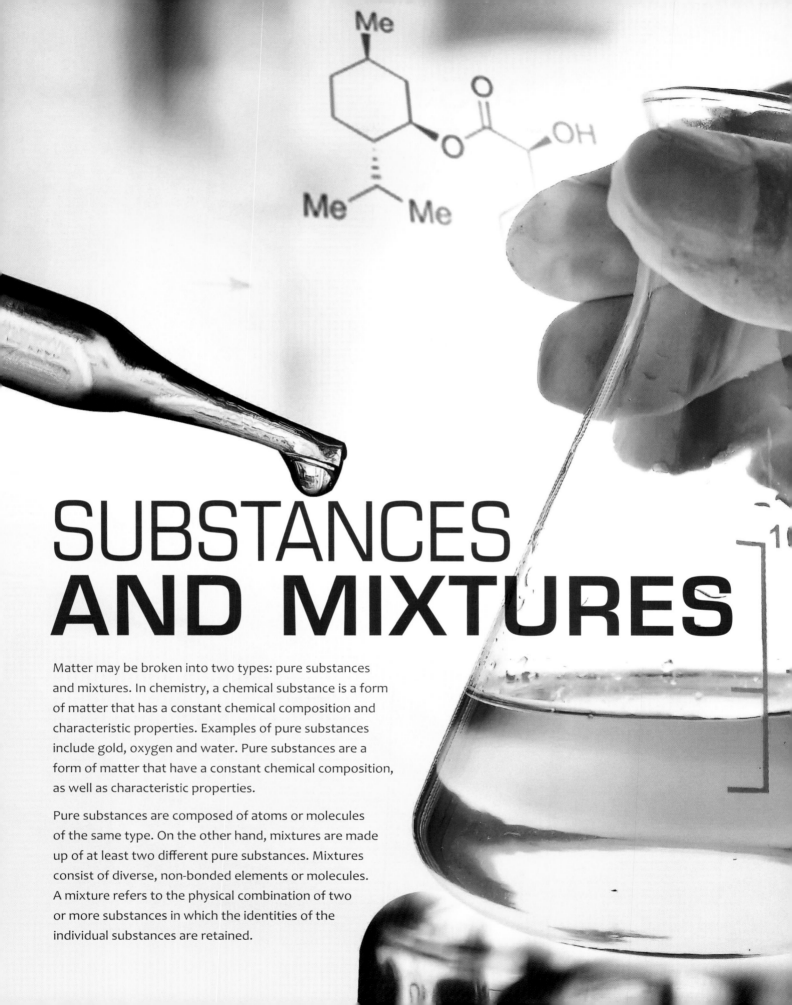

SUBSTANCES
AND MIXTURES

Matter may be broken into two types: pure substances and mixtures. In chemistry, a chemical substance is a form of matter that has a constant chemical composition and characteristic properties. Examples of pure substances include gold, oxygen and water. Pure substances are a form of matter that have a constant chemical composition, as well as characteristic properties.

Pure substances are composed of atoms or molecules of the same type. On the other hand, mixtures are made up of at least two different pure substances. Mixtures consist of diverse, non-bonded elements or molecules. A mixture refers to the physical combination of two or more substances in which the identities of the individual substances are retained.

What is a Substance?

A substance is a matter that bears a specific composition with specific properties. Any pure element can be a substance. Any pure compound can also be a substance. Chemical substances may be in the solid, liquid, gas or plasma state. Change in pressure or temperature may cause these substances to alter between different phases of matter.

Chemical substance

A chemical substance is a type of matter that has a constant chemical composition and characteristic properties. In order to break a chemical substance into its components, one must separate its components or break its chemical bonds. Chemical substances can occur in solid, liquid, gas or plasma state. Substances can shift between the different phases of matter due to changes in temperature or pressure.

Pure chemical compound

A pure chemical compound is a chemical substance that comprises a specific set of molecules or ions that are chemically bonded. When two or more elements are combined into one substance through a chemical reaction, such as water, a chemical compound is formed. All compounds are substances, but not all substances are compounds. A chemical compound could either be various atoms bonded together in molecules, or crystals in which atoms, molecules or ions form a crystalline lattice. Compounds made mainly of carbon and hydrogen atoms are called organic compounds while all others are called inorganic compounds.

Why are some substances called "pure"?

Chemical substances are often called "pure" to distinguish them from mixtures. Pure water is an example of a chemical substance. It has the same properties and ratio of hydrogen to oxygen whether it is isolated from a river or made in a laboratory. Other chemical substances commonly witnessed in their pure form are diamond (carbon), gold, table salt (sodium chloride) and refined sugar (sucrose).

Steam and liquid water are two different forms of the same chemical substance, water.

Gold is a pure substance.

What is a Mixture?

When two or more substances are mixed together but not chemically combined, the result is called a mixture. It is the physical combination of two or more substances, where their identities are retained and can be seen in the form of either suspensions, solutions or colloids. They are the end product of mixing chemical substances, such as compounds and elements by a process called "mechanical blending".

Azeotropes

Some mixtures may be separated into their components by applying physical, thermal and mechanical means. Azeotrope is the mixture that usually poses certain difficulties regarding the separation process required for obtaining their constituent (physical or chemical process or a blend).

Distillation and chromatography

On heating a liquid mixture, the liquid with the lowest boiling point is transformed into vapour and the other liquid is left behind. This process is called distillation and is used to separate alcohol from water.

Paper chromatography is used to isolate coloured mixtures, such as dyes or inks. In this method, coloured mixtures, travel at various speeds along the paper when a solvent is applied to them, thereby separating them from each other.

Separating mixtures

Several methods have been devised to separate mixtures. A common experiment performed in schools to test this approach is that of magnet and sand. The magnet attracts the iron filings to it, thus separating the iron filings from sand. Another separation method is called "centrifuging", which is used to separate particles or liquids from other liquids. This method uses the different densities of the substances that are present in the mixture as a means to separate the particles. The liquids in the mixture are separated into layers based upon their densities. This process uses a machine called a "centrifuge", which spins the test tubes containing the liquids at great speed.

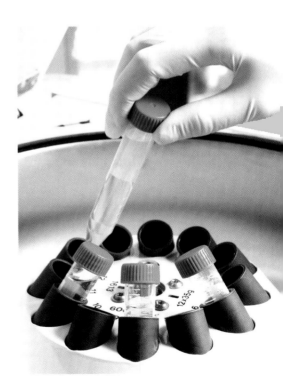

Samples in a centrifuge.

Types of Mixtures

A mixture is a substance in which two or more elements mix but don't chemically combine. Mixtures are usually classified into two broad groups: homogeneous or heterogeneous.

Homogeneous mixtures

When the components of a mixture are uniformly distributed, it is called a homogenous mixture. The chemical compositions of such mixtures are the same throughout. A single phase or state of matter is observed in a homogeneous mixture. Air, sugar, water, vinegar, detergent and steel are some examples of homogenous mixtures.

In a homogenous mixture, two or more components cannot be easily distinguished by sight. The composition of such mixtures is constant. It is more challenging to separate the components of a homogeneous mixture than to separate the components of a heterogeneous mixture.

Heterogeneous mixtures

A heterogeneous mixture is a mixture of two or more chemical substances, where different components of the mixture can be distinguished easily. These components can then be separated without much effort. Mixtures of sand and water or of sand and iron filings are examples of heterogeneous mixtures.

Homogeneous mixture of a detergent.

Heterogeneous mixture of water, oil and sand.

Heterogeneous vs homogeneous

Homogeneous and heterogeneous mixtures can be distinguished based on the scale of the sample. Any mixture is said to be heterogeneous on a small sampling scale because a sample could be as small as a single molecule. Practically speaking, if the property of interest is the same, irrespective of how much of the mixture is taken, then the mixture is a homogeneous one. We cannot pick out the components of a homogeneous mixture or use simple mechanical means to separate them. We cannot see or physically separate the components of a homogenous mixture, nor do they exist in various states of matter. On the other hand, in a heterogeneous mixture, the components of a mixture are not at all uniform, nor do they possess localised regions and distinctive properties like homogenous mixtures.

The terms "heterogeneous" and "homogeneous" are used to refer to the mixtures of materials. The difference among the two is the degree at which these materials have been mixed together along with the uniformity of their composition. Various samples from a mixture are not identical to each other. There are two or more phases in any heterogeneous mixture in which you can recognise a particular region with the properties that are different from those of a different region, even if they are the same form of matter (an example of this is a liquid or a solid). Examples of heterogeneous mixtures are vegetable soup, blood, the ice in soda, mixed nuts and soil.

Suspension mixture

A suspension mixture is created by mixing together two or more ingredients where the particles are large enough to be seen by the naked eye or with the use of a simple magnifying glass. The ingredients of a suspension mixture are heterogeneous. In fact, most heterogeneous mixtures are suspension mixtures.

• Solid–solid mix

These suspension mixtures consist of solids mixed with other solids. Bread mix is an example of visible solid particles that are stirred and mixed together. Soil is another example of a solid–solid suspension mixture as it contains dead organic matter, rocks, stones and pebbles. These mixtures can be separated by the simple process of sifting.

• Solid–liquid mix

If solid particles are mixed with a liquid to form a suspension mixture, the ingredients will separate with the heavier solid particles settling at the bottom. For example, if you mix sand and water, the sand would eventually sink to the bottom of the container. In case the solid particles are lighter than the liquid (as seen in the mixture of sawdust and water), they will separate and float to the top.

These mixtures can be separated by the processes of settling and filtration.

• Liquid–liquid mix

If drops of a liquid are mixed with another liquid or a gas solvent, the components can be separated. Once separated, if the droplets are heavier, they will settle at the bottom. If the droplets are lighter, they will float to the top.

• Size of particles

The size of solute particles in a colloidal mixture is much smaller than the particles in a suspension mixture. However, these particles are not as small as the particles in a solution. The particles in a colloidal mixture are typically as small as a clump of molecules that may not be visible even with a common microscope. What makes this kind of mixture rare is that the solute particles do not break down any further into single molecules. Thus, they form a solution.

• Blending

The blending of materials in a colloidal mixture is more forceful than the basic stirring done in a suspension mixture. Often, the materials of a colloidal mixture are violently mixed together. A good example is the concrete mixer machine that actively shakes the materials to minimise the particles settling to the bottom. Some examples of colloidal mixtures are mayonnaise, jello, fog, butter and whipped cream.

Solution

A solution is a homogeneous mixture, where one substance is dissolved in another substance. The solute dissolves in the solvent. Solutes may be solids, liquids or gases. The solvent is usually a liquid or a gas.

Solubility

In simple words, "solubility" is the ability of a substance to dissolve in water or another liquid. A more precise definition would be that solubility is the maximum amount of solute that can be completely dissolved in a solvent under a given set of conditions.

Addition of salt in water.

Principal of solubility

On adding sugar or salt to a glass of water, the sugar or salt dissolves. If we continue to add more sugar or salt to that glass, there will come a point where no more sugar or salt can dissolve in it. This means that when an equilibrium is established between the solute (the component that dissolves in a solvent) and the solvent (able to dissolve a substance), then no more solute can dissolve in it. A solution that reaches this stage is called a "saturated solution". The excess of solute added to the solvent gets collected at the bottom of the solution.

Saturated solution

A solution that becomes saturated is said to have reached its limit or its "saturation point". Any more solute put into the solvent will not dissolve under normal conditions. There are many factors that can increase the limit of solubility such as temperature, pressure, the nature of its intermolecular forces or interionic forces of the solute and the solvent. When the solubility of a solute is increased, the solution is called a "supersaturated solution". Solubility gives us an insight into the properties of the substance we are dealing with. It also tells us the polarity that distinguishes the substance from other substances in a mixture and enables us to understand its applications.

Potassium permanganate dissolved in water.

FUN FACT

If you have a saturated solution of sugar, heating it will enable you to dissolve more sugar in it.

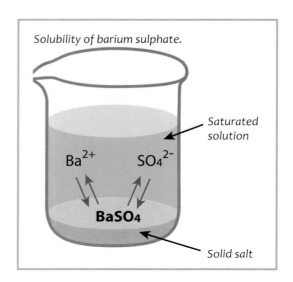

Solubility of barium sulphate.

Ba^{2+} SO_4^{2-}

Saturated solution

BaSO$_4$

Solid salt

Solid Solution

A solid solution, as the name suggests, exists in the solid state. It is a solution composed of single or multiple solutes in one solvent. This variety of a mixture is regarded as a solution instead of a compound when the crystal construction of the solvent remains the same by inputting the solutes and when the mixture remains in a distinct homogeneous phase.

Coins made of copper (alloy).

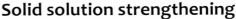

Strengthened metals have multiple uses.

Ability to mix

A solid solution can be distinguished from a manually made mixture of powdered solids, such as sugar and salt or salts. These manual mixtures have complete or limited ability to mix in the solid state. Instances of solid solutions mostly include moist solids, alloys and the crystallised salts in their liquid mixture.

Solid solution strengthening

With respect to alloys, intermetallic compounds (substances composed of definite proportions of two or more elemental metals) are frequently formed. The solute may include the solvent crystal lattice, by substituting a solvent particle in the lattice by adjusting itself into the gap between the solvent particles. Both these varieties of solid solutions influence the characteristics of the substance by altering the crystal lattice and interrupting the electric and physical homogeneousness of the solvent material. Solid solutions, according to the Hume-Rothery laws, are formed only if the solute and solvent have analogous atomic radii (15 per cent or less apart), identical crystal structure, similar electro-negativities and comparable valences. Thus, solid solutions are a blend of two crystalline solids that co-exist as a crystal lattice or a new variety of crystalline solid. Quite frequently, metal is strengthened by solid solution alloying and the mechanism is known as solid solution strengthening.

Key Properties of Substances

Substances are used for many types of applications, specifically because of their unique properties. Substance selection criteria entirely depends on the required key properties of a specific application. Some of the properties of substances are described as follows:

Copper wires can conduct electric currents.

Conductivity

It is the fundamental property of matter that determines the ability of a substance to conduct an electric current through it. Its International System of Unit (SI unit) is Siemens per metre (S/m).

Density

It is the mass per unit volume of a substance. Mathematically, it is expressed as a ratio of mass and volume. Its physical system of unit or SI unit is kg/m³. Density is the key property that we need to check for structural applications where lighter materials with more strength are preferred. Materials with higher density also find applications in various fields including military applications.

Resistance

It is the basic property of matter that determines how strongly a substance opposes the flow of current through it. It is the reciprocal of conductivity. Its SI unit is ohm-metre (Ωm).

Ductility

The ductility of a substance is its ability to be stretched into a wire under tensile stress. It is a very important property to construct desired shapes.

Elasticity

It is the tendency of a solid matter to return to its original shape after being deformed by external forces. Mathematically, it is defined as the ratio of stress and strain.

Toughness

Toughness is the ability of a substance to absorb energy and transform without fracturing itself. Mathematically, it can be defined as the amount of energy per unit volume that a material can absorb before it is fractured. Its SI unit is Joule per cubic metre (J/m³).

Malleability

It is the ability of a substance to be hammered into sheets under compressive stress. This property is found only in solids.

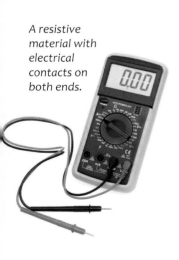

A resistive material with electrical contacts on both ends.

Gold sheets can be produced owing to gold's malleability.

THE PERIODIC
TABLE

The first ever element was discovered by a man named Hennig Brand in 1649. He had discovered phosphorous. Within the following two centuries, many other scientists discovered and expanded the knowledge base on various other elements. By 1869, a total of 63 elements were discovered by various scientists around the world.

With each new discovery, scientists realised that the elements fell under a certain pattern. The periodic table was born from a desire to list and explain each of the discovered elements as well as to relate them to these patterns. The father of the periodic table according to some is a German chemist named Lothar Meyer, while for others, it is a Russian chemist named Dmitri Mendeleev.

The Periodic Table

The periodic table is one of the most powerful tools in the hands of chemists. It is a systematic tabular arrangement of all the 118 chemical elements currently known to humans in order of increasing atomic number, that is, the total number of protons present in the nucleus of the atom.

Structure of the table

The usual format of the table consists of a grid of elements represented in 18 columns (called groups) and seven rows (called rows) with a separate double row of elements below. The table can also be interpreted by breaking it up into four rectangular blocks: the s-block on the left, the p-block on the right, the d-block in the middle and the f-block below that.

Arrangement of elements

When chemical elements are slotted into the aforementioned arrangement, a recurring pattern called the "periodic law" is formed as per their properties. Because of this, elements in the same column usually display similar properties while elements in the same row display a predictable variation in certain properties. This is extremely useful for scientists because it allows predictions to be made about a certain element based on its position in relation to another element. For example, if we know the properties of carbon, we can also make certain estimates about the behaviour of silicon (which falls right below carbon in the table). Without this arrangement, an experimental approach to the knowledge we seek about the chemical elements would give us very little insight.

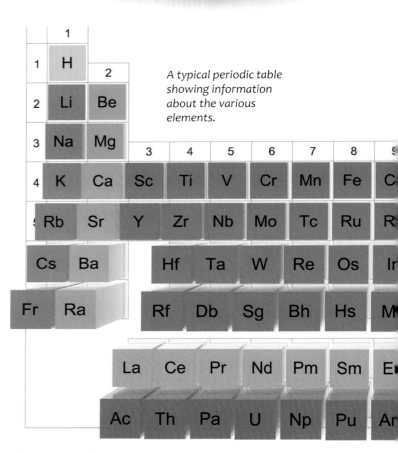

A typical periodic table showing information about the various elements.

Alkali metals

Alkali metals are the first group in the periodic table. This group includes lithium, potassium and the most commonly found alkali metal, sodium. These metals get their name because of their reaction with water, as a result of which they form alkaline solutions. However, metals such as caesium (Cs) and rubidium (Rb) have a volatile interaction with water. These metals are soft, white and are seldom found in their unadulterated form in nature.

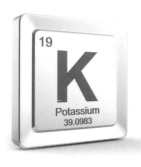

Beryllium is a steel-grey, lightweight and brittle alkaline-earth metal.

Alkaline-earth metals

Calcium, magnesium, barium and radium are all alkaline-earth metals that are found in compounds in Earth's crust. For example, beryllium (Be) is found in gemstones such as beryl and emeralds. Alkaline-earth metals react with water, although less violently than alkali metals and oxygen. Magnesium burns bright and has white ashes due to the presence of oxygen in the air. It is used to produce flares and fireworks.

Transition metals

Transition metals consist a large group of elements which include the most common metals such as copper and chromium. Some of these elements have the ability to create a magnetic field, such as nickel and iron, and the densest, naturally occurring element, osmium (Os). With the exception of mercury, which is in the liquid state at room temperature, transition metals have high melting point. They are hard metals and their electrons are capable of flowing, making them good conductors of heat and electricity.

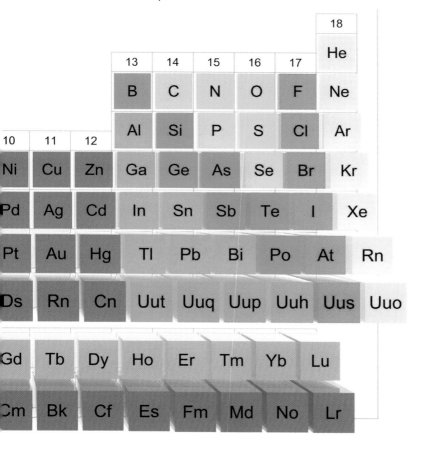

Poor and semi-metals

Metals that fall under this group are lead, tin, aluminium and bismuth. These metals are soft and have a lower melting point when compared to transition metals. These metals are extremely useful when mixed with another metals in an alloy. For example, bronze is made from an alloy of copper and tin. Semi-metals are those that have a few, but not all the properties of a metal; for example, arsenic (As), antimony (Sb) and boron (B).

Noble gases

Noble gases are odourless, colourless and unreactive to a significant extent. However, it does not mean that they do not have any properties of note. They are useful gases. The second lightest gas after hydrogen is helium. Helium does not burn. This makes it safe to use in airships and in the tanks used by deep-sea divers. All noble gases (except helium) radiate light if electricity is passed through them. Therefore, they are used for lighting.

Non-metals

This refers to the common gases found in the atmosphere, such as oxygen, nitrogen and also carbon and sulphur (S). They are poor conductors of heat and electricity, and become fragile when in the solid state. There are certain non-metals called "halogens" that form salts with other elements such as chlorine.

Chlorine gas filled in glass container.

History of the Periodic Table

Professor Dmitri Mendeleev, a Russian chemist, first published his periodic table in 1869. He then published an elaborated version in 1871. This version of the periodic table is generally regarded as the most influential and accurate one. Later, this was slightly reworked and extended by American chemist, Horace Groves Deming.

The monument honours Professor Dmitri Mendeleev. It shows his sculpture with the periodic table.

Telluric helix

In 1862, Alexandre-Emile Béguyer de Chancourtois, a French geologist, first published the basic and elementary form of the periodic table, which he called the "telluric helix". Here, the elements were arranged in a spiral on a cylinder in order of their increasing atomic weights. An English chemist named John Newlands wrote a series of papers from 1863 to 1866, where he found that when the elements were arranged in order of their increasing atomic weights, equivalent physical and similar chemical properties recurred at intervals of eight. He compared such periodicity to the octaves of music. This was called "the law of octaves".

Contributions by other scientists

Many chemists had tried their hand at classifying the elements before Mendeleev. In 1789, Antoine Lavoisier published a list of 33 chemical elements, arranging them into gases, metals, non-metals and earths. In 1817, Johann Wolfgang Dobereiner showed that the atomic weight of strontium lies midway between the weights of the elements calcium and barium. Some years later, he showed that other such "triads" exist. These are chlorine, bromine and iodine (halogens) and lithium, sodium and potassium (alkali metals).

Use in schools

Horace Groves Deming's 18 column table, first published in 1923, soon became standard study material in American schools. This was because a handout version of Deming's table was published by Merck and Company. Glenn T. Seaborg, an American chemist, won the Nobel Prize in 1951 as he had added the actinide block below the lanthanides. The award was also presented in recognition for his work on synthesising these elements.

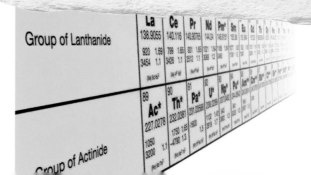

Periodic Trends

The great utility of the periodic table lies in how easily it makes predictions about the properties of a certain element based on its position with relation to some other element. Many chemical properties of elements show a certain periodicity.

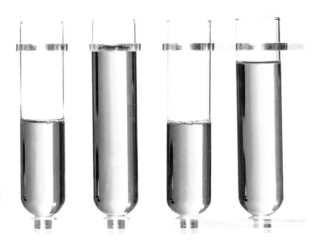

Electronegativity

Electronegativity is the measure of the tendency of an atom to attract electrons. An atom's electronegativity is affected by both, its atomic number and the distance between the valence (or outermost shell) electrons and nucleus. The higher the atomic number, the greater is the electrostatic attraction between an electron and a nucleus.

Ionisation energy

The ionisation energy of an element is the minimum energy required to displace a single electron from the outermost shell of an atom of that element in the gaseous state. It is dependent on the atomic number of the element and the size. Therefore, we see that ionisation energy increases along a period and decreases along a group. Some elements show slightly uncharacteristic ionisation energies.

Atomic radius increases

As we proceed down a group, the valence electrons will fill up higher electronic levels and the outermost shells spread further and further away from the nucleus. The intermediate electrons create a shielding or screening effect between the valence electrons and nucleus, thereby reducing the electrostatic interaction between them. Thus, these valence electrons are loosely held and the atomic radius, as a result, is large.

Atomic size decreases

Across a period, the atomic size gradually decreases. This is due to the fact that along a period, all the electrons are added to the same valence shell. However, simultaneously, the number of protons in the nucleus increases, making it more positively charged. The effect of the increasing atomic number outweighs that of the increasing electron number. Therefore, the nucleus attracts the electrons more strongly, drawing in the atom's valence shell closer to the nucleus.

The figure schematically shows the atomic size of the elements in the periodic table.

Valency

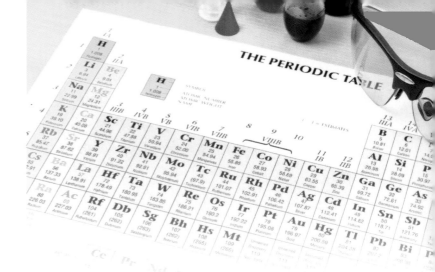

Valency is a property of an element that can estimate the number of other atoms with which the atom of the given element can bond with, simultaneously. Valence is at the very theoretical basis of the periodic table.

Theory of chemical valencies

The theory of chemical valencies may be traced back to an 1852 paper by Edward Frankland, where he used both theoretical and empirical evidence to demonstrate how atoms of certain elements would most likely bond with a given number of other atoms. Initially, the valency of an element was given by the number of univalent hydrogen atoms that it combined with.

Understanding valencies

The octet rule explains valency to a significant extent. According to this rule, all atoms aspire to the stable electronic configuration of the inert elements. Therefore, they either give away their valence electrons or bond with the requisite number of electrons to accommodate the difference. For example, elements in group one and 17 have valency one, elements in group 14 have valency four, those in group 15 have valency three and so on.

Facts about valency

In the periodic table, elements that are arranged in the same group have the same valency. The first group of elements has a valency of one, the second group has a valency of two, the third group has a valency of three and the fourth group has a valency of four. The fifth group in the periodic table has a valency of three, while the sixth group has a valency of two. The seventh group in the periodic table has a valency of one. However, the eighth group has a valency of zero.

FUN FACT

Frankland's discovery and study of the bond between atoms laid a foundation to modern day structural chemistry. He was eventually knighted for his work.

The two children are like two atoms and the apples are like electrons. They create a bond by sharing two apples, so that each has 6+2=8 shared apples.

6 apples

2 apples shared

6 apples

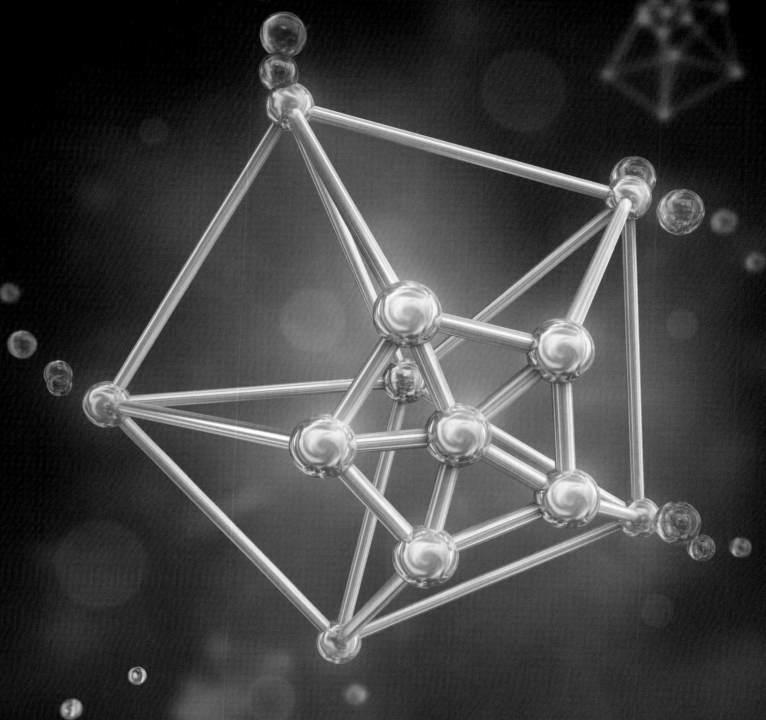

COMPOUNDS

In chemistry, a compound is a substance that is formed from the combination of two or more different elements in a way where the atoms are held together by chemical bonds that are tough to break. The resulting bond yields because of the sharing or exchange of electrons among the atoms.

The smallest, unbreakable unit of a compound is called a "molecule". The two types of chemical bonds that are common in compounds are the covalent bonds and the ionic bonds. The elements in any compound are always present in fixed ratios. Compounds can be decomposed chemically into their constituent elements.

What is a Compound?

A compound can be defined as a substance that is formed by the atoms of two or more elements reacting chemically. Iron, copper, gold, carbon and hydrogen are all elements found in nature. But water is not an element. It is composed of two atoms of hydrogen and one atom of oxygen. These types of substances are called "compounds".

Characteristics of compounds

The characteristics of chemical compounds are different from the constituent elements from which they are formed. Some characteristics of compounds are as follows:

- The elements are present in a definite proportion in a compound and this proportion cannot be changed.

- A compound can be broken up into its constituent elements by various chemical reactions. But they cannot be broken up physically or mechanically.

- Compounds possess a definite and fixed chemical structure.

- Many types of bonds are found between the elements in a compound. These are covalent bonds, ionic bonds, coordinate bonds and metallic bonds.

- Most compounds are formed naturally as the elements are combined as a result of gaining stability.

Compounds have a specific chemical formula

Compounds are designated with a specific chemical formula. The hydrogen element is shown by the formula H_2 and oxygen by O_2. Water, a compound formed by hydrogen and oxygen, is shown by the formula H_2O. Compounds differ greatly from mixtures. The properties of a compound are completely different from its constituent elements. A mixture has the properties of its constituents. The constituents of a mixture can be separated by simple physical methods, whereas we cannot separate the constituents of a compound. Compounds are widely used in our daily life. They range from drinking water, salt, baking powder, bleaching powder and sugar to the gasoline that we use as fuel; the list is endless.

FUN FACT

We know that the chemical formula of water is H_2O. However, how many of us know its chemical name? The chemical name of water is dihydrogen monoxide denoting two atoms of hydrogen and one atom of oxygen in a molecule of water.

Types of compounds.

Classification and Structure of Compounds

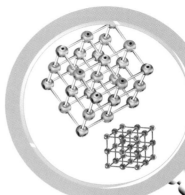

Chemical compounds encompass a wide spectrum of substances; there are multiple ways of organising and classifying them. A primary way is by finding which compounds are formed by living organisms and which are not. The compounds that are synthesised as a product of the activity of living organisms are called organic compounds and those that are not, are called inorganic compounds. This classification has a number of notable exceptions, hence, they are now defined as compounds with significant carbon–carbon bonds.

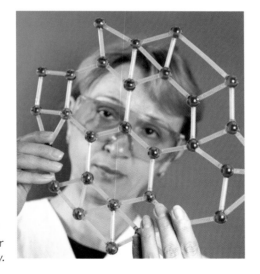

Scientist studying molecular geometry.

Chemical structure

The chemical structure of compounds can be analysed on three levels: molecular geometry (the structure of the microscopic molecules that constitute the compound), electronic structure (the configuration and the state of motion of the electrons forming the chemical bonds) and crystal structure (the comparatively large-scale systematic arrangement of the groups of molecules that recreate the entire macroscopic structure of the compound on repetition). On the microscopic level, it is often best approximated by its molecular geometry, which can be of many types, depending on the atoms forming the molecule, that is, their respective sizes, electronegativity, atomic number, etc.

Carbon dioxide (CO_2) is a naturally occurring chemical compound composed of oxygen atoms.

VSEPR

As per the quantum mechanical theory called the VSEPR, the bond length and the bond angle parameters can be used to classify molecular geometry into approximately 18 groups, such as linear, trigonal planar (carbon dioxide), trigonal pyramidal (boron trifluoride), octahedral (sulphur hexafluoride), etc.

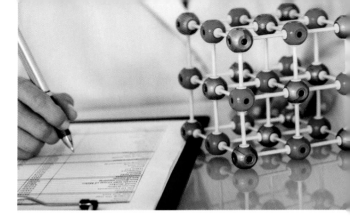

Organic and Inorganic Compounds

The field of chemistry that analyses organic compounds is called organic chemistry. The question that arises is – what are organic compounds? Compounds can be classified into organic and inorganic compounds. Organic compounds possess at least one carbon atom covalently bonded to another atom, preferably hydrogen, oxygen or nitrogen. All the compounds in which the C–H bond is found are called organic compounds, while the others are called inorganic compounds.

The definition

There is no accurate definition for organic compounds. Initially, it was believed that all compounds containing carbon atoms are called organic compounds; but there were many exceptions, like metal carbonyl, carbonates and cyanides, that were considered to be inorganic compounds. Subsequently, the "C–H" definition was found to be correct to a major extent. Organic compounds can be classified on the basis of the presence of the hitherto atoms or on their occurrence, namely, natural or synthetic. These compounds can also be classified into aliphatic and aromatic compounds. Aliphatic compounds are those possessing an open chain (C–H) structure and aromatic compounds are those possessing a carbon ring.

Methane is one of the simplest organic compounds. This image shows a methane burner with a flame used for cooking.

FUN FACT

Organic chemistry can be understood by studying carbon in nature as it is present in all the living beings present on Earth. Carbon is a non-metal.

Diamond is an inorganic compound.

The difference between organic and inorganic compounds

The presence of carbon atoms in organic compounds is the basic difference between organic and inorganic compounds. Organic compounds are mainly associated with living organisms. These primarily include nucleic acids, carbohydrates, fats, proteins, enzymes, DNA and methane. Inorganic compounds primarily include salt, diamond, carbon dioxide and metallic substances.

Inorganic Compounds

Inorganic chemistry is the study of elements and their properties from the periodic table, as well as the reactions and compounds formed among them. Fundamentally, all compounds that lack the presence of carbon atoms are called inorganic compounds. Berzelius depicted inorganic compounds as those that are not biological in origin and are inanimate.

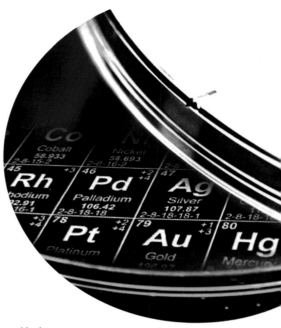

A fire alarm that detects carbon monoxide.

Nitrous oxide is also used in surgery and during pregnancy.

Some of them are listed below:

- Compounds like sodium, chloride, phosphate ions, carbonic acids, nitrogen, water, oxygen, carbon dioxide, etc., are essential for life.

Metal halide lamp.

- Coordination compounds have a wide variety of applications in various fields like photography, electroplating of silver, as oxidising agents, in estimating the hardness of water, in extraction, as dyeing agents, etc.

- Hard compounds like aluminium, copper, steel and bronze are used for making kitchen utensils.

- Oxides are also very useful. Nitrous oxide is also known as laughing gas. Water is a universal solvent.

- Many halides are used in greenhouse lamps and street lights. Sodium chloride is used in the common salt that we eat. Potassium chloride is used during cardiac surgery and in medicines.

- Carbonates are used in carbonated beverages, soaps, detergents, etc. They are also used in surgeries.

- The fields of applications of inorganic compounds are not limited and range from mining to medicine, from agriculture to fuel industries.

Oxides

Oxides are a commonly found and important class of chemical compounds on Earth. They are made of molecules that have at least one oxygen atom and one other element, if not more. Oxygen is a highly electronegative element, which means that it has a high affinity to bond with other substances. The process by which an element or compound reacts with oxygen to form an oxide is called oxidation.

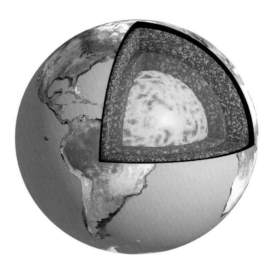

Oxides have many uses, from fire-proofing to vulcanising of rubber to being used as a colour pigment.

Uses of oxides

Some of the compounds that we encounter most commonly in our daily life are oxides. For example, the principal waste product of human respiration and an important constituent of plant nutrition is an oxide – carbon dioxide (CO_2). The reddish rust that develops on iron poles when exposed to open air for long periods is a hydrated oxide – ferric oxide (Fe_2O_3). Other important oxides are water (H_2O), without which life on Earth would have been impossible, calcium oxide (CaO), which is used to make mortar and concrete that holds buildings together, and nitrous oxide (N_2O), which is used as an anaesthetic during medical operations and for many other purposes.

Oxidation of metals and non-metals

It is possible for metals and non-metals to attain their highest oxidation states (donate their maximum number of available valence electrons) in compounds with oxygen. Ionic oxides (compounds that contain the O_2) anion is formed by alkali metals and alkaline earth metals, as well as the transition metals and post-transition metals (in their lower oxidation states).

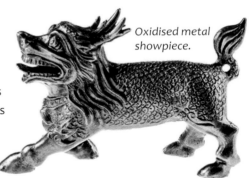

Oxidised metal showpiece.

Rusty oil lantern.

Transformation from ionic to covalent bonds

Metals with high oxidation states form oxides whose bonds have a more covalent nature. Non-metals also form covalent oxides that are usually molecular in character. As you navigate the periodic table from the metals on the left to the non-metals on the right, a variation from ionic to covalent bonds in oxides is observed. A similar variation is observed in the reaction of oxides with water and the resulting acid-base character of the products. When ionic metal oxides react with water they produce hydroxides (compounds that contain an OH– ion). Most non-metal oxides react with water to produce acids .

Ores and Minerals

Chemical compounds are not found in their pure state in nature due to a large number of adulterating influences present in the natural environment. Instead, they are found in other crystalline naturally occurring inorganic compounds called minerals. These minerals are generally formed by large-scale geological processes rather than through the actions of living organisms.

All about the ore

Ores are a special category of minerals; they usually have a high percentage of a certain element, usually a metal, as one of their constituents. As such, it is often economically viable to isolate pure elements from particular ores rather than just any mineral that contains the element. For example, while aluminium is present in both clay as well as bauxite, only bauxite is used as an ore of aluminium because it is feasible to extract aluminium from it easily, cheaply and in large quantities. Therefore, every ore is a mineral, but every mineral is not an ore. Some very important ores are galena (PbS) for lead, acanthite (Ag_2S) for silver and magnetite (Fe_3O_4) for iron. The process of extracting pure elements from ores is called mining.

Difference between ores and minerals

- Ore comprises minerals; thus all the ores are minerals, but not all the minerals are ores.

- Ores are mineral deposits, whereas a mineral is a natural form in which the metals exist.

- Ores are used to extract metals economically. Therefore, in ores, a significant amount of metals are present.

- Ores can be defined as having an economical importance, whereas minerals are more scientifically important.

A crane digging at a mining site for ore.

Basics of Ions

Atoms are the basic unit of an element. Electrons that revolve around the atoms in a circular path are sometimes lost or gained. This is when the atoms become positively or negatively charged and a positive or negative ion is formed. Thus, we can say that a charged atom, group of atoms or molecule is called an ion. It gets charged because the number of protons are not equal to the number of electrons.

Types of ions

There are two types of ions:

- **Cation** – When an atom loses an electron, it gets positively charged. When this happens, a positively charged ion called cation is formed. For example, Na^+, Ca^+ and Fe^+.

- **Anion** – When an atom gains an electron, it gets negatively charged. When this happens, a negatively charged ion called anion is formed. For example, Cl^- and P^-.

Atom is Neutral	Negatively Charged Atom, Negative Ion, (Anion)	Positively Charged Atom, Positive Ion, (Kation)
6 Protons 6 Neutrons 6 Electrons	5 Protons 6 Neutrons 6 Electrons	6 Protons 6 Neutrons 5 Electrons
Same number of protons and electrons	More electrons then protons	More protons then electrons

Types of Ions.

Classification of ions

Ions are classified depending on the number of atoms present, for example, monatomic, if one atom is present and polyatomic, if two or more atoms are present. English experimental physicist Michael Faraday introduced the term "ion" in 1834. If we look around, ions can be found everywhere, from thundering and lightning to salt dissolving in water. How we perceive the things that happen around us depends upon us.

Charge of an ion

In order to figure out what the charge of an ion should be, one must remember the following:

- The number of charges on an ion formed by a metal is equal to the group number of the metal.

- The number of charges on an ion formed by a non-metal is equal to the group number minus eight.

Ionic bonds

When metals react with non-metals, there is a transfer of electrons from metal atoms to the non-metal atoms, forming ions. As a result, an ionic compound is formed. Let us consider some reactions between metals and non-metals:

Sodium + chlorine = sodium chloride

Magnesium + oxygen = magnesium oxide

The metal atoms give electrons to the non-metal atoms in each of these reactions; the metal atoms become positive ions and the non-metal ones become negative ions. When a non-metal forms a bond, the ending name changes. In these reactions, the ending is "–ide", showing that only one element is present. If the ending was "–ate", it means that oxygen is also present in the molecule of the element.

FUN FACT

While mentioning an ionic compound, the positive ion is named first, followed by the negative ion. That is why table salt is written as $(Na^+$ and $Cl^-)$ NaCl.

All batteries run on ionic reactions.

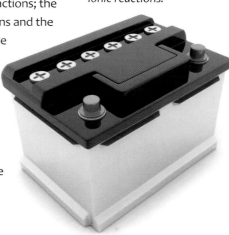

Ionic Structures and their Relevance

An atom consists of three types of particles: protons, neutrons and electrons. The negatively charged electrons, revolving around the atom in circular paths called orbits, can be very easily subtracted or added to an atom. When this addition or subtraction of electrons from an atom occurs, charged particles called ions are formed. The numerous arrangements of these ions form different ionic structures having different physical, chemical and electrical properties.

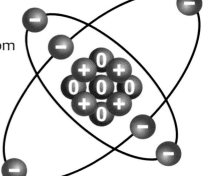

Example of ionic compounds

Magnesium oxide (MgO), calcium chloride ($CaCl_2$), sodium fluoride (NaF) and potassium oxide (K_2O) are a few examples of ionic compounds. These compounds are very easy to identify as they are metal and non-metal bonded compounds. When an atom loses its electrons, it becomes positively charged, forming a positively charged ion and when electrons are gained by an atom, a negatively charged ion is formed. The attraction between the positively and negatively charged ions form ionic compounds having different ionic structures. Different arrangements of ions are possible to create ionic structures.

Pink crystal salt.

Abstract geometric lattice with the scope of molecules.

Co-ordination number

The number of cations (negatively charged ions) around each anion (positively charged ions) is called its co-ordination number. In addition, the coordination number depends on the stoichiometry (the relationship between the substances forming a compound) and the size of the atoms; for example, Na^+Cl^-, in which Na^+ has a co-ordination number of six as there are six anions around a sodium cation. The bonding forces between the positive and negative ions in ionic structures result in different properties. Few properties of the ionic compounds are that they have high melting and boiling points due to the strong attraction between the ions. They have high enthalpies of fusion and vaporisation, again due to bonding forces. They are usually tough to break. Ionic solids like Na^+Cl^- do not conduct electricity, though they can conduct it in an aqueous solution or molten form. They mostly exist in crystalline form, such as KCl.

Lattice

Metals form structures that are packed spheres. The different arrangements of atoms, ions or molecules in solid state substances are called lattice. Mostly, in ionic compounds, anions are larger than the cations. In such cases, we consider a close packed arrangement of anions. These arrangements are cubic close packing (ccp) and hexagonal close packing (hcp). The radius ratio determines the position of the cation in the ionic structures. A radius ratio is defined as the ratio of the radius of the cation to the radius of an ion.

Process of Ionisation

The formation of ions by the loss and gain of electrons is called ionisation. The amount of energy required to remove the electrons from a neutral atom in the gaseous state is called ionisation energy. The unit of ionisation energy is not fixed. There can be many levels of ionisation energy; first level "i1", second level "i2" and so on.

Ionisation energy

The energy required to remove the second electron from an atom is more than removing the first electron. Electrons that have small orbits and are closer to the protons experience more force of attraction. Thus, they require more ionisation energy. Hence, it is concluded that as we move right in the periodic table, ionisation energy gradually increases. It decreases as we move from top to the bottom in the periodic table because the nuclear radius decreases and hence, more energy is required to remove the electrons. The process is very commonly used in numerous instruments in the research field, like mass spectrometer, and the medical field, like radiotherapy.

Electron capture ionisation

Anions are produced when free electrons collide with any atom and get trapped in the barrier caused by the electric potential, by releasing the excess energy. This process is commonly known as electron capture ionisation. Cations are formed by transferring the energy to the bound electron to release it. Threshold energy is required to knock out the electrons and is known as the ionisation potential.

An ionic chamber.

FUN FACT

Crystallisation occurs because of ionisation as well. When water is supersaturated with alum, a lot of ions are formed that float freely. In this saturated solution, if you were to suspend a thread, the alum ions would deposit on it, forming a string of crystals.

Ion formation.

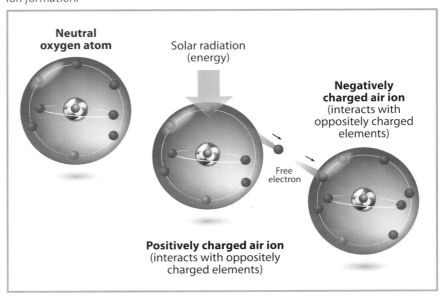

Neutral oxygen atom

Solar radiation (energy)

Negatively charged air ion (interacts with oppositely charged elements)

Free electron

Positively charged air ion (interacts with oppositely charged elements)

CHEMICAL
REACTIONS

The atom is the smallest unit that any element is made up of. A bunch of atoms is called molecules. Transformation of molecules from one form to another is called a chemical reaction. A chemical reaction occurs when two different molecules of two different elements interact with each other. The bonding forces that bind two atoms are broken and new bonding forces are created, resulting in the formation of a whole new compound having totally different properties as compared to the substances with which it was originally made up.

Endothermic Reaction

The reactions that absorb heat or energy from their surroundings are called endothermic reactions. When they absorb heat from the surrounding, the surrounding temperature decreases. A simple example of endothermic reactions is the process of photosynthesis. This is where plants prepare their own food by taking in atmospheric carbon dioxide and giving out oxygen. This not only creates oxygen for everyone but also brings a drop in the temperature of the surroundings.

Basic principle

The process of photosynthesis requires heat and light energy from the Sun. It is said that we must not go near plants during the night as they release carbon dioxide, which is harmful for human beings. The binding forces between two atoms of an element or compound is so strong that they cannot be easily broken, so during a chemical reaction, they absorb heat energy that breaks the bonding forces and forms new products. Endothermic reactions are not spontaneous reactions. Work needs to be done for these types of reactions.

In endothermic reactions, the change in the temperature of products is much higher than the reactants. That is why they absorb heat. Enthalpies of both products and reactants are greater than zero.

Melting of ice.

Application

When it is very hot and the Sun shines brightly, we see that the water from lakes and ponds begins to evaporate. When this happens, the water is actually absorbing the heat from the environment in order to bring about the evaporation of water. That is the reason why the hotter the days, the cooler are the nights. The water vapour in air contributes to the temperature drop as well.

Water evaporation.

Endothermic reaction formula

A system of reactants that absorbs heat from the surroundings in an endothermic reaction causes cooling as the heat in the products is higher than the heat in the reactants of the system.

$$N_2(g) + O_2(g) = 2NO(g) \qquad (\Delta H = +180.5 \text{ kJ} > 0)$$

$$C(s) + 2S(s) = CS_2(l) \qquad (\Delta H = +92.0 \text{ kJ} > 0)$$

As the enthalpies of these reactions are greater than zero, they are endothermic reactions.

Exothermic Reaction

When a chemical reaction between two substances occurs, energy is released in the form of light, heat, sound or electricity. When large amounts of heat or energy are released after a chemical reaction, such reactions are called exothermic reactions. As exothermic reactions release heat, they raise the temperature of the surroundings around them.

What is an exothermic reaction?

An exothermic reaction is any reaction that releases energy during chemical reactions. The word exothermic can be broken into "exo", which means to exit, and "therm", which means heat. The opposite of an exothermic reaction is an endothermic one, where "endo" means to absorb or let in. In an exothermic reaction, the energy released can be in multiple forms, including heat, light, sound or electricity. This is because when old bonds of the reactants are broken in exothermic reactions, they hold the two atoms together and energy is released in different forms. Based on the reactants that are involved, the heat released can be more or less; however, there will be a certain output of energy for certain.

Exothermic reactions

Exothermic and endothermic reactions result in energy level differences and thereby differences in heat (ΔH), the sum of all potential and kinetic energies. ΔH is calculated by the system, not the surrounding environment in a reaction. A system that releases heat to the surroundings has a negative ΔH by convention as the enthalpy of the products is lower than the enthalpy of the reactants of the system.

$$C(s) + O_2(g) = CO_2(g) \qquad (\Delta H = -393.5 \text{ kJ})$$

$$H_2(g) + 1/2\ O_2(g) = H_2O(l) \qquad (\Delta H = -285.8 \text{ kJ})$$

The enthalpies of these reactions are less than zero and are therefore exothermic reactions. For example, when a nail rusts, heat is released into the surroundings.

Rusting nails.

Snowing, precipitation.

Kinetics of Reaction

Chemical kinetics is taking into consideration the rate of the reaction. It is defined as the study of the rate at which a chemical reaction occurs. As it examines how different conditions affect a chemical reaction, it can also be called reaction kinetics. The speed at which products are formed in a chemical reaction is affected by many factors like temperature of the surroundings, catalyst and air pressure.

Adding salt to ice helps it to melt faster.

Rate of reactions

Rate of reactions is the rate of change in concentrations or the amount of either reactants or products. With respect to reaction rates, we may deal with average rates, instantaneous rates or initial rates depending on the experimental conditions. Thermodynamics and kinetics are two major factors that influence reaction rates. The study of energy gained or released in chemical reactions is called thermodynamics. However, thermodynamic data has no direct correlation with reaction rates, for which the kinetic factor is perhaps more important.

Factors affecting kinetics

The rate of reaction is the rate at which the concentrations of reactants and products change. Catalysts play a very important role in determining the speed of the reactions. These are the substances which help in completing the reaction faster. By introducing a catalyst, the rate of reaction increases. Furthermore, temperature acts as a catalyst. Higher the temperature, the faster is the rate of reaction.

Hydrochloric acid (HCl)

Hydrochloric acid is a strong acid. It ionises almost completely in water. It is colourless in appearance but has a very strong, irritating odour. It exists in liquid form. It is formed by dissolving hydrogen chloride (a colourless gas) in water. As soon as the gas comes in contact with water, it sinks and mixes well with it.

A physical example of external factors affecting a process.

FUN FACT

Hydrochloric acid is sometimes called the "workhouse" chemical because of its many applications. It is used to make various products like batteries and fireworks. It is also used in the processes that make sugar and gelatin.

Order of Reaction

Changing the concentration of the reactants usually changes the rate of the reaction. A rate equation shows this effect mathematically. The order of reaction is a part of the rate equation. Orders of reaction are always calculated by performing experiments. One cannot deduce anything regarding the order of a reaction just by looking at the equation for the reaction.

A scientist adding a catalyst to a reaction.

Different orders of reaction

First order

If a reaction rate depends on a single reactant and the value of the exponent is one, then the reaction is said to be first order. In organic chemistry, first order reactions are the class of SN1 (nucleophilic substitution unimolecular) reactions. Another class of first order reactions are radioactive decay processes.

Second order

A second order reaction is when the overall order is two. The rate of a second order reaction may be proportional to one concentration squared or to the product of two concentrations. The second type has examples such as the class of SN2 (nucleophilic substitution bimolecular) reactions.

Pseudo-first order

If the concentration of a reactant stays constant, its concentration can be included in the rate constant, obtaining a pseudo first order rate equation. An example for pseudo first order is the hydrolysis of sucrose in acid solution.

Zero order

In zero order reactions, the reaction rate is independent of the concentration of a reactant; so that altering its concentration has no effect on the rate of the reaction. An example of zero order reaction is the biological oxidation of ethanol to acetaldehyde by the enzyme liver alcohol dehydrogenase in ethanol.

Redox Reaction

The word "redox" is made up of two words; reduction and oxidation. Redox reaction doesn't have a meaning on its own; it's a combination of oxidation and reduction process. In redox reaction, gain as well as loss of electrons occurs within substances. Oxidation and reduction reactions can occur alone too and are called half reactions, and these two half reactions combine to form one full redox reaction.

Rusted iron, oxidation of iron.

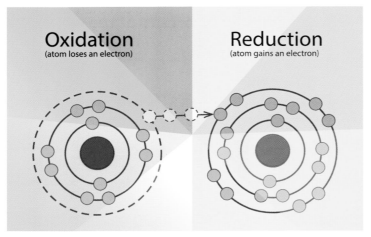

Oxidation
(atom loses an electron)

Reduction
(atom gains an electron)

Diagrammatic representation of a redox reaction.

Redox pairs

Oxidation-reduction reactions are similar to acid-base reactions. Oxidising agents are those substances, which gain electrons and reducing agents are those substances, which lose electrons. Both oxidising and reducing agents form redox pairs.

Applications

Redox reactions are very useful in industrial processes. They are used to extract iron from the ore and also to coat the discs. For example, when we drive in our car the gasoline (which is made up of heptanes) in our car gets burned. In this reaction, the heptane atoms get oxidised and oxygen atoms are reduced. The process of photosynthesis is also an example of a redox reaction. This happens in two parts. The first part is when the oxygen present in the water that is absorbed by the plant is oxidised with the help of sunlight. The second part is where the remaining H ions from the H_2O molecules react with the carbon in the CO_2 molecules and reduce it. This is an example of a redox reaction that is carried out by the agents of nature.

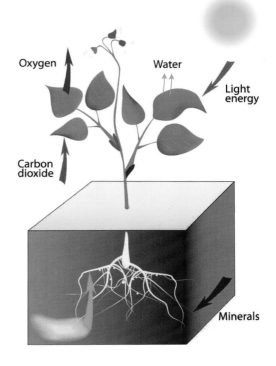

Oxygen

Water

Light energy

Carbon dioxide

Minerals

Reduction

Reduction is one half of a redox reaction. It is defined as the gain of electrons and decrease in the oxidation state. It is defined in terms of hydrogen, that is, gain of hydrogen, which is exactly the opposite of oxidation. The word reduction refers to a loss in weight, especially the loss of oxygen atoms. Reducing agents are those substances which lose electrons in a chemical reaction.

Sodium reduces silver ions to form silver.

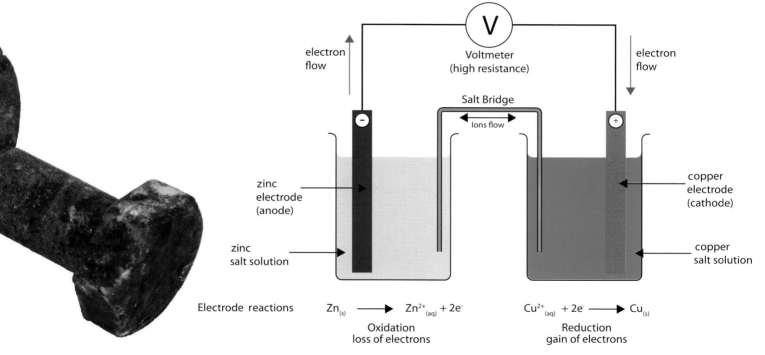

electron flow

Voltmeter (high resistance)

electron flow

Salt Bridge

Ions flow

−

+

zinc electrode (anode)

copper electrode (cathode)

zinc salt solution

copper salt solution

Electrode reactions

$Zn_{(s)} \longrightarrow Zn^{2+}_{(aq)} + 2e^-$

Oxidation
loss of electrons

$Cu^{2+}_{(aq)} + 2e^- \longrightarrow Cu_{(s)}$

Reduction
gain of electrons

Natural reduction

A simple, natural example showing oxidation process is the rusting of iron. When the iron surface reacts with the oxygen a chemical named "rust" is formed. We largely consider the rusting of any metal as oxidation and this is correct. However, the other part of this reaction is that the oxygen in the air gets reduced. This second part of the reaction counts as a reduction reaction. Chemically speaking, the oxygen atom gains electrons from the iron atoms and gets reduced.

Application

Since reduction means the gain of electrons, the major application of reduction reaction is found in the battery industry. Whether it is the little round cell that you insert in the back of your watch or the AA batteries that you put in the remote or the huge one that goes in the car, all batteries work on the principle of reduction reaction. Since the purpose of a battery is to create electricity, it works mainly by the transfer of electrons from one place to another. A battery consists of two poles, the cathode (positively charged) and the anode (negatively charged). This is surrounded by electrolyte, a liquid full of free flowing electrons. When the circuit is connected, the electrons accumulate at the anode.

Reversible Reaction

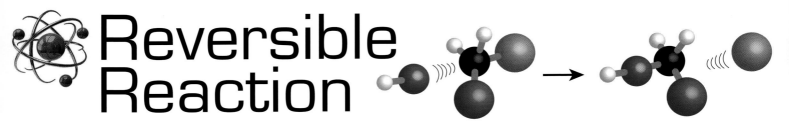

Chemical reactions form new products from the reactants. Reactions in which we are able to reverse the process and able to get the reactants back from the products are called reversible reactions. It was earlier believed that all the reactions are irreversible, but later on, with new discoveries and new concepts, it was found that it is possible to get the reactants back from the products after the chemical reaction is done.

The duality

All the reversible reactions, when written chemically, contain two arrows in the middle of the product and the reactants that face both sides. This is different than the unidirectional arrow that you will find in the middle of irreversible reactions. This type of equation shows that the reactants can't be obtained back once they have reacted with one another. The two arrows in the reversible reactions denote that even after the reaction has taken place, it is still possible for the original reactants to be obtained from it. However, they require the breaking up of the bonding forces between the atoms. In order to easily break the forces, heat energy, pressure and many other changes are introduced in the chemical reaction. This additional energy causes the molecules of the product to become unstable and break into the molecules of the reactants.

The haemoglobin that reacts with oxygen to carry it to the rest of the body is a reversible reaction.

The discovery

A scientist named Berthollet gave the concept of reversible reactions in 1803. He knew that calcium chloride and sodium carbonate react to form sodium chloride (salt) but one day, beside salt lakes, he found the formation of sodium carbonate, which was formed by the reverse reaction of the salt left after the evaporation of lake water and calcium carbonate.

Sodium carbonate deposits after the evaporation of the lake.

FORCE

Force is described by intuitive concepts, such as a push or pull. In physics, a force is any interaction that tends to change the motion of objects. In contrast, a force may cause the object with a certain mass to change its velocity (which involves moving the object from the state of rest). Since force exhibits both magnitude as well as direction, it is a vector quantity.

Force is measured in the SI unit of Newton and represented by the symbol F. Force helps objects to slow down or accelerate. Ice-skating, skydiving or any other physical activity, all use force.

Besides a simple push or pull, force also has further applications. Force can be of different types, magnitude or direction. In physics, force refers to the interaction between two objects to change the motion of an object.

Types of Forces

In science, force is not limited to only one definition, but is generally defined as something that causes the motion of an object. There can be two cases on the application of force. One case can be when force is applied to a stationary body; it sets the stationary body in motion in the direction of the force applied. In the second case, the body could be moving with uniform velocity and with the application of force, it gets accelerated in the same direction as earlier.

Types of forces

An object is simultaneously affected by different types of physical forces like thrust, drag and torque. Force can fundamentally be of three types; nuclear, electromagnetic and gravitational. As a consequence of these forces, some other forces are generated, which are called non-fundamental forces. These include normal force, friction, tension, elastic force, fictitious force, torque and applied force, among others. Applied force is the force applied to an object or body, where a frictional force is used to stop a body in motion.

Calculating force

The interaction between two objects to change the motion of an object is called force. As this interaction stops, there remains no force. Sir Isaac Newton, with his laws of motion, and Einstein, with his theory of relativity, made the concept of force clear. Force can be calculated by,

$$F = m \times a$$

where, m = mass of the object, which is considered constant and a = acceleration.

FUN FACT

The unit of measure for force is newton (N). This is indeed named after Sir Isaac Newton, who laid down the Newton's laws of motion.

Monorail works on electromagnetic force.

Stretch and Pull

Elasticity is the ability of a distorted material body to return to its original shape and size when the forces causing the distortion are eliminated. A body with this ability is said to perform elastically. The force you use to stretch an elastic body is the same with which the body snaps back to its original size. That's why a rubber band hurts!

Elastic limit

Many solid materials exhibit elastic behaviour; however, there is a limit to the amount of force and distortion till which the elastic recovery is possible for any given material. Elastic limit is the maximum stress or force per unit area that a solid object can withstand before the start of permanent distortion. Beyond this limit, stress causes a material to yield or flow. The elastic limit denotes the end of elastic behaviour for these objects and the beginning of plastic behaviour. For most fragile materials, stress beyond the elastic limit results in a fracture. If you consider different types of rubbers, some rubbers have a high elastic limit; for example, a balloon. You can blow it up to a certain extent and yet, it will retain its original shape when deflated. However, consider a rubber band. If you try to stretch it to the size of a balloon, it may snap. This is because its elastic limit is lower than that of a balloon.

Girl doing elastic rope exercise.

Variation in elastic limit

The elastic limit varies from object to object. Some forms of rubber can be stretched up to 1,000 per cent of their original size. In contrast, a steel wire can be stretched by only about 1 per cent of its original length. This is because their structures are different and the tensile force required for elastic extension in rubber is less than that required for steel.

The molecules in a piece of elastic are coiled. When the elastic is pulled, the molecules uncoil and the elastic stretches. When released, the molecules coil again and the elastic comes back to its original shape.

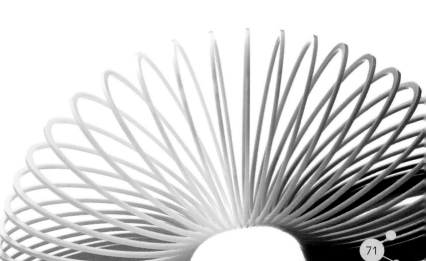

Turning Forces

The turning effect by a force around a fixed point or pivot is called a moment. For example, this could be a door opening around a fixed hinge or a spanner turning around a fixed nut. The size of a movement depends on two factors: the size of the force applied and the perpendicular distance from the pivot to the line of action of the force.

Force requirement

Why is less force used to open a door when we push it at the side furthest from the hinge rather than at the side closest to the hinge? Pushing a door open closer to the hinge requires more force to be exerted because the distance of the force from the hinge is smaller.

Now consider opening the door by pushing towards the outside of the door, the point furthest away from the hinge. It requires lesser force because the distance of the point of force applied is further away from the pivot point, that is the hinge.

When a body under the influence of a net external force is rotated about a pivot, the body tends to move in the direction in which the force is applied. Examples of the turning effect of force are the force applied to a door knob that makes it open on its hinge and a driver steering the wheel by applying a force on its rim.

Balancing moments

When an object is not turning around a pivot, the total clockwise moment should be exactly balanced by the total anti-clockwise moment. It is said that the opposing moments are balanced, where the sum of the clockwise moments equals to the sum of the anti-clockwise moments. Let us take the example of a see-saw. It has a pivot in the middle. The person on the right exerts a force downward that causes a clockwise moment. The person on the left exerts a force downward that causes an anti-clockwise moment. If both the people have similar weights and sit at equal distances from the pivot, then the see-saw will balance. This is because the total clockwise moment is balanced by the total anti-clockwise moment.

However, the see-saw can still balance if the people weigh differently. To do this, the person who weighs more must sit closer to the pivot. This reduces the size of the moment, so the opposing moments get balanced again.

A see-saw can still balance if the people weigh differently.

Tension

When we stretch an object, a force called tension is generated as in a spring; it is the opposite of compression. In physics, the best example is that of the tension in a rope and pulley system. This is a force that is transmitted along a string, wire, rope or cable that is imagined as a weightless, frictionless object that cannot be broken or stretched when it is pulled tightly by the forces at opposite ends.

Importance of tension

Similar to all forces, tension can hasten objects or cause them to bend. Being able to calculate tension is an important skill for physics students, as well as for engineers and architects. They need to know if the tension on a given rope or cable can withstand the strain caused by the weight of the object before yielding and breaking in order to construct safe and strong buildings.

Uses of tension

This can be better understood by simply taking the example of an object being pulled by a rope. We do not apply force on an object directly, but it is applied through the rope. Here, the object being pulled also exerts an equal and opposite force. The magnitude of the force remains directly proportional to the tension magnitude. If objects are placed at both ends, there are two possibilities. Either the acceleration is zero and the system is at equilibrium, or there is some force and acceleration.

Tension is created in the rope when playing tug of war.

Is it a force?

Weightlifter

It is debatable whether tension is a type of force, but it has the SI unit of Newton. "Tension" as a force has many applications in our day-to-day life. Even in biological science, it has many uses, such as:

1. Cell membrane tension causes changes in the cell shape and its motility.

2. Tension in the land causes rocks to break down.

3. In DNA, it is found that tension stabilises the chromosomes.

4. Tension works in the body of a weightlifter while practising with weights.

Torsion

Torsion is a type of force that can be called as the twisting of an object. It can be defined as a moment applied along the longitudinal axis of any object. On the upper and lower parts of an object, force is applied equally in opposite directions. It is measured in Newton metres (N.m) or foot-pound force (ft.lbf).

Rear wheels of a car.

Applications of torsion

Torsion has many important applications. Some of them are as follows:

1. Shafts loaded with torsion have application in engineering. It is used in the rear wheels of automobiles and in almost all rotating machineries.

2. It comes to use when we tighten a nut using a wrench.

3. It is also useful for opening the cap of a bottle.

4. A wide variety of torsion springs are used for door handles and clipboards.

5. The concept of torsion is applied in running shoes to avoid the chances of foot injuries for runners.

Effects of torsion

The effects of a torsional load applied to a bar are given as follows:

1. To impart an angular displacement of one end of a cross-section with respect to the other.

2. To setup shear stresses on any cross-section of the bar perpendicular to its axis.

FUN FACT

A catapult works because of the force of torsion. A rubber band and paper clip act as a simplification of the process. When the band is pulled back, torsion propels the clip into motion.

Unscrewing a bottle cap is an example of torsion.

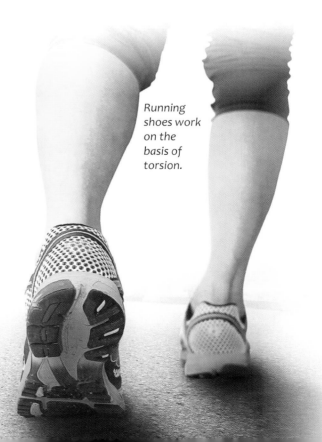

Running shoes work on the basis of torsion.

Torque

Torque refers to the measure of how much a force acting on an object causes that object to rotate. The object rotates about its axis, which is called the pivot point "O". The force is denoted as "F". The distance between the pivot point and the point where the force acts is termed as the moment arm, it is denoted by "r". Note that this distance, r, is also a vector and points from the axis of the rotation to the point where the force acts.

How it works?

Consider a heavy box on the ground that you want to turn. You can either push it or take a wrench and try to turn the box. It depends on the length of the wrench and the force required to turn that box. The longer the wrench, the lesser the force that will be required. This force is called torque. It can be defined as a force used to rotate or turn things. Torque is the product of the lever arm distance and the force applied. The symbol of torque is τ. Torque depends on the force applied, the length of the lever arm and the angle between the force applied and the lever arm. The length of the lever arm is an important factor. Choosing it appropriately can greatly reduce the amount of force that is applied. The unit of torque is Newton Metre (N•m). A crowbar, used to open jammed doors or boxes that have been nailed shut, works on the principles of torque.

Application of torque

There are many applications where torque is very important, some are given as follows:

1. Levers, pulleys, gears and other simple machines.
2. Automobiles.
3. Hand pumps and doors.

Torque force is applied to change the tyre with a wheel wrench.

Stress

Stress is the physical quantity used to express the internal forces that the neighbouring particles of any continuous material exert on each other. Stress and strain are very closely related. Strain is the result of stress and any internal movement because of stress is strain.

How is it expressed?

Mathematically, stress is measured as the force per unit area. Thus, the unit of stress becomes Newton per square metre, which is also called a pascal. The area that is used in stress is the cross-sectional area. Strain on the other hand is the change in the length of a certain continuous material divided by the original length. So, strain has no unit and is simply the ratio. Therefore, if you stretch a rubber band, you can easily calculate the strain on it by comparing its initial length with the change in its length.

Importance of stress

Stress and strain are very important for measuring the elasticity of a material. The stress versus strain graph tells us if a material is brittle, ductile or elastic. The very fundamental law that relates stress and strain is called the Hooke's law. Hooke's law states that stress is directly proportional to the strain. The slope of the linear region, that is, the constant for the proportionality is known as Young's modulus.

Different material strength

A ductile material fails at a much higher strain as compared to a brittle material. The area under the curve is called the toughness of the material, which is basically a measure of the ability of the material to absorb energy before breaking when external stress is applied. Thus, the toughness of the ductile material is much higher than that of the brittle material.

Stress force in pole vault.

Pressure

Pressure is a physical quantity derived from force and area. Pressure is normally expressed as the force exerted per unit area. This means that the force or the component of force that is applied perpendicularly to a certain area is the force in that area. Force is measured in Newton and the area in meter square. Thus, the pressure becomes Newton per metre square.

How it works?

The unit of pressure is called pascal. Pressure is also measured in relation to the atmospheric pressure. The other commonly used unit of pressure is Psi, which refers to pound per square inch. Pressure is also measured in nanometric units.

Exact and opposite reaction

Pressure is highly dependent on area. For example, if you push your thumb against the wall, the wall will not be damaged. However, if you push a board pin with the same amount of force, it might penetrate the wall. Pressure acts equally on all surfaces. It comes from Newton's third law of motion. Hence, when you are pushing that pin into the wall, the pin is also exerting pressure on your finger. However, because the head of the pin has a larger area, the same force gets distributed over a larger area and thereby does not hurt your finger.

Water pressure used for cleaning.

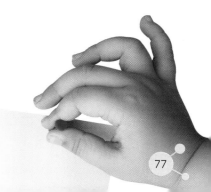

The more the weight, the higher the pressure.

Momentum

Momentum is the result of the second law of motion as proposed by Newton. The second law of motion states that the vector sum of all the forces acting on an object is equal to the mass multiplied by the acceleration of that object. In other words, we get the definition of force from this law. The force acting on an object for a certain time gives us the momentum. Or, momentum is force multiplied by time.

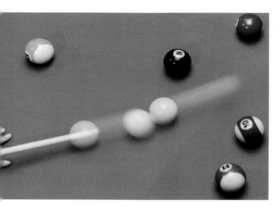

Momentum is observed in a game of pool; that is, if one ball stops dead after the collision, the other ball will continue away with all the momentum.

It is a vector

Momentum is a vector quantity; it is conserved and dependent upon a reference frame. First, it is a vector as force is a vector quantity. Rather, velocity is a vector and momentum is mass times velocity. Next, momentum is conserved. This means that the net change in the momentum of a closed system is always zero. Again, momentum is dependent on a reference frame because velocity is dependent on a reference frame.

Measure of motion

Momentum is also said to be the measure of motion. It is a very casual definition. This explains why a truck and bicycle, both travelling at the same speed, have different stopping distances. The truck goes on for a long distance before coming to a halt, whereas a bicycle will stop within just a few feet. The matter of fact is that a huge truck, even if it moves at a very low speed, has a very high momentum as compared to a small car with very high speed, simply because the truck is very heavy and has a higher mass.

Conservation of momentum

The momentum of any collection of objects is equal to the vector sum of the momentum of the individual objects. In accordance with Newton's third law of motion, these particles apply equal and opposite forces on each other, so any variation in the momentum of one particle is exactly adjusted by an equal and opposite variation in the momentum of another particle. Thus, when there is no net external force acting on a collection of particles, there is never a change in their total momentum, which is what the law of conservation of momentum states.

Newton's cradle displays how the momentum from one object can move to another.

Electromagnetic Forces

Electromagnetism is the study of the electromagnetic force, that is, a type of physical interaction, that occurs between electrically charged particles. The force experienced due to the electromagnetic fields, like electric or magnetic, is called electromagnetic force. It is one of the four fundamental interactions that exist in nature. Strong, weak and gravitational are the other interactions.

Infinite range

Electromagnetic force is the force exerted by the electromagnetic interaction of electrically charged or magnetically polarised particles or bodies. It is one of the four fundamental forces, and manifests itself through the forces between the charges (Coulomb's law) and the magnetic force. These forces are described through the Lorentz force law. Theoretically, both magnetic and electric forces are manifestations of an exchange force that involves the exchange of photons. Electromagnetic force has an infinite range, which obeys the conventional, inverse-square law.

An electromagnetic crane used in a metal scrap yard.

Electromagnetic induction

Electromagnetism is a manifestation of both electricity and magnetism. Both fields are different aspects of electromagnetism and hence are intrinsically related. Therefore, an altering electric field creates a magnetic field; conversely, an altering magnetic field creates an electric field. The effect is known as electromagnetic induction. This principle is the basis of the operation of electrical generators, motors and transformers. Magnetic and electric fields are convertible with relative motion. In quantum electrodynamics, electromagnetic interactions between charged particles can be calculated using the method of Feynman diagrams.

Centrifugal Force

Centrifugal force is an outward force that draws a rotating body away from the axis of rotation. This force is mainly caused by the inertia of the object. In physics, centrifugal force is the tendency of an object that follows a curved path to fly away from the centre of curvature. It is basically not a true force but a form of inertia.

A centrifuge rapidly rotates containers to apply centrifugal force to its contents.

FUN FACT

A slingshot used to scare away birds on farms makes use of centrifugal force. The farmer places a stone in the centre of a rope and rotates it overhead before releasing it.

Force for convenience

This force is described or grouped as a force of convenience because it balances the centripetal force that is described as a true force. If a ball is swung at the end of a rope, the rope exerts a centripetal force on the ball and causes it to follow a curved path. During the rotation, the ball exerts centrifugal force on the rope, which tends to break the rope and fly off on a tangent path. The effects of centrifugal force can be controlled and even harnessed for various useful applications. This force is applied in centrifuges and engine governors. Highway curves are tilted to prevent the centrifugal force from forcing the cars outwards off the road.

Increasing the force

Centrifugal force can be increased by increasing either the speed of rotation, mass of the body or radius, that is, distance of the body from the centre of the curve. Increasing either mass or radius will increase the centrifugal force equivalently, but increasing the speed of rotation will increase it in proportion to the square of speed. For instance, a 10 times increase in speed, say from 10 to 100 revolutions per minute, will increase the centrifugal force by a factor of 100. This force is expressed as a multiple of "g", the symbol for normal gravitational force.

Formula and units

Centrifugal force if measured in pounds can be calculated by the formula $wv2/gr$, where "w" stands for the weight of the object in pounds, and "v" represents the velocity in feet per second. The acceleration of gravity (32 feet per second) is "g". "r" is the radius of the circle in feet. There are many instances where centrifugal force is necessary. Children love to see the juggler's tricks in the circus. These could only be possible because of the existence of centrifugal force. In the dairy industry, cream is extracted from milk on the basis of centrifugal action. Besides these, there are numerous examples where centrifugal action is used for a beneficial reason in life.

Centripetal Force

Centripetal force is a force that allows a body to keep moving in a curved path. Its direction is always at a right angle to the velocity of the body and towards the fixed point of the instantaneous centre of curvature of the path. Any motion in a curved path represents accelerated motion, which needs a force that should be directed towards the centre of the curvature. This force associated with it is known as the centripetal force, meaning "centre-seeking" force.

Acceleration

An object moving in a circle experiences acceleration. Even if the object is moving along the perimeter of a circle with a fixed speed, the velocity still changes and subsequently, the object attains acceleration. The direction of this acceleration is towards the centre of the circle. In accordance with Newton's second law, any object that experiences acceleration must also experience a force in the same direction as the direction of the acceleration. Thus, for an object moving in a circle, there must be an inward force acting upon it in order to cause its inward acceleration. This is sometimes referred to as the centripetal force requirement.

A Ferris wheel uses centripetal force.

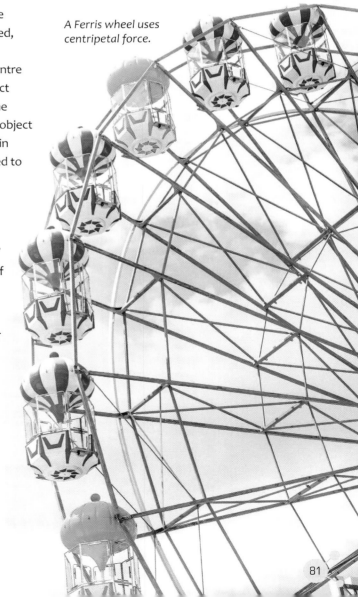

How is it expressed?

The effective centripetal force on any object having a mass "m" moving at a tangential speed "v" along a path with the radius of curvature "r" is given as:

$F = mv^2/r$

Without a net centripetal force, no object can travel in a circular motion. In reality, if all the applied forces are balanced, then the object in motion continues in a straight line at a fixed constant speed.

Factors affecting centripetal force

The centripetal force required to keep an object moving in a circle increases if:

- the mass of the object increases
- the speed of the object increases
- the radius of the circle in which it is travelling decreases

Equilibrium of Forces

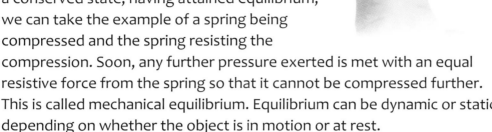

To consider a rigid body with its momentum in a conserved state, having attained equilibrium, we can take the example of a spring being compressed and the spring resisting the compression. Soon, any further pressure exerted is met with an equal resistive force from the spring so that it cannot be compressed further. This is called mechanical equilibrium. Equilibrium can be dynamic or static, depending on whether the object is in motion or at rest.

Dynamic equilibrium

Dynamic equilibrium is a condition, where in a reversible process, the reaction is proceeding at an equal rate in both forward and backward directions, and the net change in the reaction is zero. In simple words, it refers to a state of balance that is achieved by two forces in motion. We can take the example of the opening of a soda bottle or the dissociation of acetic acid. If we open a soda bottle and take out half of the liquid, then, after some time, equilibrium is attained as some molecules of carbon dioxide go from liquid to gaseous state and an equal amount of molecules transform from gaseous to liquid phase. Both reactions occur at the same rate and the state of equilibrium is attained.

Dynamic equilibrium.

Static equilibrium

Static equilibrium is a condition where a body is static; force will have to be applied in order to move the object. For an object to be in static equilibrium, there should be no net forces or torques and also no acceleration, whether translational or rotational. The best example of static equilibrium is why the leaning tower of Pisa does not fall down. This is because the static force balances it.

FUN FACT

Consider a flowing river. The flow of a river is subject to two forces in equilibrium. The first is the force that accelerates it and the second is the resistance created by the objects in its bed.

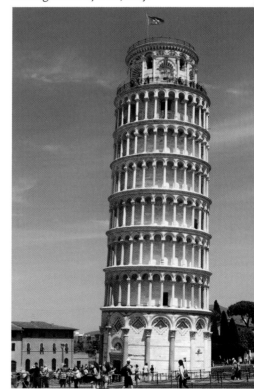

Static force balancing the leaning tower of Pisa, Italy.

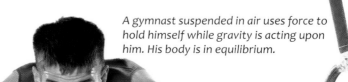

A gymnast suspended in air uses force to hold himself while gravity is acting upon him. His body is in equilibrium.

Elastic Forces

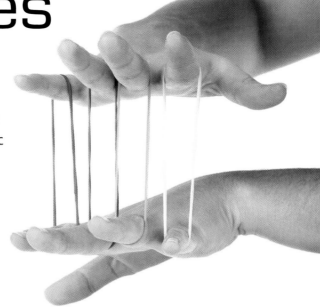

Have you ever thought about why, when we stretch and release it, a rubber band tries to regain its shape? It is because rubber has elastic properties. There is a force that acts on the molecules of a rubber band that resists on being stretched. This force is called an elastic force. It can be defined as a conservative force that arises in an object during its deformation and resists the change in all directions. This force is transmitted through the molecules of the object.

Tension force.

Types of elastic forces

There are two types of elastic forces. One is tension and the other is compression. If any object is stretched, there is a tension force in its molecules and when any object is compressed, there resides the compression force.

A catapult makes use of elastic force to set a body in motion.

Applications

There are many applications of elastic forces. The bow and arrow functions on the basis of elastic force. Elastic property is used in clothing, hair bands, bracelets and for art and craft.

When engineers build huge bridges and flyovers for heavy traffic to pass through, it is not possible for them to create the entire structure out of stone. The foundation is usually industrial quality metal. However, they have to leave gaps in the bridge. This is because they have to consider the temperature. Metal contracts in the cold and expands in the heat. If the foundation of the bridge were to contract and expand, the bridge would crumble away. Hence, gaps are left in the bridge held together with a metal that has a good amount of elasticity. This elasticity allows the metal to expand when heated and contract to its original shape when cooled. Usually, steel is used.

Types of inelastic forces

The types of forces that do not possess elastic property are called inelastic forces; for example, torque, magnetic forces, electrostatic forces or gravitational forces. Inelastic forces are also very important. Inelastic forces are responsible for changing the shape of any object permanently.

How to Measure Forces?

Force, in simple words, is the push or pull of an object. It is measured by many available instruments; whether it is a contact or non-contact force, static or dynamic. By measuring force, we can also measure torque, acceleration, weight and other quantities. Several types of gauges are available for measuring forces.

Apparatus to measure force

Different types of force gauges, spring scales, load cells, mechanical test stands, pneumatic testers, motorised test stands, digital force testers, grips and fixtures, sensors and many accessories are now available in the market for measuring force. The allowable range to measure force using these instruments varies from 103 to 109 newtons. The instruments used are based on the principle that a transducer is made that accepts the force and then changes it into some output, that is, a measurable physical quantity. Instruments from simple technique dial gauge to complex digital converters are now accessible.

A hand compresses the force measurement device, which, in turn, measures the force applied.

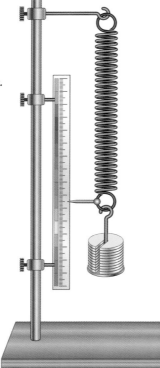

Hooke's law apparatus to measure force.

Force measurement devices

A load cell is a common force measuring unit. In general terms, a chain of transducers is called a load cell. Force is calculated by the electrical signal of the magnitude equal to that of the force applied. Hydraulic load cells, pneumatic load cells and strain gauge load cells are some types of load cells. The spring balance is another force-measuring device that is frequently used for various applications. A spring balance is an instrument with a spring and a hook on it that measures the weight of an object very accurately by opposing the gravitational force. It works on the basis of Hooke's law and measures weights from a few newtons to thousands of newtons. Mainly, it is used in industries for measuring heavy loads and as accelerometers.

ENERGY

Energy is simply the capacity to perform a task. To accomplish any task, be it lifting a suitcase, rotating a fan or heating a bucket of water, a body/machine requires a certain amount of energy. Energy can exist in many forms; potential, kinetic, thermal, electrical, nuclear and so on. These forms of energy can be converted from one form to another (although with varying degrees of efficiency, depending on the particular pair), but energy can never be destroyed. The sum total of energy in the universe or in an isolated body is always constant, which is a property called the conservation of energy.

Potential Energy

Potential energy is the energy that a body has because of its position or configuration in a force field. Depending on the kind of force field, potential energy is of several types: electrical, gravitational, nuclear, etc. These fields must necessarily be conservative, that is, an energy type that is conserved and recoverable during any work done by this force alone.

Elastic potential energy

Elastic potential energy is the second form of potential energy. It refers to the energy that is stored in elastic materials as a result of their stretching or compressing. It can be stored in rubber bands, bungee cords, trampolines, springs and an arrow drawn into a bow among others. The amount of elastic potential energy stored in such a device is related to the amount of stretch of the device, that is, the more the stretch, the more the stored energy. Springs are an excellent example of a device that can store elastic potential energy due to either compression or stretching.

Gravitational potential energy

Gravitational potential energy is the energy which is stored in an object because of its vertical position or height. The energy is stored due to Earth's gravitational attraction on an object. The gravitational potential energy of the massive ball of a demolition machine depends on two variables: the mass of the ball and the height to which it is raised. There is a direct relation between the gravitational potential energy and the mass of an object. The more massive the object, the greater the gravitational potential energy. Furthermore, there is a direct connection between gravitational potential energy and the height of an object. Similarly, the higher an object is elevated, the greater is the gravitational potential energy.

An object at a height has potential energy as gravity is acting on it and can cause the object to fall.

Latent energy

Potential energy represents the latent energy in a system. It can be converted into an active energy or motion when required, in relation with the conservation of energy, so that the energy is retained. For example, if we release a ball from a height of 15 m above the ground, it steadily loses its potential energy but gains kinetic energy as it comes down.

Kinetic Energy

Kinetic energy is the energy that a body possesses by virtue of its motion; a body at rest has zero kinetic energy. Mathematically, it is defined as half the product of the mass and the square of its velocity. Therefore, a body with a mass of 2 kg moving at a speed of 3 m/s has kinetic energy that is equal to 9 joule.

Change in kinetic energy

The mechanical work performed on a body is entirely revealed by the change in its kinetic energy. The type of motion involved may be translational (motion along a path from one place to another), rotational on an axis, vibrational or any combination of motions. The total kinetic energy is the sum of the kinetic energies associated with each kind of motion.

Forms of kinetic energy

Kinetic energy comes in different forms. Energy due to vibrational motion is called vibrational energy. Rotational energy is the energy due to rotational motion, while the energy due to motion from one location to another is called transitional energy. The translational kinetic energy that an object possesses depends upon two variables namely the mass and speed of an object.

A falling object has kinetic energy as it is in motion.

Electrical Energy

Electrical energy is a kind of kinetic energy that is formed because of the movement of electric charges. It is a form of kinetic energy because the electric charges are continuously in motion. The speed of electric charge determines the amount of electrical energy.

Power grid supplies electricity everywhere.

Uses of electrical energy

By virtue of the ease with which it can be transported from one place to another, or converted into other forms of energy, electrical energy holds enormous importance in the fields of technology and engineering. For lighting, operation of electronic equipment, automotive engines, entertainment applications and a variety of other uses, electric energy has no rival. Electric power is produced by generators, which work on the induction principle proposed by the legendary English experimental physicist Michael Faraday in 1831. The power is usually supplied to homes and businesses by the means of a power grid.

Sources of electrical energy

Traditionally, there have been two sources of electricity generation – hydro and thermal. Hydroelectricity involves creating massive dams across rivers and harnessing the kinetic energy of the flowing river water to run the electric generator and generate power. The thermal alternative basically depends on burning fossil fuels like coal or petroleum to produce heat that runs the electric generator. Nowadays, due to concerns over the environmental cost of thermal power plants in particular, that supply a lion's share of worldwide electricity demand, other sources of electricity generation are also coming into vogue, such as nuclear energy, solar plants, wind turbines and geothermal power stations.

Hydroelectric power plant.

Renewable Energy

Renewable energy is also known as alternative energy. It is made from sources of energy that are infinite or replenishable. Renewable energy makes use of the energies of the Sun, wind, tides, flowing water and so on.

The need for renewable energy

At the beginning of the twenty first century, fossil fuels contributed to approximately 80 per cent of the worldwide power demand. However, burning fossil fuels has a grave environmental impact as the by-products of the combustion reaction wreak havoc on Earth's weather patterns, causing global warming and respiratory diseases in animals and human beings. Also, these fossil fuels are a finite and fast-depleting resource. They have been formed by long-term decomposition of organic matter and cannot be created at will. The world's oil deposits are estimated to run dry by the middle of this century.

Windmills and solar panels; sources of renewable energy.

Types of renewable energy

To counter this problem, we have resorted to using resources that are not so finite, like the Sun (solar energy), wind (wind energy), hot springs and geysers (geothermal energy), tides (tidal energy) and rivers (hydroelectricity). However, there are a lot of problems associated with trying to utilise these forces of nature for our energy needs, all of which revolve around the unpredictability of these sources. If the Sun is blocked out by clouds, solar power is unfeasible. If winds are negligible, wind turbines become useless. Hot springs are too rare. Despite these hurdles and the need to optimise these technologies for maximum yield, these resources hold the promise of a cleaner future for us all.

Nuclear Energy

Nuclear energy can be harvested, at least in theory, from two types of reactions – nuclear fission and nuclear fusion. In fission, a large nucleus is bombarded with a much smaller particle to break it into two smaller nuclei. The process is accompanied by a large amount of energy. In nuclear fusion, two small atoms combine to form a larger atom, like helium, with the release of enormous amounts of energy.

Uses of nuclear energy

Both fission and fusion have been used in weapons of mass destruction. Scientists have only been able to extract energy in a controlled manner from fission. Although fusion is theoretically a far more productive and exciting source of energy, it is difficult to attain because of the high temperatures (up to 6 times the temperature at the centre of the Sun). Also, because it is difficult to confine the reaction, it continues by itself.

Nuclear explosion.

Problems with nuclear energy

While nuclear fission is used as a source of energy even now, there are certain problems associated with it – mainly due to the highly toxic, radioactive nature of the waste produced in a fission reactor. There are almost no suitable ways to safely dispose of this waste and they cause severe environmental degradation, and can cause a number of diseases in animals and humans who are within range of the radiation emitted by these wastes. Nuclear energy still remains a technology of the future.

Radiation supervisor checks the level of radioactive radiation in the danger zone.

Solar Energy

Solar energy is one of the most promising, effective and cleanest renewable energy alternatives currently available to humankind. It is rapidly becoming popular across the world. Sunlight is the largest source of energy received by Earth – despite the diffusion of the light caused by atmosphere, the light that is incident on Earth's surface is still more than enough to satisfy worldwide energy demands.

Uses of solar energy

Solar energy is utilised in two ways – to produce heat or to generate electricity. Solar thermal energy has been used to heat water, for space heating, space cooling and to process heat generation. Electricity generation is mainly done through solar cells or photovoltaic cells. In such cells, a small electric voltage is generated when light falls upon the junction between a metal and a semiconductor (such as silicon) or the junction between two different semiconductors. Solar energy is also used to drive chemical reactions to produce what is known as solar fuel.

Solar heater.

Disadvantages of solar energy

While solar energy is hugely promising, it has two major disadvantages. One – it is still costly and inefficient as most photovoltaic cells only have approximately 15–20 per cent conversion efficiency. Two – places with less sunlight or cloudy climates cannot effectively use solar energy.

Solar energy is used today, mostly in low-power, small scale applications, but this is bound to change in the future.

Solar cooking oven.

FUN FACT

If we were to use all the solar energy that Earth receives every year, we would be able to create energy that will be 8000 times the total world energy consumption.

Food and Chemical Energy

In biology, one thing that unites all living organisms, from the smallest amoeba to the largest blue whales, is their need for energy. In green plants, this energy is provided by the Sun. In animals, this energy is provided by consumption of plants or other animals. This is called an energy or food chain.

Energy sources

More complicated living organisms obtain their energy from a wide variety of nutrient groups, such as fats, carbohydrates, proteins and a few other chemicals. In humans, for example, these nutrients are simplified inside the body by the digestive system (using various enzymes) into a more manageable form like glucose and are later converted by the respiratory system into ATP in the presence of oxygen.

Various sources of nutrition.

The energy of food is generally measured in terms of the oxidative energy of food particles (using a bomb calorimeter and making corrections for the efficiency of digestion and absorption) and the unit used is a kilocalorie. This system was pioneered in the late nineteenth century by American chemist Wilbur Atwater and this method of measuring food energy is called the Atwater system.

Energy in plants

Sunlight provides the thrust for photosynthesis reaction, where water, carbon dioxide and certain other minerals like potassium and phosphorous are converted with the help of sunlight (and the green chemical chlorophyll acting as a catalyst) to produce adenosine triphosphate, which is a sort of energy currency in living organisms. It can be utilised as and when necessary, through cellular respiration. Plants being the only living organisms capable of creating energy from the sun, the rest of the living organisms have to depend upon them for their energy requirements. Hence, plants alone are the energy providers for all the organisms on Earth.

Fuel Cells

A fuel cell is a class of devices where fuel is converted directly into energy by means of electrochemical reactions. The difference that these cells have in comparison to normal batteries is that while the batteries start off with a fixed amount of fuel material and oxidants that are slowly depleted to zero with use, the fuel material and oxygen in a fuel cell are constantly supplied, similar to how a DC generator system works.

Types of fuel cells

A fuel cell may be considered as a transducer that converts chemical energy to electrical energy. The primary fuels currently used are hydrogen, reformed natural gas (methane CH_4 transformed into hydrogen-rich gas) and methanol (CH_3OH). Depending on the kind of electrolyte used, these cells are classified into three categories: (i) alkaline fuel cells that use an aqueous solution of sodium or potassium hydroxide; (ii) phosphoric acid cells that use orthophosphoric acid (H_3PO_4) and (iii) molten carbonate fuel cells that use molten potassium lithium carbonate.

Uses of fuel cells

Fuel cells have been widely used for a long time in space probes and satellites, and are now finding wide acceptance as an energy source in hospitals, schools, hotels and waste-treatment plants. They are used to derive energy from the methane produced by decomposing garbage and in automobile engine units.

First certified fuel cell boat in the world.

Energy Technology

Energy technology is currently one of the most exciting fields of scientific research – its goal is to figure out ways of extracting energy from various fuel sources in a way that optimises its efficiency, minimises its costs and reduces its adverse impact on the environment, while also devising effective mechanisms for the transportation, distribution and storage of this energy. Energy is a scant resource, and has been the source of conflict and war many times in human history.

Energy researchers

Humans have been experimenting with energy ever since the discovery of fire. There have been many legendary scientists and engineers who have made their mark in this field, for example, James Watt (inventor of the steam engine), Alessandro Volta (inventor of the battery), Frank Shuman (solar energy pioneer), Enrico Fermi (developed the first nuclear fission reactor based on the ideas of Szilard, Meitner, Strassmann and Hahn) and Nikola Tesla (pioneer of the alternating current). Moreover, as we head into the age of renewable energy and maybe even nuclear fusion, we will add to this list of luminaries with the next generation of energy researchers.

Reconstruction of the first electric battery.

Steam engine.

Electric power engineering

Electric power has become an indispensable part of our daily life. It is hard to imagine a day without electricity, let alone a lifetime. Hence, there are scientists who are studying the sources of electricity and their uses. There are two parts to this study. The first one deals with efficient and economic ways of creating electricity, while the second one deals with building machinery that uses less electrical energy or can run on alternate energy efficiently. People who study this field are called electrical engineers and the field of study is called electrical or electric power engineering. With energy resources depleting at the current rate, this line of study becomes more and more important.

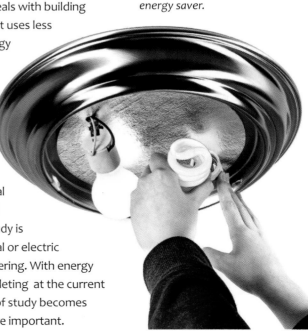

CFL bulb is an energy saver.

Conversion of Energy

Energy cannot be put to useful work in every form, so we usually convert it from one form to another as and when required. However, all these transformations are not equivalent, that is, energy transforms from one form to another with a range of efficiencies.

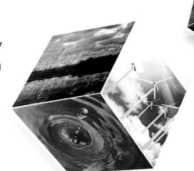

Laws of conversion

There are rigid limits imposed on the maximum efficiency with which work can be extracted from a given amount of energy, according to two theorems called the Carnot's theorem and the Second Law of Thermodynamics. The degree of efficiency of transformation between any two types of energy is determined by entropy considerations. Entropy is a measure of the randomness or disorder of a system and according to the Second Law of Thermodynamics, the entropy of the universe always increases in every natural physical process. Only those types of transformations are more likely to occur on a larger scale, where the overall disorder or entropy of a system increases; for example, electrical energy to heat.

Daily application

Many events happen during our day when we don't realise that energy is being converted. When you eat and work out, the food energy is getting converted into kinetic and muscular energy. Energy gets converted every day all around us.

Conversion of chemical energy to heat energy.

Transducers

Devices that transform one kind of energy into another are called transducers; for example, windmills that convert wind energy to mechanical energy for grinding grain and pumping water or the engine of a car that utilises the chemical energy of fossil fuels to generate kinetic energy.

Windmill is one of the best transducers.

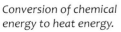
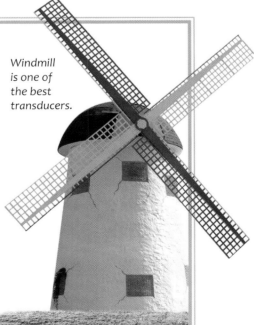

Mass-Energy Equivalence

In physics, the mass-energy equivalence is the concept that the energy content of a body also depends upon its mass rather than simply being a function of its speed, temperature or configuration in a force field. A ball with smaller mass will have less impact than one with more mass when dropped from the same height.

Albert Einstein

The discovery

Albert Einstein put forward this radical re-imagining of energy in his 1905 paper, "Does the inertia of an object depend upon its energy content?", one of the three papers that he published that year (called the *Annus Mirabilis* or *Year of Miracles* papers) that led to a paradigm shift in modern physics and laid the foundation for three hugely important disciplines – relativity, quantum mechanics and statistical mechanics.

$E = mc^2$

In this paper, Einstein showed that the energy content due to the mass of a body can be calculated by the formula $E = mc^2$, where c is the velocity of light, 3×10^8 m/s. Mass and energy are interchangeable and always connected by the same proportionality equation. This radically changes our idea of the universal conservation of energy, as now the quantity to be conserved is not just energy as we thought previously (let us call it E) but the sum total of E and the new-found mass energy. This is also the explanation of how, in nuclear bombs, a small amount of matter can produce so much energy, because a small part of the mass of the parent nuclei is converted to energy. Therefore, the statement of the conservation of energy postulate may now be defined as follows: The sum total of energy and mass in the universe or in any isolated physical system is constant.

A person using the same amount of energy to drive a small nail using a small hammer will have less impact than someone using the same energy to hit a spike with a sledgehammer.

Law of Conservation of Energy

The total energy of the universe or of an isolated physical system is always constant. This is the law of conservation of energy. It's one of the most important postulates and calculation tools in physics. According to Noether's theorem, the conservation of energy is a mathematical consequence of the fact that the laws of physics do not change with time; another foundational axiom.

Conversion of energy

In some cases, the notion of conservation of energy might seem counterintuitive. When we set a ball rolling on the ground, sooner or later, it will come to rest. Therefore, not only does it lose its kinetic energy, but its potential energy also shows no corresponding increase. However, the energy is only redirected elsewhere, as heat generated by the friction force exerted by the ground on the ball. To date, no exception to this law of energy conservation has been observed. If there was, everything we know about our universe would be brought into question.

Einstein's theory

Einstein postulated a now widely-accepted notion of how the mass of a body also contributes to its energy content, which is called the mass-energy equivalence. In general, if we're trying to be very precise in our definition, the sum total of energy and mass in the universe or in any isolated physical system is constant. This becomes the basis of the conservation of energy.

Conservation of energy can be understood by a simple example of a motorcycle, where the fuel acts as potential energy, which is consumed to impart kinetic energy to the motorcycle.

Fuel (potential energy)

"converted into"

Rotation (kinetic energy)

International Energy Law

The arena of international energy legislation is a complicated one. Every country has a different agency (and sometimes two or three), which controls the energy production and distribution within that country; for example, the Oil and Natural Gas Commission of India, the Australian Petroleum Production and Exploration Association, etc. These agencies also determine the overall energy policy.

Global energy consumption

Although most countries recognise the danger that rampant fossil fuel consumption poses to the environment, and the fact that fossil fuel deposits are fast depleting and will soon hit rock bottom, many countries, especially developing ones like China or India, often rely extensively on fossil fuels to power their high economic growth (as this form of energy is cheap and easy to generate). Nevertheless, almost all countries have some form of renewable energy programmes; some of them are highly successful.

FUN FACT

The total energy that the TV sets in the USA use when they are switched off can power a nuclear plant. This is because the TV sets use electricity to put them on standby so that they can instantly turn on when switched on.

Geothermal power plant in Iceland. Here, the thermal energy is generated and stored in Earth.

Alternative energy

Iceland's 80 per cent of energy needs are met by their own indigenous geothermal energy programme and more than 50 per cent of Germany's energy requirements are met by solar power. In addition, laws on carbon footprint and emission trading have made it cost-effective for most industries to use more renewable energy resources rather than oil or coal-based energy.

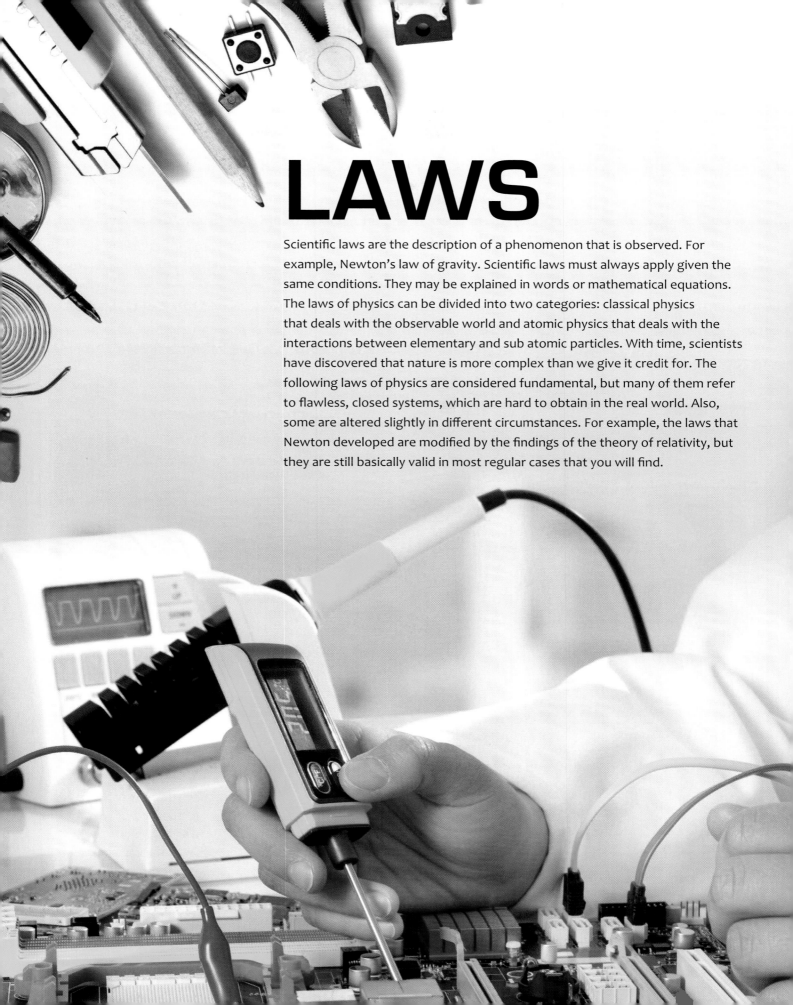

LAWS

Scientific laws are the description of a phenomenon that is observed. For example, Newton's law of gravity. Scientific laws must always apply given the same conditions. They may be explained in words or mathematical equations. The laws of physics can be divided into two categories: classical physics that deals with the observable world and atomic physics that deals with the interactions between elementary and sub atomic particles. With time, scientists have discovered that nature is more complex than we give it credit for. The following laws of physics are considered fundamental, but many of them refer to flawless, closed systems, which are hard to obtain in the real world. Also, some are altered slightly in different circumstances. For example, the laws that Newton developed are modified by the findings of the theory of relativity, but they are still basically valid in most regular cases that you will find.

Archimedes' Law

When asked by the king to measure the mass of an object without weighing it, Archimedes came up with the idea of immersing the object in water and measuring the amount of water it displaces. Archimedes got this idea when he was in his bathtub!

The level of water in a tub rises when a body is placed in it.

Archimedes' principle

The buoyant force is basically an upward force exerted by a fluid that causes the object to float. Therefore, gravity is always pushing down upon the object and the buoyant force is pushing up the object, causing the object to float in the fluid. Based on the Archimedes' principle, the weight of the object floating in the fluid is equal to the weight of the buoyant force. Objects that have a total density greater than that of the density of the fluid, have a negative total force. The object that is unsupported, gradually sinks and can also become totally submerged.

For example, a wooden boat floats on the water in a pool until the weight of the water that it displaces is just equal to its own weight. As the boat is loaded, it sinks deeper, displacing more water, so the magnitude of the buoyant force continuously matches the weight of the boat and its cargo.

Application of the principle

1. Fish have a swim bladder that allows them to reach equilibrium in water. Without the help of the swim bladder, the density of the fish would be lesser than that of water, which would cause it to float.

2. The human brain is suspended in static equilibrium within the skull. In case of an accident, where there is a loss of fluid around the brain or an excess of fluid due to swelling, a problem could occur, causing great pain or permanent brain damage.

3. Hydrometers are used to measure the density of liquids. It is a tube with a bulb at one end with lead shots in it to weigh it down and allow the hydrometer to float vertically in a liquid. In a low density liquid, a greater volume of liquid must be displaced for the buoyant force to equal the weight of the hydrometer. So it sinks lower in it.

Coulomb's Law

In 1785, Charles–Augustine de Coulomb, a French physicist, published the actual and exact mathematical relation between two electrically charged bodies and also derived from that relation an equation for the repulsion or attraction force between them, which later came to be known as Coulomb's law.

First law

Like charge particles repel each other and unlike charge particles attract each other.

Second law

The force of attraction or repulsion between two electrically charged particles is directly proportional to the magnitude of their charges and inversely proportional to the square of the distance between them.

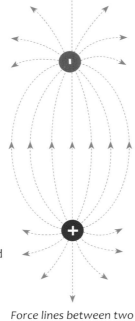

Force lines between two unlikely charged particles.

Salient points

The force between the charged bodies is directly proportional to the charge of the bodies.

Again, the force acting on both the bodies is inversely proportional to the distance (r) between them.

Therefore, the total development of the force is not at all the same for all the mediums. As we have discussed in the law above, their force would change for a different medium.

For example, if the charged particles are present in air, their charge would be more as compared to if they were present underwater.

The limitations of the Coulomb's law

1. Coulomb's law is only valid if the average number of solvent molecules between the two different charge particles is large.

2. Coulomb's law is valid only if the point charges are at complete rest.

3. It is very difficult to apply Coulomb's law on a body when the charges are in an arbitrary shape. Therefore, we cannot confirm the value of the distance "r" between the two charges when they are in that arbitrary shape.

4. Coulomb's law does not provide a constant universal answer. Depending upon the medium, the derived solution will be different.

Hair charged by the same polarity repel each other.

Joule's Law

We have studied that when current flows through a wire, heat is generated. This forms the basis of many household appliances and industrial machinery. But how much heat is generated and on what conditions does it depend can be answered by studying Joule's law.

What is Joule's law?

Joule's law can be written mathematically as the amount of resistance that can convert electrical energy into heat energy. In 1840, English physicist James Prescott Joule gave us the law of heating that the amount of heat produced per second in a current-carrying wire is directly proportional to the electrical resistance of the wire, time of the current flow and square of the current flowing through the circuit. These three conditions can be written as:

1. $H \propto i^2$ (When the resistance of the wire and time of the current flow is constant)

2. $H \propto R$ (When the current in the circuit and time of the current flow are constant)

3. $H \propto t$ (When the current flowing in the circuit and resistance is constant)

By summing up all the three conditions, we get a final equation for Joule's law, which is $H \propto i^2 Rt$

Here, H is the heat generated in a system that is measured in joules.

This equation can be written as;

$$H = \frac{1}{J} i^2 Rt$$

where J is Joule's mechanical equivalent of heat.

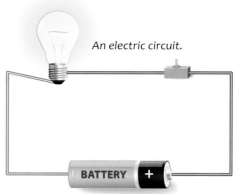
An electric circuit.

Applications

Any electrical appliance that generates heat makes use of Joule's law of heating. The common household iron that is used to iron clothes makes use of this law. Other such appliances include the toaster, electric kettle, etc.

Other appliances use this heat to create light. For example, in an electric bulb, a thin filament of metal wire exists. When electricity is passed through this wire, heat is generated and the heated wire filament begins to glow. This is how a bulb works.

Joule's Law of heating also comes to use in a circuit fuse. It consists of a thin wire with a low melting point. Hence, when too much electricity passes through it, the thin wire heats up and melts, breaking the circuit.

A common household iron.

Newton's Laws of Motion

Issac Newton observed an apple fall from the tree and it set him thinking. That led to the discovery of gravity, and the relation between the forces acting on a body and the motion of the body. By observing, experimenting and researching, he arrived at three basic laws.

First Law: Law of Inertia

According to Newton's First law of Motion, every object in a state of uniform motion tends to remain in that state unless an external force is applied to it.

Burning fuel releases energy that lifts off a rocket.

Second Law: Law of Force and Acceleration

Newton's second law can be put into a simple equation:

Force = (mass X acceleration)

When a force acts on an object, that object will accelerate in the same direction as the force.

The net or total force applied is directly proportional to the mass; however, mass and acceleration are inversely proportional.

Third Law: Law of Force Pairs

For every action, there is an equal and opposite reaction.

Newton's first law tells you how the forces act and what they do. Newton's third law, however, tells you what forces are and how they react.

One falling domino transfers its energy into the next, which transfers it into the next one, causing all of them to cascade.

How does a force affect an object's motion?

The second law describes how velocities change when forces are applied.

Therefore, this law explains how an object's motion totally changes when an external force is applied to the object, hence causing motion. Hence, mass and acceleration each play a role in how force affects an object's motion.

Example: If you consider the mass of a book in relation to that of a truck, then the book's mass is much smaller than the truck's mass. If an equal force is applied to both the objects, which object will have less acceleration or accelerate slower? The answer will always be the heavier object (truck), which accelerates slower than the lighter object (book).

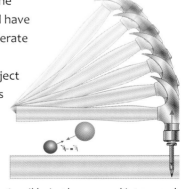

A nail being hammered into wood.

Ohm's Law

Ohm's law relates current, voltage and resistance, which are the three basic quantities of electricity. Hence, this is considered as the most basic law of electrical engineering.

What is Ohm's Law?

Ohm's law states that the current flowing through a conductor is directly proportional to the potential difference across its two points. By naming the proportionality constant as R in this equation, we will get,

$$I = \frac{V}{R}$$

where, I = current flowing, V = potential difference, R = Resistance

This is Ohm's law.

Resistance came to be measured in ohms after the name of its discoverer. In 1827, German physicist Georg Simon Ohm described how applied voltage and current are mathematically related through simple electrical circuits using different lengths of wire. This law was then modified by Gustav Kirchhoff to determine the conductivity of a conductor.

$$J = \sigma E$$

where, J = current density in a resistive material, E = electric field, σ (Sigma) = conductivity

Ohm's law is an empirical equation. It has a broad area of scope from a wide range of length scales , which can work even for silicon wires that are four atoms wide. Materials that obey Ohm's law are called Ohmic or linear. This law can be used to solve simple circuits and for calculating the EMF, that is, the electromotive force of a cell. By applying Ohm's law, we can find out the value of resistance in a circuit, by knowing only the values of the current flowing and the potential difference in a circuit.

The circuit shows the relationship between current, voltage and the resistance, following the Ohm's law.

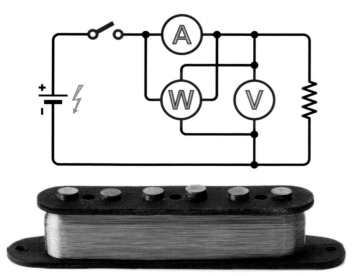

Molecular explanation

At the molecular level, a solid conductor contains free electrons that carry negative charge. The atoms and ions are heavier in weight as compared to electrons. Therefore, they do not contribute towards the flow of the current and become barriers to the path of electron flow. These barriers create resistance in a circuit. When we apply a voltage, V, between the leads of a resistor, we can expect a current, I = V/R, to flow through it. The electrons keep being accelerated by the applied static electric field or voltage. Thus, they acquire some kinetic energy as they move towards the positive end of the piece of material (resistor). However, before moving away, they collide with an atom or ion and lose some of their kinetic energy and bounce back. Due to the presence of a static electric field, the free electrons accelerate again. This method of drifting or diffusing electrons in the presence of static atoms and ions is the simple physics behind Ohm's law.

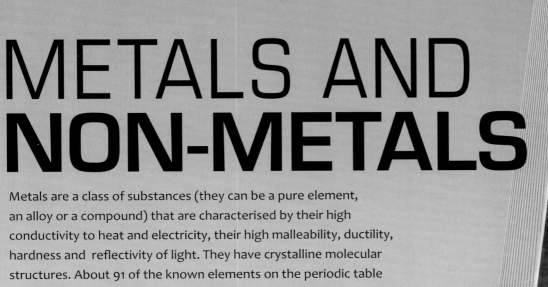

METALS AND
NON-METALS

Metals are a class of substances (they can be a pure element, an alloy or a compound) that are characterised by their high conductivity to heat and electricity, their high malleability, ductility, hardness and reflectivity of light. They have crystalline molecular structures. About 91 of the known elements on the periodic table are metals, and are arranged on the left side and the centre of it.

Non-metals share none of the distinctive characteristics of metals. They are poor conductors of heat and electricity, and are amorphous, non-malleable and highly volatile. There are 17 elements on the periodic table that are classified as non-metals and they are found on the right-hand side of the table.

Alloy

An alloy is the combination of two or more metals or a metal and a non-metal. Alloys, such as brass (copper and zinc) and bronze (copper and tin) were known since the ancient ages. Once an alloy has been formed, it cannot be separated by physical means. Over 90 per cent of the metals we use are alloys.

Making of alloys

Cutting process of hard alloys.

The properties of alloys are quite distinct from their constituents. For example, although aluminium and copper are both very soft and ductile, the resulting aluminium–copper alloy is much harder and stronger. Similarly, the addition of a small amount of non-metal, "carbon" to iron yields an alloy called steel, which is much harder and tougher. Any alloy consists of two constituents, the matrix (primary element) and the alloying elements (the additional element needed to make the alloy). Alloys are generally produced by co-melting the mixture of ingredients. The alternate route for producing alloys is the powder metallurgical route. Alloys are designed with respect to the selection of alloying elements. Their composition is a very difficult and challenging task. Different alloying elements are added to impart specific properties.

Ferrous and non-ferrous alloys

On the basis of commercial importance, alloys can be classified into two groups, ferrous alloys (the primary element is iron) and non-ferrous alloys (the primary element is not iron). Among ferrous alloys, the most important ones are steels. The main alloying elements of steel are Cr, Ni, Mn, Mo, Si, W, V, etc. Steels exhibit a wide range of desirable properties, including hardness, toughness, ductility and corrosion resistance. Copper-nickel, copper-zinc, aluminium alloys, magnesium alloys and nickel alloys are examples of non-ferrous alloys, which are widely used for various engineering components. On the basis of the atomic position of the alloying element, the alloy may be categorised into two groups – atom exchange (substitutional alloy) and interstitial alloy. The relative size of the constituent element of the alloy plays the main role in determining the type of alloy. When the constituent atoms are similar in size, usually, the substitution mechanism takes place, whereas if a wide difference in size exists, interstitial mechanism takes place to form the alloy. Classic examples of substitution alloys are bronze and brass, where some of the Cu atoms are substituted with either Sn or Zn atoms. Fe–C alloy steel is an appropriate example of interstitial alloys.

Alloy wheel caps are used in a car.

# Iron

Iron, which has the symbol Fe for its Latin name Ferrum, is one of the oldest elements known to man. Iron is highly valued for its strength and its ability to provide much stronger alloys, such as steel. Iron has hugely contributed to the evolution of the civilisation and shaped it into its current form. Iron is the 26th element on the periodic table.

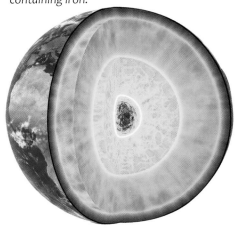
The core of Earth containing iron.

Pyrrhotite is a rare iron sulphide.

Iron in nature

It is the most common element on Earth. It is also common in other planets that have a rocky surface. Earth's inner and outer core is made out of molten iron. Other than iron, even nickel is present in Earth's core. In nature, iron is found to be combined with oxygen molecules to form oxides of iron. These are the most common substances found in Earth's crust. Iron combines with oxygen in different ratios to give different oxides – hematite, magnetite and wustite. Iron oxides are found in abundance in meteorites too.

Reactivity

Iron forms compounds by sharing a multiple number of electrons. Those with a valence of two are called ferrous and those with three are called ferric. Likewise, we have ferrous and ferric oxides. Iron reacts with halogens like chlorine, fluorine or bromine to create halide salts. At high temperatures, iron reacts with sulphur to form iron sulphide, which is commonly known as pyrite or fool's gold.

Steel

Iron is the most common element in Earth's crust. It is vastly used in manufacturing and industries. However, iron is not directly used because of its many drawbacks. It is a relatively soft metal. Also, pure iron combines with atmospheric oxygen in the presence of humidity to form oxides of iron or rust, which makes it weaker. The solution is steel. Steel is an alloy of iron that contains around one per cent carbon. Sometimes, a little manganese is also added. Based on the percentage of carbon and manganese, we get different types of steel that we see around us every day.

Carbon steel is the most widely used version of steel containing one per cent carbon. Stainless steel, contains 12–30 per cent chromium. It also contains traces of nickel.

FUN FACT

Stainless steel is so versatile that it's not only used in making household utensils, ornamental mirrors, photo frames, and imitation jewellery but also in the construction of bridges, buildings and skyscrapers.

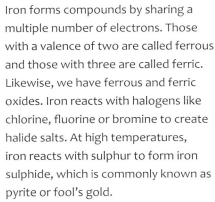
Stainless steel kitchenware.

Superalloys

Superalloys are high-performance alloys that are utilised in extreme situations. These alloys have brilliant mechanical strength; they do not distort under pressure or influence of extreme temperatures and are corrosion, rust or oxidation resistant.

Jet plane engine.

Uses of superalloys

High-performance alloys are primarily utilised in engines that are used in the aerospace and marine industry. Some examples of high-performance alloys or superalloys are Inconel, Hestelloy, TMS alloy, MP98T, RB199 and CMSX single crystal alloys. Superalloys are heavily dependent upon chemical and process inventions. New superalloys are being devised occasionally and have various applications. Nickel-based and cobalt-based superalloys are mostly in demand because of the various advantages they offer.

Elements used

The elements utilised in superalloys have high melting points because the resulting alloy must withstand high temperatures. Nickel is commonly used as the base for such alloys. We also have carbon, tungsten, vanadium, molybdenum, chromium, hafnium, boron and even more elements that are incorporated in these alloys. These alloys experience multi-phase coating. Pack cementation process is a stage conducted at lower temperatures, where the coating material is diffused inwards through the surface. The gas phase coating occurs at thousands of degrees centigrade. Then, the bond coating is performed, which is an adhesive form of coating.

Extreme use

A superalloy is also known as a high-performing alloy. The arms and weapons manufacturers of many countries use this material to create weapons that are easier to carry by soldiers and can withstand the elements of nature at the same time. Scientists are always in the process of developing superalloys that are cheaper to create and lighter in weight, and yet strong enough to survive extreme conditions.

A yacht makes use of superalloys so that it can float as well as avoid rust.

Silicon

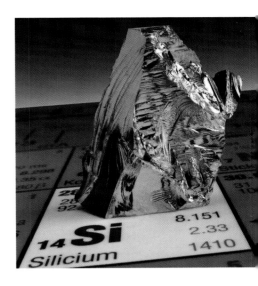

Silicon is the second most abundant element in Earth's crust. Earth's crust is made of 28 per cent silicon. It is also the most abundantly found element in the universe. Planetoids and comets, even dust and sand, contain silicon. However, silicon is not present in a free state in nature. Sand is an oxide of silicon. Silicon is a metalloid. It is also a semiconductor and can act as a conductor or a resistor. By nature, silicon is inert but can react with halogens and dilute alkalis.

Process of controlling the manufacture of microcircuits on a wafer of silicon.

Glass

Silicon is a major component of glass. If you pick up a handful of sand, half of it is made up of silicon. It is said that glass was invented when ancient Egyptians had studied the effects of lightning striking the sand. Of course, it took many years of experimenting before we arrived at the glass that we use today.

Silicon sand, also known as quartz sand, is melted with carbon up to 2205° C to create glass. As the glass forms, the by-products get released in the form of carbon monoxide gas.

In today's day and age, glass is not only an intricate part of modern architecture; most scientific apparatus are also made of it. We also use it in our daily life for drinking, eating and cooking.

Use in electronics

Silicon has a huge contribution to this era of information. Every single electronic and logic device, even a pocket calculator relies on silicon for functionality. It is extensively used to make transistors, which are electronic switches. These switches can collectively build logic gates. These logic gates successively form complicated microprocessors, microcontrollers and flash memory, all of which are essential in today's world. The silicon used to make electronic devices are known as electronic grade silicon. Electronic grade silicon is very pure; more than 99.9 per cent pure. Silicon is also used to make solar cells.

Solar cells made of silicon.

Light Alloys

Light alloys are based on aluminium, titanium, beryllium and magnesium. These alloys are light, but they also have great mechanical strength. This means that they have a good strength to density ratio. They are commonly used in building vehicles like cars, rockets and aeroplanes. They are also used in the shipbuilding industry. The commonly used alloys in the construction industry are iron and nickel based.

The body of a metal flashlight is made from light alloys.

Electronics are also made from light alloys.

Electronics

Usually, magnesium alloys are used to make chassis for electronic goods. Expensive professional cameras use magnesium alloy chassis to withstand rough usage. For such alloys, magnesium is mixed with lithium and a few other elements. Other expensive electronics like flagship tablets and smartphones also have metallic bodies that are crafted from aluminium or magnesium alloys. These make the devices lighter and portable. Also, because of their high tensile strength, they are resistant to drops and bumps. In larger scales, light alloys are used extensively in automotive engineering. Making cars lighter gives them more mileage. They are also used in nuclear power engineering and civil engineering.

Aviation

Aluminium alloys are majorly used in the construction of aeroplanes. This is because this alloy is light, economical and a bad conductor of electricity. Due to this, it does not put a lot of pressure on the engines while flying, subsequently consuming less fuel. Since the material is cheap, it tends to be economically feasible. Also, there is very less chance of the plane being hit by lightning when in flight due to the non-conducing properties of the alloy. There are other materials that are being developed to replace aluminium in the aviation industry; however, they still have to prove their reliability.

Other applications

Other than electronics and aviation, light alloys are also used in many other items of our daily use. Some household utensils, mostly the ones that are large in size, are made of light alloys. They are also used in the manufacturing of bicycle parts, as it makes it easier for the rider. Daily items like soda cans and metal flashlights are also made from these. Also, a lot of costume jewellery makes use of light alloys. As this type of jewellery is usually elaborate, the light alloys ensure that not only do they look ornamental but also don't cause undue discomfort to the wearer.

A soda can made from a light alloy.

FUN FACT

The pens that were used in olden days were made from metals. Hence, they were quite difficult to write with and even caused injury. Today, there are many light alloys that are used to make the pens that we use, and they are almost weightless!

MACHINES

A machine is defined as a system that makes the life of human beings easy. Every machine in this world requires energy to work; this energy can be thermal, mechanical, electrical, light or any other form. The complexity of machines varies with the functions that they are made to perform. Simple machines like the pulley (a wheel rolled around a rope or chain that raises the load), lever (rigid bar on which the load rests), wedge (an object with one sharp end used to cut objects), wheel (the simplest machine that helps to move a load), inclined plane (an inclined surface at any angle used for lifting heavy objects at a height, e.g. ramps) and screw are very less complex as compared to machines, such as the computer, automobile or radio.

These simple machines don't require much force and energy to work. They just require a single human force and they work against this force, which is when we say that work is done.

Efficiency of Machines

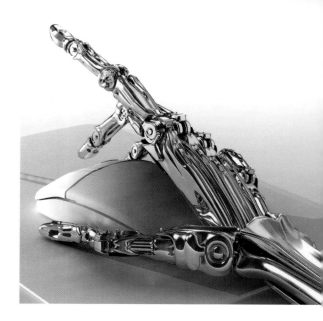

Machines convert input energy into motion. Electrical motors used in household chores require high voltage of power supply to be able to extract underground water. The efficiency of machines is a useful element as it compares the input and output of energy.

What is a machine's efficiency?

A typical machine helps in changing the direction or magnitude of a force using the force that has been provided from a specific input. This input is in the form of energy. The work done by the machine is the creation of a motion against a resistive force. The efficiency of the machine helps in conserving energy as well. If a machine is highly efficient, it will make use of minimum energy to give maximum output. Hence, while judging any machine, its efficiency is used to rate its quality. Therefore, when buying a machine, for example, a refrigerator, we consider the amount of energy it consumes and the amount of cooling it provides. If the cooling is greater than the energy consumption, then the machine is efficient.

Light weight machine parts are used for efficient running of the aircraft.

Increasing efficiency

Engineers, scientists and designers keep looking for ways to increase the efficiency of engines. Efficiency can be enhanced by many innovative ways. However, the simplest way to do this is by reducing the weight of the machine. This can be achieved by choosing lightweight material for its construction. Therefore, the strength to weight ratio of any material is an extremely important parameter. Operating the machine at a higher temperature is another way to increase efficiency. Similarly, choosing other design parameters can improve efficiency. But the fact is that conceptualising or incorporating changes to enhance efficiency is not an easy task.

FUN FACT

The efficiencies of different machines are different. The amount of energy that you use to heat water using an electric geyser for one bath is enough to keep the bulb in your house lighted for 3 months!

Barometer

A barometer is an instrument employed to measure atmospheric pressure, also known as air pressure or barometric pressure and the weight of air.

Invention

In 1643, Italian physicist and mathematician Evangelista Torricelli invented the barometer. He started by inverting a simple glass test tube (4 feet in length) filled with mercury into a dish. He realised that the mercury did not flow out of the tube, but a small amount of vacuum was created in the tube. He further observed that the amount of vacuum created varied from time to time and place to place. He was able to relate this change in vacuum to the atmospheric pressure at the given point of time. The Fortin Barometer is an improved version of the barometer. It has been proven that this advanced version of the barometer gives a clearer result than any other.

An old barometer.

Principle of working

The barometer is a glass tube that is 3 feet tall, open at one end and sealed at the other. This tube is filled with mercury and placed inverted in a container known as a reservoir. It basically contains mercury that falls into the tube and creates a vacuum at the top. To properly operate the barometer, it is given a balanced weight. If the weight of mercury is less than the level of air pressure, the mercury level rises in the tube and vice versa. Thus, to check the proper measurement, it is important to keep the mercury and vacuum weight balanced.

An old glass barometer showing air pressure with the help of dials.

Applications

Aneroid Barometer is a type of barometer that does not make use of any liquid. Thus, this kit is mainly used as an altimeter in aircrafts. A low pressure or sudden fall of pressure indicates uncommon weather, whereas a high pressure indicates fine weather.

The change in atmosphere pushes the top of the metal box upwards or downwards. This is rigged into a circular dial with a hand that magnifies the movement of the box and points to a number around the circumference of the dial.

Altimeters can be seen in the cockpit of an aircraft.

Induction Heater

Induction heating is a process that bonds, hardens or softens metals or other conductive materials. Induction heating offers an attractive combination of speed, consistency and control.

Invention

In 1831, Michael Faraday discovered the principle of induction heating. When an alternating electrical current is applied to the primary of a transformer, an alternating magnetic field is generated. According to Faraday's law, if the secondary of a transformer is located within the magnetic field, then an electric current would be induced.

Initially, this discovery was simply used to avoid the overheating of motors and transformers. However, by the twentieth century, the need arose to find more efficient ways of generating heat, mainly in order to melt industrial steel. This is when the laws of Faraday were brought into use and induction heating took main stage. Today, we use induction heating in our daily household appliances as well.

Passing a current through the metal coil causes the formation of a magnetic field, which, in turn, generates heat.

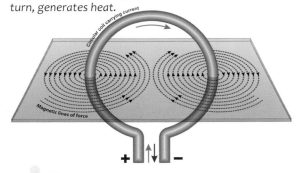

Principle of working

Induction heating relies on the unique characteristics of radio frequency (RF) energy, which is a part of the electromagnetic spectrum below infrared and microwave energy. As heat gets transferred to the object through electromagnetic waves, the object never witnesses direct contact with any flame. Also, the inductor does not get hot and there is no product contamination. If the process parameters are standardised, the process can be replicated and controlled. In basic induction heating, a solid state RF power supply transmits an AC current through an inductor (often a copper coil) and the part to be heated (the work piece) is placed inside the inductor. The heating usually occurs with both magnetic and non-magnetic parts, and is often denoted as the "Joule effect".

An AC electric induction machine.

Applications

One of the major applications of induction heating is in vacuum furnaces. Induction cookers are widely used for cooking purposes. Sometimes, induction heating is also used to expand an item to fit it at a specific spot. Presently, induction welding, brazing and furnaces are also used.

Induction heating furnace used for heating steel.

Furnace

The furnace is used as a heating element at a very high temperature. It is built to produce useful heat by combustion or other means. Coal furnaces, gas-fired furnaces and electrical furnaces are widely used in many industries.

Invention

The German-born British inventor Sir William Siemens first demonstrated the arc furnace in 1879 at the Paris Exposition by melting iron in crucibles. In 1906, the first commercial arc furnace was installed in the USA; it had a capacity of four tonnes and was equipped with two electrodes.

Melting Iron.

Principle of working

Furnaces can be distinguished based on their uses. The basic principle of a furnace is that chemical energy is converted into heat by burning fuels, such as coal, wood, oil and hydrocarbon gases. In an electric furnace or burner, electrical energy is converted into heat.

A furnace that uses coal as fuel.

Applications

Electric furnaces produce roughly two-fifths of the steel made in the USA. They are used by speciality steelmakers to produce almost all the stainless steel, aluminium alloy, cast alloy and special alloys, which are required by chemical, automotive, aircraft, food processing and other industries. Electric furnaces are also employed exclusively by mini-mills and small plants that use scrap charges to produce reinforcing and merchant bars.

FUN FACT

The Romans were the earliest humans to use a furnace around 1200 BCE. They called it "hypocausts". They used it to heat their houses, quite like the central heating systems that we use today.

Electric burner.

Hot steel in a furnace.

Generator

It is difficult to imagine our life without electricity. What happens when there is a power failure? We use a generator. The generator is a device that converts mechanical energy into electrical energy.

Industrial power generator.

Invention

In 1831, English chemist and physicist Michael Faraday and American physicist Joseph Henry almost simultaneously discovered the principle of operation of generators.

Principle of working

There is a basic principle on which different types of generators work, but the details of construction may differ. A coil of wire is placed within a magnetic field, with its ends attached to an electrical device, such as a galvanometer. When the coils are rotated within the magnetic field, the galvanometer displays a current being induced within the coil. Generators can be sub-divided into two major categories depending on whether the electric current generated is alternating current (AC) or direct current (DC). An AC generator can be modified to produce DC electricity as well. The change requires a commutator, which is a slip ring. The brushes are attached to both halves of the commutators. They are placed in such a way that the brushes slip from one half to the other the moment the direction of the current in the coil is reversed.

Applications

In an electrical generator, the galvanometer is substituted by an electrical device. Electrical generators are used to power many electrical systems, like those within a car. One of the major practical applications of generators is in the production of prominent amounts of electrical energy for industrial and residential use.

Electronic galvanometer.

Electric Motor

A machine that converts mechanical energy to electrical energy is called an electric generator. On the other hand, an electrical machine that converts electrical energy into mechanical energy is called an electric motor. Electric motors are a part of every electrical appliance, that we find around us, whose output is mechanical energy in some form.

Invention

In the 1740s, the first ever electric motor, a simple electrostatic device, was invented by a Scottish monk, Andrew Gordon. In 1827, Hungarian physicist Ányos Jedlik invented the electromagnetic self-rotors that delivered relatively weak electric currents. In May 1834, the first actual electric motor that could deliver a significant amount of mechanical output power was invented by Prussian engineer and physicist Moritz von Jacobi. The present day electric motor was invented in 1886 by American inventor Frank Julian Sprague and can produce a considerable amount of power under various amounts of electrical loads.

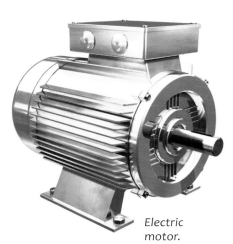

Electric motor.

Principle of working

An electric motor generally runs on the principle of Fleming's Left Hand Rule. An armature is placed between two magnetic poles. When an electric current is passed through the armature, they create a rotating magnetic field. This rotating magnetic field takes hold of the rotor and makes it spin around. Any form of machine that runs on an electric motor is then physically built around this rotating rotor.

For example, let's take a look at a toy car. When you put batteries in the car, an electric current gets passed through the rotor in the electric motor of the car. This will create rotating magnetic energy, causing the rotor to rotate. When the rotor begins to rotate, a network of wheels connected to the rotor will begin to rotate, which in turn will make the wheels of the toy car rotate. This is how the toy car ends up running on a pair of batteries.

Applications

Electric motors have a wide range of applications. They are used in water pumps, refrigerators, vacuum cleaners, cars, fans and so on.

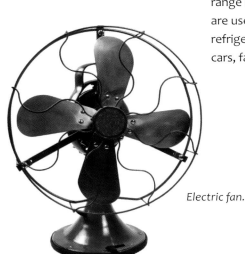

Electric fan.

Electric car at a charging station.

Steam Engine

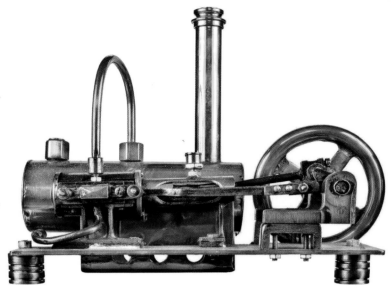

Every machine requires energy to work. The steam engine is a type of machine that requires steam to work. In this machine, heat energy is converted into mechanical energy.

Old style steam machine.

Furnace in steam train.

Invention

The steam engine was first brought into existence in the first century by Hero of Alexandria, but it was not used commercially back then. In 1698, English engineer Thomas Savery invented the steam engine that could pump water. In 1712, English inventor Thomas Newcomen developed the steam engine with a piston. In 1781, Scottish mechanical engineer James Watt gave us the first steam engine that worked with continuous rotary motion. Separate condensing techniques were used to avoid the heating of the cylinder in each cycle. They slowly became a primary source for the production of power and electricity. Initially, steam engines were used in rotary machines, power looms, automobile industries, mills and agriculture. With advancements in science and technology, the steam engine was improvised and steam turbines started being used for the generation of electricity. Commercially speaking, the first steam engines were used only to pump water.

Principle of working

Steam engines supply steam using boilers that expand in the presence of pressure and transform heat into work. The remnant heat energy is allowed to escape. The steam engine has maximum efficiency when the steam is condensed. The condenser temperature should be very low and the pressure should be high. To raise the temperature of steam, it is passed through the super heater; which has a few parallel pipes containing hot gases.

Applications

Steam engines are used in railways, ships and for various other purposes. They have a widespread industrial use as well.

Microwave Oven

The microwave oven has become a household device because of its many advantages over conventional ovens. It uses microwaves to create heat within the item that is kept inside it. Depending upon the amount of food, you can adjust the amount of time that you want to heat it for.

Invention

The first microwave oven was unexpectedly discovered by Percy Spencer during World War II as a byproduct of radar research using magnetrons.

Principle of working

Microwave ovens are devices that are used to cook or heat food by using microwaves for their operation. This appliance cooks food by means of high-frequency electromagnetic waves, that is, microwaves, instead of any sort of flame or heat. A microwave oven is a relatively small, box-like oven containing magnetron. Magnetron is responsible for the generation of microwaves, which interact with food particles, primarily water molecules, and increase the temperature of the food. Like all electromagnetic waves, microwaves too have dual polarity and they change their polarity with respect to each cycle, every second. Food particles contain many water molecules, as well as positive and negative poles, which interact with the poles of the microwave. This interaction of the food particles and microwave particles results in the excitation of food particles. The food particles then rotate at double the speed, producing heat, which increases the temperature of the food and cooks it. Microwave particles don't interact with plastic or glass; thus, the container doesn't get affected. This is why it is always advised to use special microwave-oven utensils.

Applications

Microwaves are a form of radiation that occupy a part of the electromagnetic spectrum. Microwaves are called millimetre waves due to their small wavelength. These waves are mostly used in a microwave oven or for satellite communication, medical purposes, etc.

Food can be heated and cooked in a microwave oven.

FUN FACT

Microwave ovens were not always so compact. The first one ever made was the size of a refrigerator, about 6 feet tall. Not only that, it weighed about 350 kg!

Satellite

A satellite is a scientist's creation that moves around Earth at different velocities. Satellites vary in size and design. They can be lightweight and spherical, slightly heavier and consisting of only two radio transmitters or heavily instrumented space laboratories weighing tonnes.

Sputnik 1

Invention

The concept of an artificial satellite in orbital flight was first suggested by Sir Isaac Newton.

Principle of working

Newton remarked that a cannonball shot at a very high velocity from the top of a mountain in a direction parallel to the horizon will revolve around before finally landing. Although gravitational force makes objects fall on Earth's surface, its momentum will result in the object covering a curved path rather than a linear path. Celestial bodies like the moon have such a high velocity that it results in a complete dispatch from Earth's surface. Sputnik I, launched by the Soviet Union, circled around Earth every 96 minutes. Exactly three months later, a satellite named "Explorer" was launched. Though it was much smaller than Sputnik, it could efficiently detect radiation and discover the innermost Van Allen radiation belts.

FUN FACT

As more satellites are being sent into space, the "satellite traffic" is increasing, which could cause accidents. A Russian and American satellite had collided in space in 2009.

Applications

Satellites are used to make astronomical observations and collect experimental data. Meteorological departments make their forecast using weather satellites. Telephone, radio and other communication channels work with the help of communication satellites.

Spacecraft

Space has no limits. How nice would it be to get in a vehicle that would carry us to space! Such vehicles do exist and are used by astronauts to travel in outer space and observe, research, study, and explore space. A spacecraft is defined as any vehicle that is capable of flight in outer space.

Invention

In 1919, American pioneer Robert H. Goddard's publication got spaceflights into limelight. Later, motivated by his publication, German physicist Hermann Oberth and German-American space architect Wernher Von Braun started their work on spaceflights. Sputnik 1 became the first humanmade satellite to orbit around Earth.

Principle of working

A spacecraft has three constituents. These are, the orbitter, solid rocket boosters and external fuel tank. The orbitter is where astronauts sit in if it is a manned spacecraft. There are two rocket launchers attached to the outside of the orbitter. These help launch it into space and separate from the spacecraft. External fuel tanks provide the fuel for this liftoff to take place. Once the fuel tanks are empty, they separate from the body. As the required distance is achieved, astronauts take control of the craft.

Applications

Spacecraft applications are similar to satellites. Spacecraft are used for satellite communication. The meteorological department uses them for weather forecast and to capture images of space. A scientist uses spacecraft to know more about space and explore new things. Communication channels like television, radio or others also require spacecraft for transmission. Space tourism is one of the latest important applications of spacecraft.

Thermometer

The thermometer is very common device used in our daily lives. Over the years, its general principle was improved after experiments were carried on with liquids like mercury. A scale was also provided to measure the expansion and contraction caused by these liquids with a rise and fall in temperature.

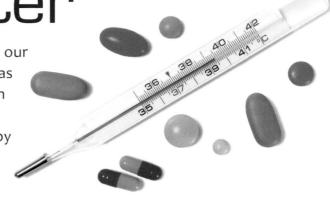

Invention

Famous Italian mathematician–physicist Galileo Galilei invented the thermometer.

Substances sensitive to changes in temperature, like mercury, are utilised in a thermometer. Different types of thermometers are available, such as gas and liquid thermometers. Gas thermometers generally work at very low temperatures. The commonly used ones are liquid thermometers that usually have mercury enclosed in a sealed glass tube with nitrogen gas around it. Mercury thermometers are simple to use, inexpensive and can be used to measure a wide temperature span.

Galileo thermometer.

FUN FACT

Thermometer is an improved product. Before it, there was a thermoscope that only indicated if the object was getting hotter or colder!

Applications

The thermometer is used mostly in industries, research and laboratories. They are used wherever we need to measure temperature.

Principle of working

There are several types of thermometers. Electrical-resistance thermometers use platinum and operate on the principle that electrical resistance varies with changes in temperature. Thermocouples are composed of two wires made of different materials joined together at one end and exposed to temperature. The other end is attached to a voltage measuring device. When there is a temperature difference, a voltage is generated between the two ends. Magnetic thermometers work best at low temperatures. As the temperature decreases, their efficiency increases, due to which they are believed to measure low temperatures with more accuracy.

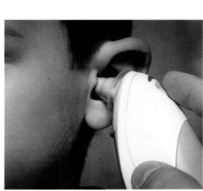

Electrical resistance thermometer.

Digital thermometer.

Clinical thermometer.

Turbines

Turbines are machines that convert the energy in a stream of flowing body into work by passing the flowing body through the blades of a rotor. When higher velocity flowing bodies exert force on the rotor, the blades move and work is performed. Turbines can be classified according to the flowing bodies used: water, steam, gas and wind.

Steam turbine.

Invention

In 1888, American engineer Lester Allen Pelton designed the first modern turbine, which was more efficient, to produce mechanical energy. When the free water stream strikes the turbine buckets tangentially, the flow of the stream gets equally divided in both directions.

Applications

Wind turbines are modified variations of windmills that have been a major source of electricity in many parts of the world, including the USA. Presently, the primary use of water turbines is for electric power generation.

Principle of working

Steam turbines are efficient machines as they produce the maximum amount of electrical energy. A steam turbine is driven by the steam produced by either fossil fuels or nuclear power. The output energy extracted from the steam is expressed according to change of temperature across the turbine. The change of temperature by steam increases with the pressure of the steam generator and with reduced turbine-exit pressure. In gas turbines, the flowing body is a mixture of air and other gaseous products of combustion. Gas-turbine engines consist of a compressor, turbine and many other complex parts. A water turbine uses the potential energy of water to provide mechanical energy.

Gas turbine.

The turbines of an aircraft.

Submarine

Submarines are machines that remain underwater. In 1578, William Bourne, a British mathematician and writer on naval topics, suggested an entirely closed boat that could remain submerged in water, as well as float on water.

Invention

Since the seventeenth century, there has been continuous progress on submarines. Submarines first became a major factor in naval warfare during World War I (1914–18) in both the Atlantic and Pacific, when Germany used surface merchant vessels. They made use of torpedoes, which are underwater missiles. Later, in the 1960s, submarines that remained under water for months or years became the sole weapon during wars. These submarines were nuclear-powered. Thus, submarines loaded with many torpedoes and nuclear missiles were used in the naval wars. Famed American inventor and artist Robert Fulton experimented with submarines for several years before his steamboat Clermont steamed across the Hudson River.

Principle of working

The submarine is a vessel that must be able to float on water, as well as completely submerge underwater. In order for a heavy vessel made of iron to float on water, it is built in a special way. The body of the submarine is made of two layers. There is an inner layer and an outer layer. The space between the inner and outer layer is the air chamber. If the submarine is floating and has to submerge, then pumps fitted on the outer layer pull in water and fill the air chamber with water, causing the submarine to sink. When the submarine has to float again, pressurised air is pushed into the air chamber, causing the submarine to come to the surface and float again.

Applications

A submarine, unlike any naval vessel, is capable of propelling itself beneath the water, as well as on the water's surface. It cannot be compared to the normal surface ships. This property of submarines makes them capable enough to be used in wars. Submarines are used to extract oil from deep sea. They are also used in the tourism sector and for exploring underwater living environments.

The crew of a submarine.

A submarine appearing at sea-level.

Periscope

It would be exciting to travel underwater by a submarine. However, how do the seamen know what is happening over the sea level? The answer is very simple. They make use of a periscope. A periscope helps one to see objects above or below their eye level.

Invention

The first periscope was marketed in the 1430s by German goldsmith Johannes Gutenberg. Furthermore, it was only in 1647 that a periscope with lenses was made by the famous astronomer Johannes Hevelius.

Principle of working

The periscope is an optical instrument, a device consisting of two mirrors or reflecting prisms set parallel to each other at an angle of 45 degrees. These two mirrors help in changing the direction of light coming from the scene observed. The first mirror deflects it down through a vertical tube while the second mirror diverts it horizontally to allow convenient viewing. If the two mirrors are placed at 90 degrees, it helps to see the view behind the viewer.

Applications

Periscopes of this type were widely used during World War II in tanks and other armoured vehicles as observation devices. When fitted with a small, auxiliary gun-sight telescope, the tank periscope can also be used for pointing and firing guns. Defence personnel also use a periscope in gun turrets. The periscope is used in naval wars when, sometimes, there is low visibility. It also enables an observer to see his/her surroundings while remaining undercover, behind the armour or submerged. In addition, periscopes are also used to see into nuclear reactors.

Soldiers using a periscope behind their bunker to scout for enemies.

Telescopes

A telescope is a typically long tube of metal with a lens at each end that helps us to see faraway objects. Telescopes are used to examine celestial bodies like the moon, Earth and stars. They are also used by sailors to search far-off horizons for the sight of land.

Invention

In the seventeenth century, Galileo was the first person to include a telescope in the study of celestial bodies called astronomy. Prior to this, no magnification instruments were used. With new progress in science and technology, more powerful telescopes have been developed that can magnify any small part of space. In addition to advancement in telescopes, there are more optical instruments like cameras, microscopes and spectrographs. Such developments have contributed a lot to the exploration of space and knowing things that would be impossible to know without their existence.

Principle of working

When light travels from one medium to another, it bends either towards or away from the focal point of the medium. This process is called refraction. Light changes path only when the densities of two mediums are different. Similarly, a telescope uses the process of refraction. There is a two-lens arrangement in a telescope: objective lens and eyepiece lens. The outer one is the objective lens from which light enters the telescope. The eyepiece lens enlarges the image of the object being viewed. The second lens is the eyepiece lens, which enlarges the image of the object.

A coin viewer.

Applications

The telescope is used to capture magnified images of bodies in space and even on Earth. It helps in space exploration. Telescope plays a key role in astronomy. They help to study the nature of various celestial bodies like comets, meteors, planets, Milky Way and other galaxies.

GRAVITY

Do you know why we can stand on Earth and why everything flies in space? This is caused by a force that attracts two things towards each other, called gravity. Our Earth has a gravitational force. That is why if we jump we are drawn back to Earth. However, in space, there is no gravity which is why astronauts can float about.

It is gravity that causes objects to have weight. When some object has weight, it means that there is a certain amount of gravity acting on that object. The Sun's gravitational pull influences our planet to orbit around it. The motion of the moon is influenced by gravity between the Sun and Earth. The moon's gravity pulls on Earth and makes the tides rise and fall every day. As the moon passes over the ocean, the sea level swells. As Earth rotates, the moon passes over new parts of Earth, causing the oceanic swells to move along with it.

What is Gravitational Force?

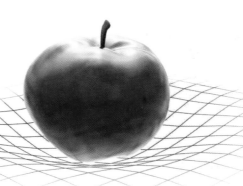

Gravitation is the force of attraction that acts to draw any body together while gravity is the force in operation between Earth and other bodies. Gravity depends on the gravitational field of Earth, as well as on other factors, such as Earth's rotation. The measure of force of gravity for any given body is the weight of that body; however, the mass of any body does not vary with its location. It is the weight that varies.

Gravitational force working on a heavy object.

Gravitational force

Did you know that the same person would weigh slightly different if weighed at different parts of the world? At a given location, objects are equally accelerated by the force of gravity. This is because Earth's rotation can spin any object into space. The gravity of Earth at the equator is 9.789 m/s² while the force of gravity at the poles is 9.832 m/s². Thus, an object will weigh more at the poles than at the equator because of this centripetal force. This means that weight is a relatively variable number.

Difference in force of gravity

The force of gravity changes depending on what lies beneath any object. Any higher concentrations of mass like high-density rocks can alter the force of gravity on an object slightly.

Calculating gravitational force on Earth

To do this, we need one more factor, a gravitational constant with the value 6.673×10^{-11} Nm²/kg². The force of gravity in our daily life is termed as "weight". Our weight is a measurement of the force of Earth's gravity acting upon us.

Objects falling to Earth due to its gravity.

Acceleration Due to Gravity

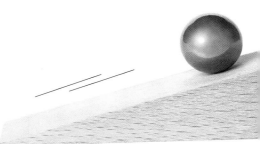

We have already learnt in the previous section that any free-falling object is under the influence of gravity. A free-falling object has an acceleration of roughly 9.8 m/s^2 towards Earth. The numerical value for this acceleration is an important value and has been referred to as the acceleration of gravity, which is the acceleration of objects moving only under the influence of gravity.

Acceleration due to gravity value

Acceleration due to gravity is the numerical value for the acceleration of a free-falling object. It is denoted by the symbol "g". The numerical value for the acceleration of gravity is 9.8 m/s^2. However, slight variations in this value are primarily influenced by the altitude, increasing or decreasing speed or changing direction of an object. Any free-falling object is always under the influence of gravity with an acceleration of 9.8 m/s^2 in the downward direction. These free-falling objects are independent from resistance of air. This is gravitational acceleration or acceleration due to gravity, denoted by "g" has a standard value of 9.8 m/s^2 but varies in gravitational environments. The gravitational field widget is used to investigate the effect of location on the value of "g".

What is acceleration due to gravity?

Among all types of forces, the most common is the force of gravity. It is experienced by us in everyday life. Also, it is present on a global scale. The reason behind objects falling on the ground is the inherent property of Earth exerting a force of attraction on objects. This force is the force of gravity and the acceleration generated on these objects because of this force is acceleration due to gravity. According to the definition of force, the equation of force due to gravity has been denoted by,

W = mg

where m = the mass of the object and g = acceleration due to gravity.

In this case, force is better known as the weight of objects. Acceleration, in this case, is acceleration due to gravity, which is constant and denoted by g. The approximate value of acceleration due to gravity is 32 ft/s^2 , or 9.8 m/s^2. These are the values of acceleration of gravity on Earth.

Application

Hence, if we want to calculate the force (weight) of a ball falling from the top of a building, we would find out its mass in grams and simply multiply this number with 9.8 m/s^2. This helps to solve a lot of physics-related problems.

Ball falling down due to gravitational force.

Newton's Law of Universal Gravitation

Newton's law of universal gravitation states that any two bodies in the universe attract one another with a certain amount of force. This force is directly proportional to the product of the two masses and inversely proportional to the square of the distance between them.

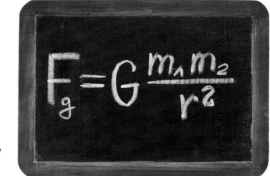

$$F_g = G \frac{m_1 m_2}{r^2}$$

Newton discovered gravity after observing an apple falling from a tree.

Newton's theory

Sir Isaac Newton discarded his old theories and put forward a new one that the amount of gravitational force on an object also depends on its distance along with its mass. However, after him, Einstein's theory of relativity describes gravitational force even more clearly. Gravitational force is the weakest of all four fundamental forces of nature. It is negligible in the case of subatomic particles, but it has great importance in case of macroscopic bodies. The effect of gravity extends from all objects in all directions, but the further you move from the object, the lesser the gravitational force one will feel.

How does Newton's law affect Earth?

Earth revolves in an orbit around the Sun because of the Sun's gravity. Why can we not feel the gravity of the Sun? This happens because of the distance between the Sun and us. The moon also exerts some gravity on Earth, which causes ocean tides on Earth. When the tides are high, we know that the moon is very close to us. On the other hand, when the tides are low, we know that the moon is far away from us.

Orbit of Earth around the Sun.

Gravity or gravitation is a natural process by which physical bodies attract one another. Gravity provides weight to the physical objects and directs them to fall towards the ground if dropped. In modern physics, gravitation is accurately described as the consequence of space-time. For most situations, gravity is approximated by Newton's law of universal gravitation, which considers that the gravitational force of the mass of two bodies will increase if the product of the masses increases and vice versa; and will decrease if the square of the distance between them increases and vice versa.

be much greater than, say, an apple. That is why the apple moves towards Earth. On the other hand, the mass of the Sun is much larger than that of Earth and so Earth rotates around the Sun rather than the other way round.

Also, gravity is everywhere. We might feel that there is no gravity in space, but gravity is present even in space. However, because it is very far away from any object having mass, the gravity there is weak. The force of gravity that an object with mass exerts on another object weakens as the distance between the two object increases.

Application

When an object falls to Earth, not only is Earth attracting that object towards itself, but the object is pulling Earth towards itself as well. However, if we compare the masses of the object falling to Earth and Earth itself, the mass of Earth will

Gravity on Moon

Gravity is the force between two objects and not simply the force between an object and Earth. It is the force between the Sun and Earth, moon and Earth and is present anywhere in the universe. The centre of our solar system, the Sun, also has gravity, because of which all the planets revolve around it.

Weight on Earth v/s moon

If we measure our weight on Earth, it can be calculated as the product of the mass of the object and the gravity of Earth, which has a fixed value of 9.8 m/s^2. If we try to measure our weight on the moon, will it be same? The answer is no, as it will depend on the gravity of the moon, which is not the same as that of Earth. The moon is 1/4th the size of Earth; thus, the moon's gravity is much less as compared to Earth's gravity. To be precise, it is 83.3 per cent less. And so, we can assume that if we were to weigh ourself on the moon, our weight would show up to be much less compared to that on Earth. Since the moon's gravitational attraction is less, we can even jump twice the height and distance as compared to that on Earth.

Differences in gravity

In a spaceship, your weight would read zero; you are weightless. If you were on any other celestial body, you would weigh a different amount than you do on Earth. The weight that you feel depends on many things, including your actual mass, the mass of the planet that you are on and how further away you are from the centre of that planet.

FUN FACT

We say that Earth's gravity is weak. But how is that possible when it holds all of us on Earth? Consider a little magnet that sticks to your refrigerator. It just takes that little magnet's electromagnetic force to cancel out the gravitational force acting on it to remain on the refrigerator.

Astronauts spacewalking, as no gravitational force is working on them.

Without gravity, the body feels weightless.

ELECTRICITY

Electricity is the set of physical occurrences related to the flow and presence of electrical charge. There are a wide variety of events associated with electricity, namely, electrical current, static electricity, lightning and electromagnetic induction. The creation of electromagnetic radiation was possible due to electricity. It produces charges which in turn produce electromagnetic fields, which act on other charges. The word "electricity" comes from the Greek word "ilektrismós" meaning amber. In traditional times, amber was rubbed together to produce electrical charges or effects. However, it is only during the second half of the nineteenth century, that its practical applications came into being.

Electricity Production

Think of your life from the time you wake up to the time you go to bed. In this modern world, we are totally dependent upon electricity from charging our mobile to entertaining ourselves with television or music systems, from adding with hot water to preparation of food items in the microwave. We use electricity everywhere.

A cellphone being charged.

Electricity production

Generation of electricity is the conversion of any one form of energy into electricity. It is not exactly the generation of energy. As the law of conservation states, energy can neither be created nor destroyed. This initial energy that is converted into electricity is often called primary energy as this sort of energy is readily available in nature. A prime example of such energy is wind energy or solar energy. These two examples are also clean energy sources as the process of converting them to electricity does not harm the environment.

In general, the term "generation of electricity" is mostly concerned with the entire process of converting one form of energy to electricity, taking it from where it is usable to an entire city and then distributing it to various homes.

Basic principle of electricity production

The basic principle that is used in these systems that help generate electricity was proposed by Michael Faraday. He stated that electricity is generated in a loop of wire when it is moved between the poles of a magnet. A more formal Faraday's Law was formulated from it too. Before transmission and distribution of electricity, the fundamental generation of electricity uses the discovery of Faraday in 1830s, that is, conversion of movement or mechanical energy into electricity. The process includes turbines that are rotated using various sources of energy like wind, water, gas and steam. It lights a spark that gets collected by a generator and distributed elsewhere as usable electricity.

A man starting a generator.

Solar and photovoltaic energy

Solar and photovoltaic cells are the best renewable source of energy. They convert solar energy to electrical energy using semiconductors. These cells turn energy from the Sun's rays directly into instantly usable energy. There are two main types: solar thermal and photovoltaic. Solar thermal panels utilise the Sun's energy to heat water that can be used in washing and heating. Photovoltaic panels utilise the photovoltaic effect to turn the Sun's energy directly into electricity.

Solar panels convert solar energy to electricity.

Fuel combustion

Traditional materials like coal and natural gas are used as fuel in many power stations. These are used to heat water and generate steam, which rotates the turbine and generates electricity. Coal is the major source of fuel for electricity generation. Most power stations require huge reserves of coal to produce electricity continuously. However, coal combustion not only leaves by-products but is also replenishable. Hence, alternative, efficient resources are being looked into.

Electricity is collected and generated from power houses.

Hydroelectricity

Hydroelectricity generation is the method used to generate electricity by harnessing the power of moving water, known as hydroelectric power. To produce electricity from the kinetic energy in moving water, the water has to move with adequate speed and volume to spin a propeller-like device called a turbine, which in turn rotates a generator. For instance, about four litres of water per second falling one hundred feet can generate one kilowatt of electricity.

Dams are used to harness water and create electricity.

Wind power

Wind power is a great source of electricity generation, currently. In the areas near the sea coast and vast deserts, this method has got great success. A wind turbine works on the principle of using wind harnessed mechanical energy to make electricity. Wind turns the blades of the windmills, which spin a shaft, which is connected to a generator that generates electricity. These turbines convert kinetic energy in the wind into mechanical energy. Wind turbines can be built on land or offshore in large bodies of water such as oceans and lakes.

Windmills are used to generate electricity.

Electromagnetism

Electromagnetism is the study of the electromagnetic force. It is a type of physical interaction that occurs between electrically charged particles. It is one of the four fundamental interactions that exist in nature, others being strong interaction, weak interaction and gravitation. It is the force exerted by the electromagnetic interaction of electrically charged or magnetically polarised particles or bodies.

What is electromagnetism?

One of the four fundamental forces, electromagnetic force manifests itself through forces between the charges (Coulomb's Law) and magnetic force. These forces are together described through the Lorentz force law. Theoretically, both magnetic and electric forces are manifestations of an exchange force involving the exchange of photons. Electromagnetic force is a force of infinite range, which obeys the conventional inverse square law.

A Magnetic Resonance Imaging (MRI) machine makes use of electromagnetism.

Where does it act?

Electromagnetism manifests as both electric fields and magnetic fields. Both fields are simply different aspects of electromagnetism and, hence, are intrinsically related. Thus, a changing electric field generates a magnetic field; conversely, a changing magnetic field generates an electric field. This effect is known as the electromagnetic induction.

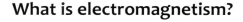

Teacher conducting an experiment on electromagnetism.

FUN FACT

A common misconception about electricity was that it was discovered by Benjamin Franklin. While he did prove the existence and science of electricity using the kite experiment, humans have known about electricity since the times of the Ancient Greeks.

Applications

The principle of electromagnetism is the basis of the operation of electrical generators, motors and transformers. The magnetic and electric fields are convertible with relative motion as four vectors. In quantum electrodynamics, electromagnetic interactions between charged particles can be calculated using the method of Feynman diagrams. It is used in scrap metal yards to pick up heavy loads of metal and in MRI machines in hospitals.

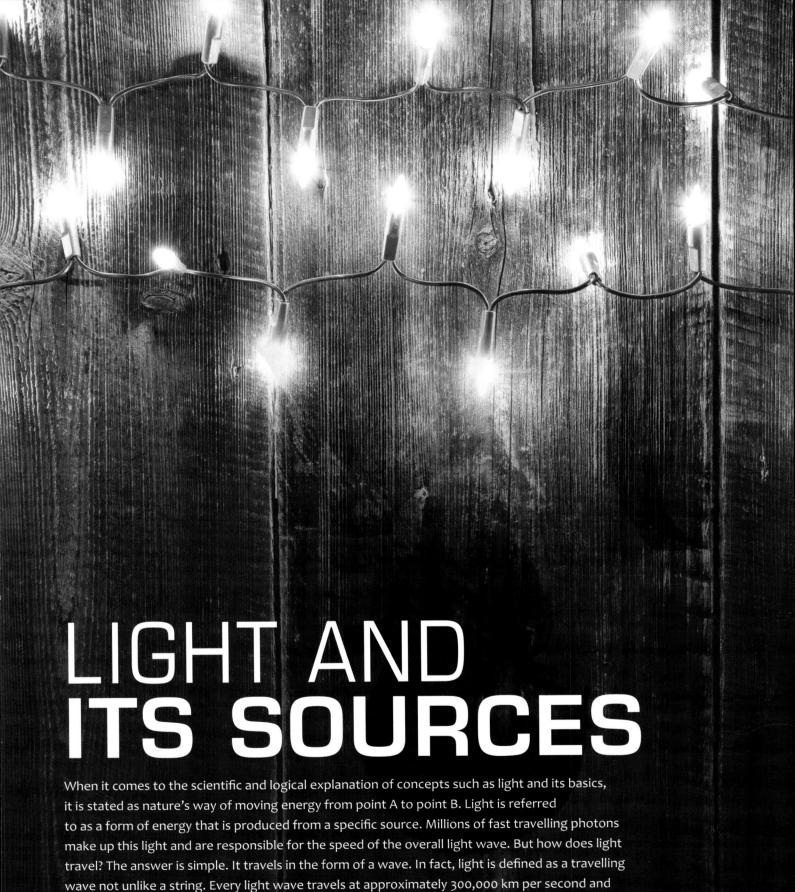

LIGHT AND ITS SOURCES

When it comes to the scientific and logical explanation of concepts such as light and its basics, it is stated as nature's way of moving energy from point A to point B. Light is referred to as a form of energy that is produced from a specific source. Millions of fast travelling photons make up this light and are responsible for the speed of the overall light wave. But how does light travel? The answer is simple. It travels in the form of a wave. In fact, light is defined as a travelling wave not unlike a string. Every light wave travels at approximately 300,000 km per second and can go through vacuum as well; for example, when it travels through space. However, when travelling through denser materials, be it from the atmosphere of a planet to a simple piece of glass, the speed of a light wave slows down considerably. Let's find out why this happens.

Visible Light

An electromagnetic spectrum is the combination of a range of different colours of lights. Visible light, that is, visible spectrum is that portion of the electromagnetic spectrum, which can be detected by the human eye. An average human eye often responds to 390–700 nanometre (nm) wavelengths of light and this is known as the visible spectrum.

The invention

In the seventeenth century, English physicist Isaac Newton first named this principle "spectrum", which is Latin for appearance, after his discovery of the concept of a prism's capacity to disassemble and reassemble white light. There are, sometimes, unsaturated colours like pink, purple or even magenta, which the human eyes and brain might not be capable of distinguishing. All those colours that contain only one wavelength are usually known as spectral colours or pure colours.

Dispersal of white light into various colours by a diamond.

Spectrum

A spectrum of pure colours is continuous as it has no clear boundaries between one colour and the next. Visible wavelength can pass through a region of the electromagnetic spectrum, the optical window, which allows it to pass largely undisturbed through Earth's atmosphere itself. Many species can see light frequencies that are beyond a human's visible spectrum. A white light, which is visible to us, is composed of seven colours of different frequencies. They are violet, indigo, blue, green, yellow, orange and red. In short, VIBGYOR. By remembering the word "VIBGYOR" (consists of the first letter of the seven constituent colours of white colour) one can remember these seven colours. These colours are often visible in nature. For example, the rainbow that is formed in the sky when we get sunshine during or immediately after the rains. This happens because sunshine is broken up into seven colours by water droplets in the atmosphere. The curvature of the rainbow is due to the different wavelengths of different colours.

FUN FACT

The human body actually emits light. However, the amount of light is so small, that it isn't visible to the eye.

Different wavelengths of colours.

10^3	1	10^{-3}	10^{-5}	10^{-7}	10^{-9}	10^{-11}	10^{-13}

Radio waves | Micro-waves | Infrared radiation | Visible light | Ultraviolet | X-rays | Gamma-rays

Frequency and Wavelength of Light

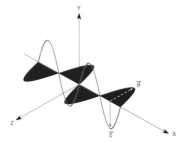

In terminologies used for light, the quantity that is known to be "waving" in the electromagnetic field can be described with a particular wavelength and wave diagram. The Greek alphabet "lambda" is normally used to notify the wavelength of light. There are many such units of length used for depicting the wavelength of electromagnetic radiation.

Wavelength of light

If we were to measure light on a scale, it would quite literally be like a wave. Consider a straight line. The wave would begin from the starting point of this line, moving upwards like a climbing graph, then downwards to intersect the straight line and continue below like a dipping graph. Eventually, the wave would again come up and intersect the straight line. The important thing to remember is, that the length the wave covers over the straight line is equal to the length that it covers under the straight line. Also, the distance between the two highest points is the same as the distance between the two lowest points. This distance is called a wavelength.

A rainbow.

Frequency of light

If we have to measure the frequency of light, we have to take another variable into consideration; time. In that case, we consider that the straight line that we spoke of earlier represents time. Now, the wave keeps rising and falling as described earlier. However, the number of times that the wave reaches a certain height in a given amount of time is called its frequency. In simpler terms, if we consider the number of times that a wave reached its highest point within 1 second, that is described as the frequency of the wave. Therefore, frequency is defined as the number of times a wave rises or falls within a given amount of time.

Measuring the spectrum

If we were to consider the spectral colours and measure their wavelength and frequency, we would see that red has the lowest wavelength and frequency. Hence, it falls on the lowest part of the spectrum and violet has the highest wavelength and frequency, putting it at the other end of the spectrum. They all lie in order of the "VIBGYOR".

A prism dispersing colours of different wavelengths.

A light meter, typically used by photographers.

Infrared/ Ultraviolet

The invisible radiant energy of electromagnetic radiation which has longer wavelengths than visible light is known as infrared. On the other hand, the invisible radiant energy of electromagnetic radiation which has shorter wavelengths than visible light is known as ultraviolet rays.

Uses of infrared light

English astronomer Sir William Herschel discovered an invisible light with a wavelength less than that of red light in 1880. This light came to be known as infrared light. There are many uses of the infrared light. One of its major properties that has been put to use is its sensitivity to heat. Hence, this light has been used in making night vision goggles that enable one to see objects in the dark based on the object's heat signature. This technology has also been used to make infrared space telescope that enables the viewer to get a better view into space. Infrared thermal imaging cameras are used to detect the overheating of electrical apparatus, detect change of blood flow in the human body, etc.

Uses of ultraviolet light

Johann Wilhelm Ritter, a German physicist, discovered violet rays with a wavelength that was more than that of violet light. This light came to be known as ultraviolet light. Ultraviolet light is available abundantly in nature. The Sun is a major source of ultraviolet light, also known as UV light. In fact, our bodies need UV light to create Vitamin D. This light has a special property of causing chemicals to react and cause certain substances to glow. UV light is used in many ways. Since it increases the rate of melanin production in our skin, it is used in tanning beds to make the skin tan faster. Because it has the ability to make certain substances fluoresce, it is used in the detection of fingerprints, bodily fluids and blood traces at crime scenes amongst many other things.

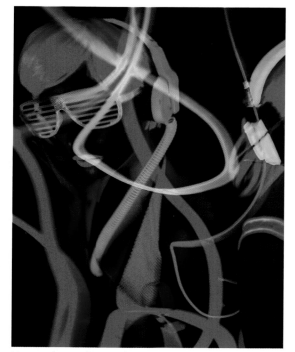

Neon colours glow under ultraviolet lights.

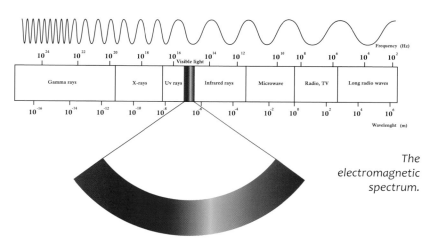

The electromagnetic spectrum.

☀ Intensity

Many aspects of light are measured as its intensity. Everything from a light's radiance to its luminosity can be measured under the umbrella of intensity. In physics, the simple meaning of the term intensity is the energy that is transferred per unit area.

What is the intensity of light?

Usually, scientists don't mention light in terms of waves and amplitude, as light by itself doesn't change when it travels through water or air. Intensity is like the brightness measure of light and can be easily measured at a rate at which light energy can be delivered to a chosen or given unit of surface area.

A light meter.

Solar panels with photoreceptor cells.

FUN FACT

Fish are more aware of their predators when there is a greater intensity of light. This is why they're easier to catch at dawn or dusk rather than in the middle of the day.

Application of intensity of light

Knowing the intensity of light can come in handy in many ways. For example, the intensity of sunlight on a solar panel when multiplied by the area of the panel can specify how much power is available to use solar appliances at home. A lot of simplified equations and formulas can help an individual calculate the energy per unit time to run different solar appliances and thus save up on a lot of energy wastage as well. Similarly, when we purchase bulbs, we look at the watts that it consumes. This gives us an indication of the amount of brightness or the intensity of the bulb. We can assume that a bulb with higher watts usage will provide more intensity of light or will be able to brighten a larger area in the house.

Different ways of measuring the intensity of light

There are several electronic components that are light-sensitive and measure the intensity of light. Photoelements or solar cells generate electricity when light shines on them. They can be present in small battery chargers and small lamps. The advantage of these photocells is that the electrical current they deliver increases strictly with the light intensity. Photoresistors are small components whose electrical resistance reduces when light shines on them. They help increase the brightness of a display in areas where there is an increase in the surrounding light. Photoresistors are usually made to have the same spectral sensitivity as the human eye. Photodiodes and phototransistors are very small components that permit a greater electric current to pass through when light shines on them. They are used to sense the movement of a computer mouse.

Photon

A photon is the basic unit of all electromagnetic radiation. It is a mass-less, charge-less, stable quantum of light. Photons exhibit the properties of both waves and particles. They are not made up of any smaller particles as they themselves are basic particles. Hence, they are also known as elementary particles.

What is a photon?

In 1900, German physicist Max Planck first suggested the existence of photons while he was working on black-body radiation. Planck proposed that the energy of electromagnetic waves is released as discrete "packets" of energy. Later, Albert Einstein suggested that electromagnetic waves can only exist as these packets of energy, which he called "light quantum".

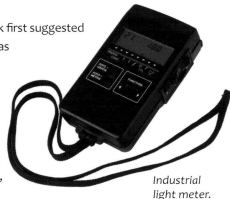

Industrial light meter.

Creative representation of a photon.

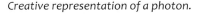
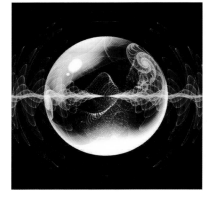

Photon properties

A photon can travel through empty space at a speed of almost 299,792 km/second. The ratio of the speed of photons in a particular medium to their speed in a vacuum is called velocity factor. It is always between 0 and 1, and depends on the wavelength to some extent. The shorter the wavelength of an electromagnetic disturbance, the more energy each photon contains. At any specific wavelength, every photon has the same amount of energy. The brilliance or intensity is a function of the number of photons striking a given surface area per unit time. Photons can be destroyed/created when radiation is absorbed or emitted.

Application of photon

Using this hypothesis, Einstein explained the photoelectric effect of electromagnetic radiation, which earned him the Nobel Prize in 1921. Einstein proved that photons are actually physical quanta of light as they show properties of both wave and particle. Accepting the dual nature of photons, it was possible to explain the photoelectric effect and other phenomena caused by electromagnetic radiation. Photons have numerous technological applications, particularly in experiments and devices that deal with the photoelectric effect.

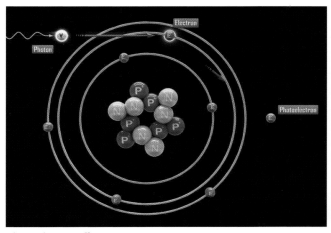

Photoelectric effect.

Optics

Optics is the branch of physics that deals with light, its properties and behaviour, and phenomena caused by or related to light. Light is an electromagnetic radiation; thus, optics also explains the generation, propagation, detection and other behaviour of electromagnetic waves like X-rays, microwaves and radio-waves. This branch of physics deals with three principal ranges of light – visible, ultraviolet and infrared light.

A camera works on the principles of optics.

What is optics?

Optics is the study of the science of light. It is an inextricable part of human life. The human eye contains photoreceptor rod cells and cone cells, which act as natural optical devices. The eye works on the basic principle of optics, which has various uses in the field of medicine, surgery and construction of optical devices like spectacles and corrective lenses. Optics is separated into two major areas: geometrical optics, which deals with how light moves and where it goes, and physical optics, which deals with the nature of light and the interaction between light and matter.

Applications of optics

Optical devices like magnifying glasses, photographic lenses, rear-view mirrors, microscopes and telescopes are all applications of optical phenomena and principles. Zoom camera with long focus is one of the modern applications of optics in the field of photography. Newer fields like opto-physics, optical-engineering and opto-electronics are coming up to encompass all phenomena and technologies involving light and other electromagnetic radiations.

Quantum optics

Most optical phenomena, like reflection, refraction and diffraction can be explained using classical electromagnetic views of light. However, some phenomena like photoelectric effect can be explained only by quantum optics that considers the wave–particle duality of light. Quantum optics have applications in the fields of physics and engineering along with practical uses. Lasers, photomultipliers, light-emitting diodes, photovoltaic cells, CCDs, etc., all function on the basic principles of quantum optics.

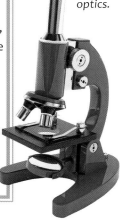

A microscope working on the basic principles of quantum optics.

143

Light-emitting Diode and Fluorescent Lamp

Light-emitting diodes or LEDs are semiconductor devices that produce visible light when an electrical current passes through them. Light-emitting diodes are basically a solid state lighting (SSL), as are organic light-emitting diodes (OLEDs) and light-emitting polymers (LEPs). LED lighting differs from incandescent and compact fluorescent lighting in various ways. In order to work, an electrical current, "I", passes through the semiconductor material, which eventually illuminates the tiny-sized light sources known as LEDs.

LED colours

Many common LED colours are available today. In reality, there is no such thing as a "white" LED. To get a white light, the type we use for lighting residential as well as industrial premises, different coloured LEDs are mixed with a phosphor material that converts the colour of light. Colourful LEDs are frequently used in traffic signals, indicators, power buttons on computers/laptops, etc.

LED applications

LEDs are now being incorporated into bulbs and fixtures for general lighting uses. LEDs can be made in various sizes and can be designed in different shapes. Some LED bulb solutions may look like the usual light bulbs. Some LEDs light fixtures can have LEDs built in as a permanent light source. LEDs are directional light sources, which means they emit light in a specific direction, unlike the incandescent and the compact fluorescent bulbs, where emission of light and heat takes place in all directions.

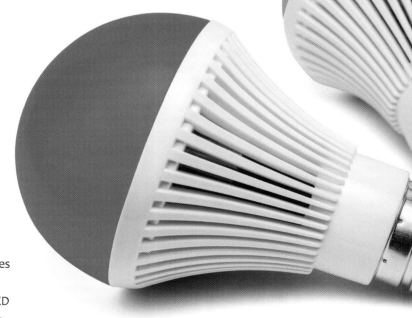

Common incandescent lights.

FUN FACT

Once used, fluorescent bulbs shouldn't be thrown into the trash. The bulbs have small amounts of mercury in them. This classifies them as "hazardous waste".

Applications of LEDs

LEDs can be divided into four major categories. First, they can be used as visual signals where light travels more or less directly from the source to the human eye. This application can be used to convey a message or meaning. Second, it can illuminate objects to provide a visual response of those objects. Third, LEDs could be used to measure and interact with processes involving no human vision. Fourth, LEDs operate in narrow band light sensors in a reverse-bias mode and respond to incident light, instead of emitting light.

Fluorescent lamp

A fluorescent lamp or bulb is a low pressure mercury (Hg) vapour gas-discharge device, which uses fluorescence to yield visible light. When an electric current is passed through the gas, the

LED lamps.

Colourful LED lights.

mercury vapours get excited and produce short-wave UV light, which then causes the phosphor coating inside the bulb to glow brightly. A fluorescent bulb/lamp converts the electrical energy to light with higher efficiency as compared to incandescent bulbs/lamps. The life of a simple white LED is forecasted to be between 3500 and 5000 hours, which is much higher than its competitor's incandescent bulb that has a life of 750–2000 hours. The lifetime of a conventional bulb is determined by the longevity of its filament; however, the lifetime of LEDs is determined differently. The lifetime of LEDs is defined as the mean number of hours till the light falls to 70 per cent of the initial brightness, in the unit of Lumens.

Efficacy of fluorescent lights

The luminous efficacy of the fluorescent light bulb may exceed above 100 Lumens/watt, which is several times higher than the efficacy of an incandescent bulb with similar light output. The incandescent and fluorescent lamps consist of filaments in glass bulbs, whereas LEDs contain small capsules/lenses where tiny chips are placed on a high thermal conductivity material (which acts as the heat sink).

LEDs, typically, just fade gradually. Conventional light bulbs waste most of their energy as heat. For example, an incandescent bulb gives off 90 per cent of its energy as heat; while a compact fluorescent bulb wastes 80 per cent as heat. LEDs remain cool. In addition, because they contain no glass components, they are not vulnerable to vibration or breakage like conventional bulbs.

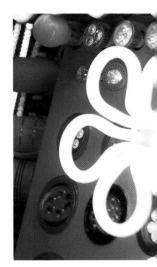

Fluorescent light inside a CPU.

Applications of fluorescent lamps

The compact fluorescent lamp utilises the auxiliary electronics into the base of the lamp, enabling them to fit into a regular light bulb socket. Fluorescent lamps can be used in kitchens, basements or garages. Furthermore, special fluorescent lights are used in stage lighting for film and video production. These lamps are cooler than traditional halogen light sources and use high-frequency ballasts.

Filament

An incandescent light globe is the most common type of lighting used in our homes. It consists of a very fine and coiled tungsten or sometimes molybdenum filaments that are raised to white heat by passing an electric current through them. The filament is held in position by two support posts that are insulated. They are supported by a glass base. The glass envelope of the globe retains an inert atmosphere around the tungsten filament so that it does not burn.

Working of a bulb

In a light bulb, an electric current is sent through a resistive material. Typically, materials will glow before reaching a melting point and most materials will glow a dull red colour when they reach around 525 °C. Filaments are made from materials that have a high melting point. Tungsten can reach up to 3422 °C before melting. The carbon arc lamp reaches the highest temperature of 3500 °C. Other materials have made good filaments or parts of filaments including tantalum, molybdenum and carbon.

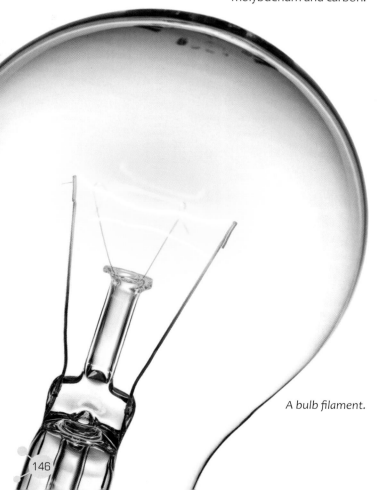

A bulb filament.

History of light filaments

Sir Humphry Davy

In 1802, Cornish chemist Sir Humphry Davy discovers incandescence in a platinum wire.

In 1841, English inventor Frederick de Moleyns patents an incandescent lamp within a glass bulb and partial vacuum.

In 1879, English physicist Sir Joseph Swan starts working with incandescent light; however, his invention is developed at the same time as Thomas Edison. Swan uses carbonised paper as a filament in a partially evacuated bulb, which lasts several hours.

In 1879, Thomas Edison is able to succeed in creating the first reliable light bulb. His bulbs last almost 600 hours.

Thomas Edison

In 1902, German chemist Werner von Bolton discovers that using tantalum for a filament increases efficiency, durability and bulb life. The age of metallic filaments begins and Siemens and Halske hold the patent.

In 1904, American chemist Willis Whitney counters the threat from the tantalum lamp with a GEM lamp: a unique process which generates a metallised filament.

In 1904, German chemist Alexander Just and Croatian inventor Franz Hanaman patent a sintered tungsten filament. Tungsten proves to be a good material; however, it is fragile and hard to work with.

In 1912, American chemist Irving Langmuir develops three important improvements to the bulb by developing an argon and nitrogen-filled bulb, tightly coiled filament and a thin molecular hydrogen coating on the inside of the bulb.

Irving Langmuir

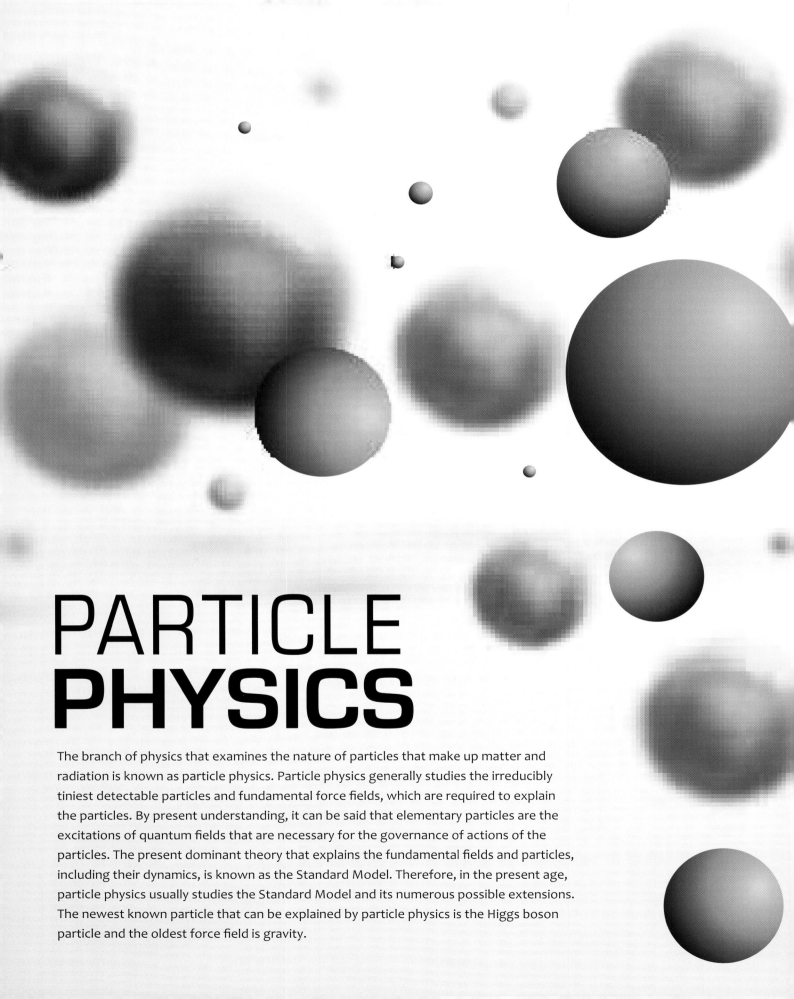

PARTICLE
PHYSICS

The branch of physics that examines the nature of particles that make up matter and radiation is known as particle physics. Particle physics generally studies the irreducibly tiniest detectable particles and fundamental force fields, which are required to explain the particles. By present understanding, it can be said that elementary particles are the excitations of quantum fields that are necessary for the governance of actions of the particles. The present dominant theory that explains the fundamental fields and particles, including their dynamics, is known as the Standard Model. Therefore, in the present age, particle physics usually studies the Standard Model and its numerous possible extensions. The newest known particle that can be explained by particle physics is the Higgs boson particle and the oldest force field is gravity.

Splitting an Atom

Splitting an atom is also termed as a fission reaction. Nuclear fission reaction is basically the splitting of any heavy nucleus, when it absorbs neutrons.

Otto Hahn, in 1938, discovered the phenomena of nuclear fission. Nuclear fission can take place naturally or heavy nucleus can be made fissionable by the bombardment of neutrons, known as induced fission.

History

In 1932, in England, James Chadwick discovered the neutron, which began the discovery of nuclear fission. Then in 1939, German physicists Lise Meitner and Otto Frisch first coined the term fission. It was used to explain the disintegration of a heavy nucleus into two lighter nuclei of almost equal size. Heavy elements, including uranium, thorium and plutonium, can undergo spontaneous fission, a form of radioactive decay, as well as induced fission, a form of artificial nuclear reaction.

A weapon of mass destruction: Nuclear bomb made from uranium.

Co-relation of nuclear fission and energy

The nuclear fission of any heavy nucleus needs an energy input of about 7 million electron volts (MeV). This is the amount of energy required to overcome the attractive nuclear forces, which hold the core, that is, the nucleus, in its shape.

The isotopes, which undergo induced fission after being struck by the free neutron are known as fissionable. They can be used as nuclear fuel to produce energy; for example, 233U, 235U and 239Pu.

The produced neutrons sustain a chain reaction because each atom that splits, releases excess neutrons, which cause the neighbouring atoms to split. The aftermath of the splits is the release of enormous amount of energy in the form of heat. This heat is utilised to heat up the coolant that goes off to the turbine and generator to produce electricity.

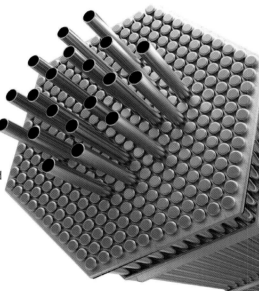

Nuclear fuel assembly.

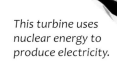

This turbine uses nuclear energy to produce electricity.

Fatal Fusion

Nuclear fusion is the method by which two atoms, belonging to elements with lower atomic number, are made to react with one another to form a heavier atom, releasing a lot of energy in the process. The amount of energy released by nuclear fusion is much higher than fission and produces fewer by-products.

History

Nuclear fusion is a very exciting field of physics that has captured the interest of scientists all over the world. However, it came into existence almost as soon as the atom was discovered. But its research and studies picked momentum at the end of World War II, when the arms race began. Nuclear fusion came to be used for battle purposes and nuclear bombs, such as Hydrogen Atomic bomb, were invented. Around the late 1940s and 1950s, the scientists got a better understanding of the process. Soon, nuclear fusion was being explored to create clean, renewable energy.

Renewable energy.

FUN FACT

Helium was discovered in the Sun as a by-product of all the nuclear fusion and was named so after the Greek Sun God, Helios.

Types of fusions

There are two types of fusion: one, where two hydrogen atoms combine and two, where one atom of deuterium and one atom of tritium combine. In 1930, German physicist Hans Bethe stated that by fusing two hydrogen atoms, energy can be released that could be harnessed and used for our benefit. However, to be able to do this practically, it would be better to use deuterium and tritium atoms as the rate of the reaction is much higher and the amount of energy released is 40 times that of hydrogen fusion.

Atom bomb used in the war.

Naturally occurring nuclear fusions

The Sun, which is the source of energy for our entire planet, is a hot ball of fire. We know this. However, how does this fire keep burning? How does it not run out of fuel? The answer is simple. The Sun is covered with nuclear fusions that have been going on since millions of years. Without any control, the reaction keeps going on, creating this hot mass of fire that is capable of running an entire solar system.

Nuclear Power

Imagine travelling with a bolt of electricity back through the wall socket, through miles of power lines into the nuclear reactor that generated it. We would find the generator that produces the spark. We would also discover the jet of steam that turns the turbine and finally, the radioactive uranium bundle that turns water into steam.

Nuclear power plants

Nuclear power plants are essentially thermal power plants, where the source of heat energy is the nuclear reaction. In a typical thermal power plant, we have coal with high calorific value as the fuel. We burn this coal to generate heat. This heat in turn converts water into pressurised steam and that does the mechanical work of turning the turbine. That way, heat is converted into mechanical energy. Then, we have the turbine's mechanical energy converted into electricity via the generator. Nuclear power plants employ exactly the same working principle. However, instead of burning coal, we have nuclear rods inside a nuclear reactor.

Control room of a nuclear power station.

Nuclear reaction

The nuclear reactor is where a nuclear chain reaction occurs in a controlled manner. Usually, uranium rods are used in the nuclear fission. A kilogram of uranium can generate three million times more energy than what we get by burning a kilogram of coal. When the nuclei collide with nearby atoms in the nuclear reactor, we have thermal energy. This is used to raise steam. Then, the process proceeds as it would have done in case of any typical thermal power plant.

Disadvantages of a nuclear power plant

Nuclear power plants also cause pollution and the waste is radioactive in nature. This means that the waste takes a very long time – hundreds of years – to lose its radioactivity. Discarding nuclear waste is a very difficult task. Again, accidents at nuclear power stations can be fatal. Chernobyl in Russia is a prime example of how bad accidents in nuclear power stations can be.

Distribution of nuclear power in the world.

What is a nuclear reactor?

Have you thought of what will happen when all the coal in the world exhausts and all the thermal power plants are forced to shut down? How will electricity be generated? To answer that, there are a few solutions that can be an alternative, such as hydro, nuclear and solar energy. Among them, the most prominent one is nuclear energy.

A nuclear power plant uses nuclear reactors for generating electricity. A nuclear reactor is also used to move spacecraft and submarines, produce isotopes for medical and diagnostic uses, and also for conducting research. A nuclear reactor is a mechanical system where sustained and controlled nuclear chain reaction is allowed to take place.

Principle of working

Fuel kept in the reactor vessel takes part in a chain reaction and yields enormous heat. This heat is extracted to produce electricity. Nuclear chain reactions are of two types through which electricity can be generated: (a) fission chain reaction and (b) fusion chain reaction. Utilisation of the released energy during either fission or fusion chain reaction is the main objective in the nuclear power generation methodology.

A nuclear reactor is a part of a nuclear power plant.

FUN FACT

As of 1st March, 2011, there were 443 operating nuclear power reactors across the world in 47 different countries.

- Operating reactors, building new reactors
- Operating reactors, planning new build
- No reactors, building new reactors
- No reactors, planning new build
- Operating reactors, stable
- Operating reactors, considering phase-out
- Civil nuclear power is illegal
- No reactors

Main components of a nuclear reactor

- **Core** – The core of the reactor contains the nuclear fuel, basically uranium, in the form of bundles.

- **Coolant** – The heat produced during the nuclear reaction is taken out by the coolant. The most common type of coolant is plain water (H_2O), heavy water (D_2O), liquid sodium and helium.

- **Control rods** – These are required for controlling the reaction and shutting down the plant.

- **Turbine** – It transforms the heat taken out by the coolant into electricity like in any other conventional power plant.

- **Containment** – This is the structure that separates the nuclear reactor from the outer environment. These are made of high density, steel reinforced concrete to conceal the harmful radiation inside.

- **Cooling towers** – These require some time to dump the excess heat, which cannot be converted into electricity because of the limitation imposed by the laws of thermodynamics.

Cooler tower on a nuclear power plant.

Quantum Physics

Quantum physics is a branch of physics, where we deal with the interactions going on inside an atom. At an atomic level, we study about subatomic particles and radiations. The word quantum means energy or unit. It is the smallest amount of energy, which can act on its own.

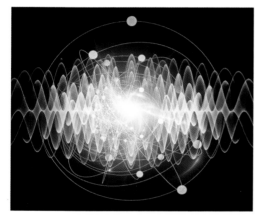

An atom with quantum waves.

Birth of quantum physics

Quantum physics originated in the 1920s to study and describe the laws of physics that are applicable to tiny objects. There were certain facts that classic physics was unable to answer and so, many theories were invented, like photoelectric effect, black-body radiation, atomic theory, corpuscular theory of light and Heisenberg's principle of uncertainty.

Principles of quantum physics

1. Quantum mechanics successfully explained the wave particle or the dual nature of matter.

2. It explained that we cannot simultaneously determine the position and momentum of a particle to high precision.

3. It also explained the basis of quanta, which is the smallest packet of energy.

FUN FACT

The nucleus of an atom is quite small. If you magnify an atom to the size of a football field, the nucleus will only be the size of a marble.

Scientists who contributed

Max Planck is known as the father of quantum theory. Many scientists were involved in the foundation of quantum mechanics. Niels Bohr, Werner Heisenberg, Louis de Broglie, Arthur Compton, Albert Einstein, Erwin Schrodinger, Max Born, John von Neumann and several other scientists made important contributions in this field.

Applications

Traditionally, quantum mechanics works in a subatomic world, but it can clearly explain the working of superconductors, super fluids and many other large organic molecules. Many modern technologies are based on this branch of physics; for example, laser, electron microscope, magnetic resonance imaging, etc.

Cutting a metal sheet using a laser beam works on quantum mechanics.

Electron microscope.

CELLS

A cell is the smallest unit of life. Every structural part of a human, animal, plant and organism is composed of cells. Living things range from simple and single-celled to complex and multicellular, such as human beings. Our human body comprises trillions of cells. These cells make up the structure of the body, absorb nutrients from food, convert these nutrients into energy and perform specialised functions.

Cells also contain the body's hereditary material and can make copies of themselves.

The study of cells began approximately 330 years ago. Robert Hooke was the first person to discover cells and coined the term "cells". In 1838, German botanist Matthias Schleiden found that all plants have cells as their basic unit. Around a year later, German zoologist Theodor Schwann discovered that all animals also have cells as the basic unit of life. In 1855, German physician Rudolph Virchow also contributed to this theory, when he found that all cells come from other existing cells.

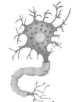

What is Cell Theory?

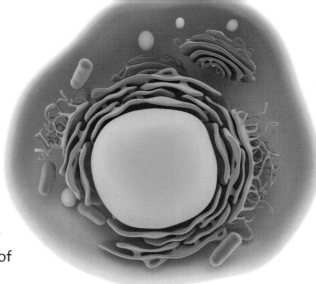

In 1838, German botanist Matthias Schleiden discovered that all plants were composed of cells. Subsequently, a year later, German zoologist Theodor Schwann discovered that all animals were composed of cells as well. These two scientists proposed the cell theory.

The basic unit

The first part of cell theory explains that all living things can be very simple, that is, composed of just one cell. There are varied structures within the single-celled amoeba that help it to reproduce, use the energy for growth, respond to the environment and let nutrients and materials enter and exit the cell. Larger organisms, such as a cat or coconut tree, are also composed of cells. If you observe a small tissue sample under a microscope, you will see one actual cell within the larger living thing. Thus, cells reproduce to form new cells, thereby explaining how organisms reproduce and grow. For example, the human skin is constantly being replenished as new cells replace the old ones. If you use a dry towel to rub down your body after a warm bath, you will see old tissue fall off your skin. This tissue is made up of millions of tiny, dead cells.

If we magnify our skin under a powerful microscope, we will be able to see cell tissues.

Modern interpretation of the cell theory

The generally accepted parts of modern cell theory include:

- All known living creatures are made up of single or more cells.

- All living cells are formed from pre-existing cells by the method of division.

- The cell is the most fundamental unit of any structure in all living organisms.

- The different activities of organisms depend on the total activities of independent cells.

- Energy flow occurs within the cells.

- Cells contain deoxyribonucleic acid (DNA), which is found specifically in the chromosome and ribonucleic acid (RNA), which is found in the cell nucleus and cytoplasm.

- All cells are basically the same with respect to the chemical composition in organisms of similar species.

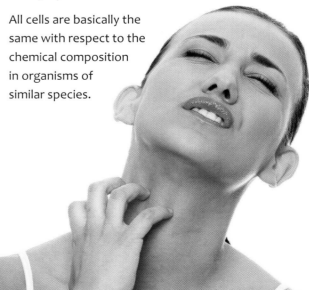

Building Block of Cells

Cell is the basic unit of living organisms. Just like a building stands by joining many bricks, our body is formed by different types of trillions of cells joined together.

What are these cells? What are they made up of? All cells are composed of some common building blocks, regardless of whether they are plant cells or animal cells or whether they have a different function or location. These building blocks are called biomolecules.

Carbohydrates

These are the major source of energy in our body. The most common carbohydrate is sugar. Carbohydrates provide structure and help in the defence mechanism of any cell. They also help in communication and adhesion.

Proteins

Different amino acids join together and form different types of proteins. We all know that protein is a body building constituent. Besides this, proteins are useful in cell transport, maintaining cell contact and controlling its activity. Membrane proteins can also function as enzymes to accelerate chemical reactions, act as receptors for specific molecules, or transport materials across the cell membrane.

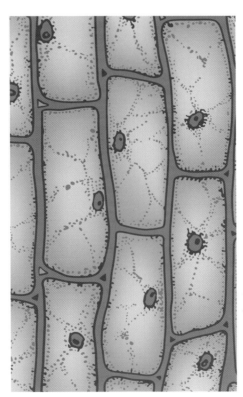

Microscopic view of a plant cell showing anatomical structures.

Lipids

A range of fats, oils, waxes and steroid hormones come under lipids that form cells. Fats also serve as a source of energy and form the cell membrane. These materials provide protection against microbes. Lipids in the form of steroid hormones regulate cell activity.

Nucleic acids

There are two types of nucleic acids found in our body. They are RNA and DNA. DNA is found in the nucleus and it carries genetic information, whereas RNA helps in protein synthesis. It is transcribed from the DNA.

Cells divide and re-divide to help a plant grow.

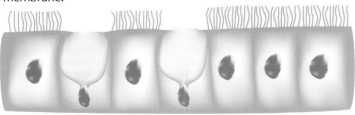

Microscopic view of an animal cell showing anatomical structures.

Plant Cell and its Structure

There are two major types of cells: plant cells and animal cells. There are a lot of differences between plant and animal cells. Plant cells are covered by a thick cell wall to give them rigidity. A plant cell can also produce its own food.

Distinctive features of plant cells

1. These cells have a large vacuole filled with water and other materials and surrounded by a membrane called tonoplast. It helps in storing and digesting materials, controlling the movement of molecules and maintaining the cell's turgor.

2. These cells are covered with a thick cell wall made up of cellulose.

3. They have plasmodesmata, which are the pores in the cell membrane.

4. Plastids like chloroplast, amyloplast, chromoplast and elaioplast are present. Chloroplast contains a green pigment called chlorophyll present in the leaves that absorbs sunlight and water, and helps in making food for the plant. This process is called photosynthesis.

5. Cell division occurs in the presence of phragmoplast.

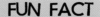

FUN FACT

Chocolate releases the hormone serotonin in the human body that makes you feel relaxed, calm and happy.

A dose of laughter can suppress the release of stress hormones like cortisol and epinephrine.

Plant cell showing anatomical structures.

Organelles

The organelles present in plant cells are different from that present in animal cells. The organelles of plant cells are cell membrane, cell wall, nuclear membrane, plasmodesma, vacuole, plastids, chloroplast, leucoplast, chrome-plated Golgi bodies, cytoplasm, nucleus, DNA, chromatin, RNA, cytoskeleton, nucleolus and mitochondrion. If you want to distinguish between animal cells and plant cells, it is very apparent. Plant cells have a particular shape and are not irregularly shaped like animal cells.

Types of plant cells

- Parenchyma cells
- Collenchyma cells
- Sclerenchyma cells

Leaf surface showing plant cells.

Parenchyma cells

These cells have thin, permeable cell membranes that are found in vascular bundles of the phloem and xylem. The same cell system is also found in leaves. Some parenchyma cells present in the stem are specialised for the absorption of light and providing support for gaseous exchange while some others are non-specialised and remain deep inside the body. Some of these cells, which possess chlorophyll, are called chlorenchyma cells. These cells perform most of the metabolic processes of the plant and also perform other functions like storage, transferring nutrients and water, nectar and some other substance secretions. For example, an aloevera leaf belongs to the cactus family and uses photosynthesis to produce energy as well as stores food in bulk.

An aloevera leaf made of parenchyma cells.

Collenchyma cells

These cells are quite elongated in appearance and can undergo division transversely, giving them a separate appearance. These cells are not hard and form the body of the soft stem and support as a plastic stem. These cells are alive at maturity and possess a cell membrane composed of pectin or hemicelluloses, which is tough at the corners.

The bark is made up of sclerenchyma cells.

Sclerenchyma cells

These are the cells that provide mechanical support to the plant in standing erect for a long time. They are the hard and tough cells of the plant. They are further divided into two types: sclereids and fibres. These cells die at maturity. They secrete a hard cell wall inside the primary cell wall that restricts the exchange of materials and water, giving them a short lifespan. For example, if you closely observe the bark of a tree, you will find that it has all the characteristics that sclerenchyma cells impart to it. The bark of a tree is tough and dry. A bark is made up of dead cells of the tree. These cells dehydrate and become hard, and enable the tree to stand erect and tall. If you pour water on this bark, you will realise that it doesn't absorb any and lets it flow to the ground, from where the roots absorb it and send it to the leaf.

A fern consisting of collenchyma cells.

Life Cycle of a Plant

Among the various systems of living organisms, the reproductive system is one by which an offspring can be produced from a living organism. Like animals, plants also reproduce. In the life cycle of a plant, a flower produces seeds, which can generate many more plants. Plants can be classified into annuals, biennials, perennials and monocarpic, depending upon their life cycle. Plants can reproduce sexually as well as asexually.

Germination

The life cycle of a plant begins with the germination of the seed. As the seed gets favourable conditions, it soon sprouts into a small seedling. Favourable conditions include moist soil, carbon dioxide and sunlight. This seedling then grows and slowly becomes a fully grown mature plant. Then, reproductive organs develop on the plant. These reproductive organs are flowers.

Reproductive parts

A flower is the reproductive organ of the plant. Some flowers have both male and female parts, whereas others may have any one reproductive part. The sterile parts of flowers are called sepals and petals. The main reproductive part of the flower is the stamen (male, also termed androecium) and carpel (female, also termed gynoecium). Each individual unit of the androecium is called a stamen that consists of a filament, which supports the anther. Pollen grains contain the male gametophyte (microgametophyte) phase of the plant. The gynoecium consists of the stigma, style and ovary which contains one or more ovules. These three structures are often referred to as a pistil or carpel. In many plants, the pistils will fuse for all or part of their length.

Anther

Stigma

Petal

Sepal

In case of flowers that have both male and female parts, pollen grains adhere to the stigma, a pollen tube grows and penetrates the ovule and fertilizes them. The cells then begin to divide. If the flowers have separate sexes, the plant has to depend on external features for the pollen to reach the ovules.

Pollination

After the plant matures, it is the time of pollination. Pollination is the process by which pollen reach into the mouth of the pistil. It makes us wonder how it is possible for pollination to take place as plants can't move like other living organisms. This process needs the help of insects, flies and bees for its completion. They visit the flowers to get nectar, during which the pollen sticks on their wings, legs and other body parts. When they go to another flower, they leave those pollen on the second flower. In this manner, pollen reach the ovary of female flowers and fertilisation occurs.

Fertilisation

Fertilisation is defined as the fusion of a male and female gamete to produce a zygote or baby seed. When a flower is fertilised, its ovary begins to swell. The petals wither and fall off the flower. Soon, only the swollen ovary is left. This is the ovary that is known to us as a fruit. The fruit is fleshy on the inside as it holds a lot of nutrition as well as many seeds, which can sprout many more plants. The outer covering of the fruit protects the newly created seed as well as nourishes it.

Dispersal by explosion.

Dispersal of seeds

There are three ways in which seeds get dispersed. The seeds are carried far and wide by water, air, explosion and animals, where they ultimately find soil and favourable conditions, and germinate. Dispersal by water happens when the seed or fruit of a tree falls in flowing water and gets carried away; for example, the coconut. Dispersal by air happens when the seed gets blown away by the wind; for example, the

dandelion. Dispersal by explosion happens when the fruit ripens too much, dries up and ultimately, bursts open and throws out all the seeds within it; for example, balsam. Lastly, dispersal by animals is when the seeds stick onto animal fur, or when birds eat the seed and their droppings are found elsewhere, or even when we eat the fruit and throw the seeds away.

Life cycle of some other non-flowering plants

There are different life cycles for non-flowering plants. In gymnosperms, their seeds are open to the air with no layer, such as the seeds of flowering plants. Conifers use cones to store their seeds. Conifers reproduce using their cones. Spores produce spores instead of seeds to reproduce. Mosses typically only grow a few inches tall and use spores to reproduce. Ferns also reproduce using spore casings on the underside of their leaves.

The stages that a seed goes through while germinating.

Dispersal by water.

FUN FACT

The attractive colours of flowers and the sweet scent that they produce, are means by which they attract birds and bees that help in pollination.

Animal Cell

In 1838, German zoologist, Theodor Schwann discovered that all animals have cell as their basic unit of life. In 1855, German physician Rudolph Virchow also contributed to this theory, when he found that all cells come from other existing cells.

An overview

What makes animals different from any other living organism? They can move around on their own. They can hunt, eat, sleep and make noise. There are so many things that they can do that plants cannot. What gives animals their unique characteristics? It is their cell structure and its constituents that make a difference. The cells present in animals are eukaryotic cells or cells with a membrane-bound nucleus. DNA in animal cells is situated within the nucleus. Animal cells have various sizes and irregular shapes. Most of the cell sizes range between 1 and 100 micrometers and are visible to the human eye only with the help of a microscope.

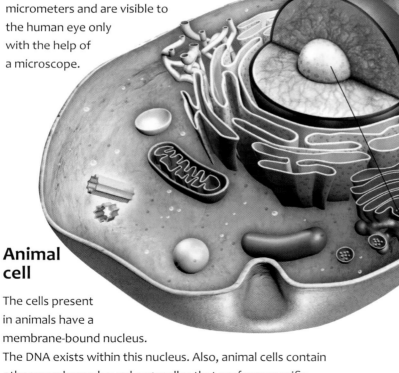

Animal cell

The cells present in animals have a membrane-bound nucleus.
The DNA exists within this nucleus. Also, animal cells contain other membrane-bound organelles that perform specific functions essential for normal cellular operation. Organelles have an extensive range of responsibilities that include everything from producing hormones and enzymes to providing energy for animal cells.

Unicellular animals

What is the smallest animal that we know? Numerous animals come to our mind. The smallest animals that our mind can imagine are insects. However, there are animals that are no more than one cell big. These are only visible to the eyes through a microscope. There are animals on this planet that consist of only one cell. These are called unicellular organisms. These can be classified into two types – Prokaryotes and Eukaryotes. We will look at some examples of Eukaryotic unicellular animals. These are many. Some of them are as follows:

The animal cell is very different than the plant cell.

The nucleus of the cell.

FUN FACT

Paramecium is considered as an animal, although it is a single-cell organism. To survive, paramecium uses a tube and a thread of its body for locomotion.

Paramecium

This unicellular organism is actually neither animal nor plant. However, when learning about unicellular organisms, it is very important to study this organism as it is a model unicellular organism. It has a single mouth that it uses to eat plant as well as small, dead animal cells. It can be found in stagnant water and ponds.

An unicellular organism-paramecium.

Amoeba

Amoeba is a shapeless organism that moves using its ability to take any shape. It basically flows from one spot to another using its flexible boundaries, also known as its pseudopods (false feet). Amoeba is actually plural for Amoeboid. It is unicellular and feeds on bacteria, algae and other microscopic organisms.

Constituents of the animal cell

Among the species living on this Earth, animals constitute three quarters of the total count. We have already established that these are very different from plants. However, in addition to cell structure, the constituents of cells also make a vast difference in their basic build-up. These cell constituents are called organelles. The ones that animal cells contain are listed below:

Cell membrane	Lysosomes
Centriole	Microfilaments
Cytoplasm	Microtubules
Cilia and flagella	Mitochondria
Endoplasmic reticulum	Nucleus
Endosomes	Peroxisomes
Golgi apparatus	Ribosomes

Scientists have revealed the mystery of the animal cell and disassembled it for further studies and investigations.

Animal cells vs. plant cells

There are many similarities between animal cells and plant cells; the foremost being that they are both eukaryotic cells and have similar organelles. Animal cells are mostly smaller than plant cells. They are also present in various sizes and tend to have irregular shapes, whereas plant cells are more similar in size and are typically rectangular or cube shaped. A plant cell contains structures that are not present in an animal cell. Some of these include a cell wall, a large vacuole and plastids. Plastids, such as chloroplasts, assist in storing and harvesting the needed substances for the plant. In addition, animal cells also contain structures such as centrioles, lysosomes, cilia and flagella that are not ideally present in plant cells.

Making their own food

Of all the differences that we find in a plant and animal cell, the most important one and the one that makes the maximum difference in their existence is the ability to make their own food. Plants can make their own food, whereas animals need to search for it or hunt it. This difference occurs because of the presence and absence of chloroplast in the cells of plants and animals, respectively. It is what gives the plants their green colour. Chloroplast helps the plants to create food from sunlight and CO_2.

A magnified image of a mitochondrion.

Life Cycle of Animals

The life cycle of a living organism means the sequence of developmental stages that it passes on its journey towards adulthood. There are thousands of animal species living on Earth, so there are a number of life cycles to observe. In some species, it is a very slow and gradual process, whereas in others, it is fast. For example, the life cycle of some insects is only of a few weeks, whereas the life cycle of sea urchins is many years.

Type of reproduction

Sexual reproduction is found in animals with separate male and female genders. Animals like slugs, snails and barnacles can reproduce asexually. Mammals have a characteristic property of giving birth to young ones, whereas birds, fishes and reptiles are egg-laying animals. In some egg-laying animals like shark, eggs are laid and incubated inside the body, and then given birth to young ones.

FUN FACT

The caterpillar attaches to a twig and sheds its outer skin, and within hours, changes into a pupa.

As tadpoles change into frogs, they slowly develop legs and their tail starts shrinking.

Camouflaging and hibernation

A chameleon is known to be the best example of an animal that uses camouflage to be safe. Chameleons protect themselves from birds of prey by changing their skin colour to that of the background so that they become practically invisible.

Bears are known to hibernate for months during the winters as this helps them conserve their energy and keep warm.

Adaptation

Environmental conditions like water, temperature and light affect the development of an organism. They have to struggle for food, safety and reproduction; thus, they get adapted to their environment. Animals spend time with other members of the same species. That helps in adaptation. Other examples of animals evolving to adapt to their environment is navigating, migrating, camouflaging and hibernation.

Navigating and migrating

Sandhoppers are small, shrimp-like animals that live on sandy beaches. This is their natural habitat. Every 24 hours, they migrate into the sea. They use the Sun to navigate themselves in the direction of the sea and out of it every day. This helps them survive the heat and cold of the day as well as guides them in the correct direction.

Some special life cycles

Virus

As we know, viruses are like parasites on other living organisms. They use host cells, energy and nutrients for nutrition replication. This is very different from symbiosis, where both the organisms benefit from each other. Viruses cause their host's health to deteriorate.

Anglerfish

In this species, the tiny male bites the female skin and fertilises the eggs in the female body. When this attachment happens, their bodies fuse to share a circulatory system, so that the female provides nutrients to the male body. The male increases in size as compared to other unattached males. Multiple males can latch onto a female anglerfish at a time.

The life cycle of a mosquito.

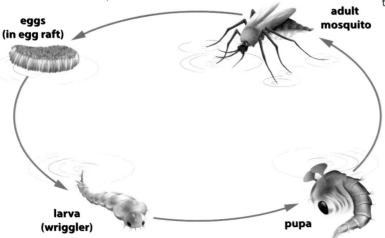

eggs (in egg raft)

adult mosquito

larva (wriggler)

pupa

Different life cycles

Some animals have very simple life cycles. They are born either from the mother or hatched from an egg to grow into an adult. Fishes, mammals, reptiles and birds have this type of life cycle. Ostrich makes a common nest, in which the male and female both incubate the eggs.

The life cycle of a bee.

Amphibians like frogs and newts have a life cycle that completes with a metamorphosis. After their birth, they can swim in water with gills and are called tadpoles that eventually become frogs. After this stage, they change into adults with lungs and can live both on land and water.

Insects have a complicated life cycle, which is completed in a few stages, namely, egg, larva, pupa and adult. The larval stage is the stage when most of the feeding is completed. They appear as worms. Subsequently, they form a cocoon and cover their body in it. This is an inactive stage of their life cycle. As the pupa hatches from the cocoon, an adult insect with wings emerges.

Some insects like cockroaches, grasshoppers and dragonflies skip the stage of pupa. They complete their life cycle in three stages– egg, nymph and adult. A nymph is the feeding stage of these insects, after which they change into adults with wings. This is the reason why these species are able to reproduce very fast and create an infestation within a matter of days. As soon as they grow out of their pupal stage, they start moving around in search of food.

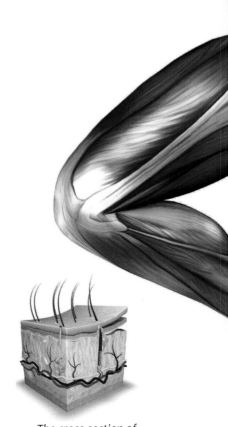

Human Body

The human body is the most intricately working living system. You would be familiar with your body parts, but do you know how many systems are working in your body? The cell is the basic unit of life. Cell combines and forms tissue, which in turn form organs, and these organs together form the structure of the body.

Anatomical structure of human body

The study of the morphology of the human body is called anatomical study. Our body is anatomically divided into many systems as given below:

Skeletal system

Bones, joints and the vertebral column constitute the skeletal system. Major functions performed by this system are support, movement, protection, production of blood cells, endocrine regulation and storage of ions.

Endocrine system

A large collection of ductless glands constitute the endocrine system. Pituitary gland, pineal gland, pancreas, ovaries, testes, thyroid gland, parathyroid gland, hypothalamus, gastrointestinal tract and adrenal gland are the major endocrine glands. They cover a wide range of functions.

Muscular system

The shape of the body is determined by the overall distribution of muscles and fatty tissues. Skeletal, smooth and cardiac muscles constitute this organ system.

Digestive system

Salivary glands, teeth, oesophagus, stomach, small intestine, large intestine, liver and the gall bladder constitute the digestive system.

Homeostasis

Our body maintains homeostasis, meaning it regulates its temperature, pH, blood flow and position at a constant level. Homeostasis is very vital for survival. For example, if the temperature is too high, we tend to sweat profusely. This is how the body gets rid of heat within so that its internal temperature is maintained. Our internal organs are very delicate and hence the temperature and vital levels of the body must be maintained at all times.

Another example is when we eat too much sugar. Our body detects this and sends a signal to our brain, who in turn activates the endocrine system and releases insulin to deal with it.

The cross-section of a sweat gland.

Integumentary system

Skin, hair and nails constitute the integumentary system. This system protects the body from damage, loss of water and abrasions. The study of the working of these systems is called physiology. All the systems in the body are mutually correlated in functioning.

The muscular system of the human body.

Excretory system

Kidney, urinary bladder, ureters and the urethra constitute the excretory system. It removes wastes from the body.

Cardiovascular system

Heart, arteries, veins and capillaries constitute the cardiovascular system. Heart, the pumping organ of the body, circulates blood continuously through the body.

Nervous system

Brain, spinal cord and a network of nerves constitute the nervous system. This system transmits signals from different organs to the brain and vice versa.

Lymphatic system

The lymphatic system is the immune system of the body composed of lymph vessels that form a network in the body.

Reproductive system

The male reproductive parts comprise the penis, testes and the prostate gland. The female reproductive parts comprise the ovary, uterus, fallopian tubes and the vagina. The organ system of the male body and the female body are quite different, also giving them secondary sexual characters.

Respiratory system

Lungs, trachea, bronchi, bronchioles and diaphragm constitute the respiratory system. This system is responsible for the intake of oxygen and releasing carbon dioxide out of the body.

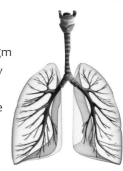

Some facts about the human body

- There are 206 bones in an adult human body. A child has more bones which then fuse as the body grows older.

- The human body can be divided into many body cavities like pelvic cavity, thoracic cavity, abdominal cavity and dorsal cavity. Many small cavities are also there, which are called sinuses.

- The red fluid flowing through the vessels in the body is called blood. An adult human body has 5 to 5.5 *l* of blood.

- The presence of red blood cells lends blood the red colouration.

- A human body contains about 75 per cent of water.

- The small intestine found in the abdomen is 6 m long.

- The human heart beats at a rate of 73 beats per minute. This is the pulse rate that we feel in our wrist.

- Copper, zinc, cobalt, calcium, manganese, phosphates, nickel and silicon are found in our body in different forms.

- Nose behaves as a natural air conditioner as it changes the temperature of the air received by the body and also removes impurities from it.

Bones

The branch of science called "biology" studies the structure of the human body. If we touch any part of our body, we will find something hard beneath the muscles. The hard organs are called bones that form the skeleton of the human body. An adult human body is composed of 206 bones that are of different shapes and sizes.

What are bones?

Bones are rigid organs that together constitute the vertebral skeleton. The red and white cells of blood are produced inside these bones. The bones consist of dense connective tissues of cortical and cancellous type. They are light in weight but strong and hard, and store different minerals. The different types of bones are flat, long, short, irregular and sesamoid bones.

Skeleton

In our body, the femur (thigh bone) is the longest bone. The stirrup inside the ear is the smallest bone. Each hand has 26 bones.

Cartilage

The nose and ears are not made of bone but of cartilage. The cartilage is not as hard as the bone and is made out of flexible bone tissue. This is the reason why we can squish our nose and bend our ears without breaking them.

Joints

If bones are so hard, how can we bend our hands or legs? Are they flexible too? The answer will be no, as a bone cannot bend. It is the joint that helps us to bend our hand or other parts. We can bend our hand at any point because there are joints like the elbow joint, shoulder joint and wrist joint.

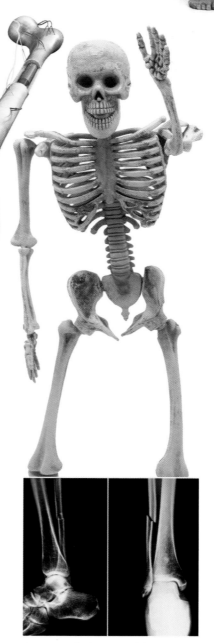

An x-ray of a human with fractured ankles.

Bone injury

When a bone cracks or breaks due to an accident, it is called a fracture. Based upon the type of damage, there are basically two types of fractures. The first one is a hair-line fracture. This type of fracture happens when the impact on the bone is not too high and hence the x-ray of the bone shows only a minor crack. The second type of fracture is called a complete fracture. This ranges from a gap between the crack in the bone to a completely snapped bone. There is also a third issue related to the bone. This is when, due to a strong impact or yank in one of the body parts, the bone slips out of its position. This is known as a dislocation. This can occur at any of the joints. The most common dislocation is of the shoulder, when the arm bone slips out of the socket. Painful as they all may sound, all these types of bone injuries are treatable and with time, can allow us complete use of the injured body part.

Fractures can occur because of car accidents, falls, sport injuries, low bone density, osteoporosis, etc., which causes the weakening of bones.

Joints

The word "joint" is derived from the Latin word Junctura that means junction or joining. Joints, also known as bony articulations, are the strongest point of meeting of two or more bones; they also attach teeth and cartilage in the body with one another. Think what would have happened, if our body would have been composed of a single, rigid bone. We would have been strong, but without any locomotion or movement. That is why joints are vital in our body.

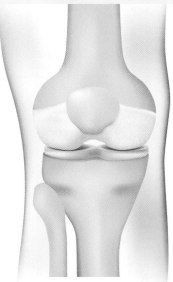

Structure of a joint

A joint is covered by a tough, fibrous capsule, which restricts its motion, and a fluid called synovium present inside the joint capsule, which provides lubrication and prevents friction.

Ligaments are muscles that give strength to the joints and avoid dislocation. Tendons are muscles that attach the bones to other muscles.

Thus, joints are parts of the body that make bending, stretching, twisting and turning activities possible.

Types of joints

Joints can be classified on the basis of their functionality or their structural composition. The functional classification of joints divides them into three types on the basis of the degree of allowed movement.

1. **Synarthrosis**

The joints where no movement is allowed are called synarthroses; for example, the joints in the skull.

2. **Amphiarthrosis**

The joints that allow little movement are called amphiarthroses; for example, the joints in the intervertebral disks of the spine and pubic symphysis of the hips.

3. **Diarthrosis**

The joints that permit a large area for movement are called diarthroses; for example, the joints in the elbow, knee, shoulders and wrists.

Structural classification is based upon the nature of binding tissues and the presence or absence of synovial cavity. On this basis, joints can be of the following types:

1. Fibrous joint
2. Cartilaginous joint
3. Synovial joint

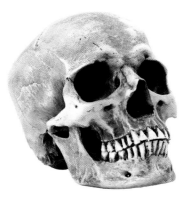

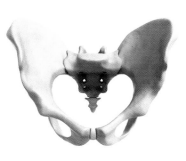

The upper bone is called a femur and the lower two bones are the tibia and fibulla.

Muscles

A total of 650 muscles constitute the muscular system of the human body. Muscles constitute approximately 70 per cent of our body weight. Our daily life activities like walking, sitting, standing, bending, drinking and eating are all controlled by muscles. There are many other functions of the muscles that go on continuously without our knowledge, like pumping of the heart, breathing with lungs and digestion by peristalsis in the alimentary canal.

Skeletal muscle.

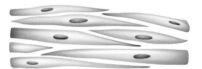

Smooth muscle.

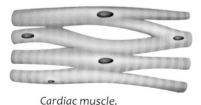

Cardiac muscle.

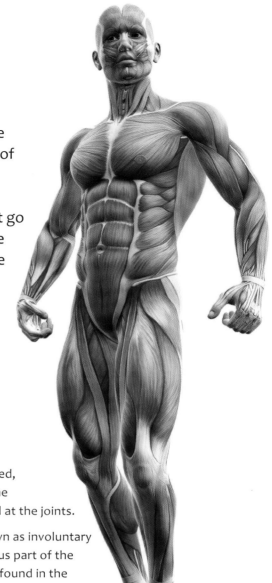

Types of muscles

There are three types of muscles found in the human body:

1. Skeletal muscles
2. Smooth muscles
3. Cardiac muscles

Skeletal muscles – Skeletal muscles are the striated, voluntary muscles of our body. They control all the consciously performed activities. These are found at the joints.

Smooth muscles – Smooth muscles are also known as involuntary muscles as these are controlled by the unconscious part of the brain. These muscles are spindle-shaped muscles found in the visceral organs of the body. Their wave-like actions generate peristalsis movement and help in passing food, blood, urine, and air from one organ to another.

Cardiac muscles – Cardiac muscles are the striated involuntary muscles found in the heart. These types of muscles can generate electrical impulses, which produce rhythmic contractions in the heart.

Functions of the muscles

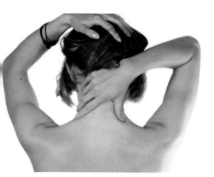

Muscles are the only part of the body possessing the ability to contract. That is why they are necessary for locomotion or movement. Besides this, muscles maintain the posture of the body and transport blood, urine, food and many other substances. Muscles are also responsible for generating body heat.

How muscles get fatigued

Our muscles get fatigued when we work excessively. This is because our muscles use energy from one or the other source of our body to work. During excessive workout, the muscles lack this energy, causing waste products like lactic acid and ADP to get accumulated, thereby making us feel tired. Our muscles feel like they are on fire.

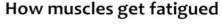

Movement

We have studied that the human body consists of many types of joints, which allow different types of movements. Movement is necessary for the human body to physically move and do a lot of things. By the term "movement", we understand the motion of organs, joints, limbs and other sections of the body. The skeleton of the human body works with 650 muscles to allow all movements.

Study of movement

A child learns movements like walking, eating and standing. As he/she grows older, he/she can learn many other activities by practice and skill.

The study of movements is based on the principles of biomechanics and kinesiology. The scientific study of movements is known as kinesiology or human kinetic.

The movement can include the study of gait, posture, sports, exercise movements and daily life activities.

Scientists study the human body in different planes and different anatomical positions. Movements in the joints can be classified into various types considering these planes and positions.

Different types of movements

The different types of movements that are allowed through various angles at various joints are flexion, extension, abduction, adduction, horizontal abduction, horizontal adduction, internal rotation, external adduction, lateral flexion, rotation, elevation, depression, retraction, protraction, upward rotation, downward rotation, circumduction, radial deviation, ulnar deviation, opposition, eversion, inversion, dorsiflexion, plantar flexion, pronation and supination.

Movements can also be classified in various categories based on the nature of the joints involved like gliding, angular and rotational movements. Movements can be either of linear or angular type.

For example, the movement of our wrist from side to side is a gliding movement, the movement of our elbow while flexing our muscles is an angular movement and our head rotating at the neck is a rotational movement.

The human body has to make use of multiple and many muscles while running.

We use the muscles of our back and stomach to bend over and touch our toes.

Nerves

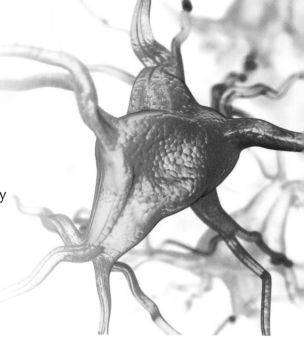

Nerves are a collection of cells called neurons. Nerves are studied under the nervous system, which is responsible for all voluntary and involuntary actions, and for every movement, sensation and thought. There are approximately 100 billion nerves in the peripheral nervous system.

If we touch a bowl that is very hot, we spontaneously remove our hand. This occurs within seconds and we don't need to think about it. Such actions are done because of nerves.

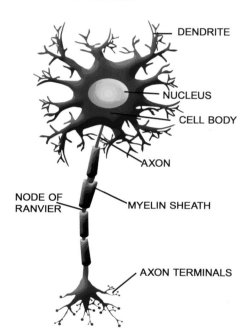

What is a nerve?

A nerve is a specialised cell or cord-like bundle of fibres that transmits nerve impulses in the form of electrochemical signals from different organs to the brain and from the brain to different organs and body parts.

The term used for diseases related to nerves is neuropathy.

Structure

A neuron comprises a large cell body with one elongated axon and many branches called dendrites. They are surrounded by the Schwann cells in the peripheral nervous system. The axon is surrounded by multi-layered sheath called myelin and/ or a membrane called neurilemma. The nerve carries information in the form of electrochemical impulses at a speed of 120 m/s. The junction between two neurons is called the synapse.

Types

There are three types of nerves based on the direction of the electrical signals they carry.

1. Sensory nerves: These nerves transmit impulses from the sensory organs to the brain.

For example, when we touch a hot utensil by mistake, the sensory nerves from the skin of our hands send signals to our brain.

2. Motor nerves: These nerves transmit impulses from the brain to organs, glands and muscles.

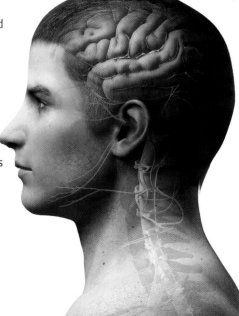

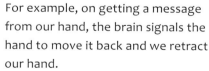
The brain is the headquarter of our nervous system.

For example, on getting a message from our hand, the brain signals the hand to move it back and we retract our hand.

3. Autonomic nerves: These nerves control involuntary actions of the body like temperature regulation, digestion, blood pressure and heart rate.

For example, our heart beats faster to pump more blood when we are active.

Senses

Aristotle described that there are five sense organs present in the human body. Sense is the physiological capacity of an organism to react to some external stimuli. The five senses that a human body has are smell, sight, sound, taste and touch.

The famous five

The five sensory organs that enable us to survive.

1. **Seeing:** A human being possesses a pair of eyes for visual perception. This is placed on the front side of our head to allow a maximum range of vision. Each eye remains connected to the brain by the optic nerve, which gives electrical impulses to the brain for detecting and forming images. Different parts of the eye include lens, conjunctiva, retina, pupil, cornea, iris and fovea. Our eyes have photoreceptor cells in them. Rods and cones are the two photoreceptor cells present in the eye.

2. **Smell:** The nose is an organ that detects smell or olfaction. It has hundreds of small olfactory receptors that get excited and signal the brain. Our brain can store memories with respect to different smells. This is why we can recognise smells.

3. **Taste:** Tongue is the sense organ of taste that has taste buds present on it for differentiating between various tastes like bitter, sour, sweet and salty. We taste these different tastes at different parts of the tongue.

4. **Sound:** Two ears present on the sides of the head are the sense organs for hearing or sound perception. There is a tympanic membrane in the ear that vibrates on hearing a sound. These vibrations reach the small bones of the internal ear that sends signals to our brain and enables us to hear sounds.

5. **Touch:** This is a perception that results from the excitation of the minute hair and various nerve endings present all over the body that communicate with the brain.

More than five

Besides these five senses, there are many other senses by which a human body can react to many changes in the environment, like temperature, pain, balance, vibration, time, thirst, hunger and many other internal stimuli.

The big boss

Brain has the capacity for perceiving, interpreting and organising the data received by sense organs. Sensing initially occurs at the cellular level, which then goes to the brain by the nervous system.

Blood and Circulation

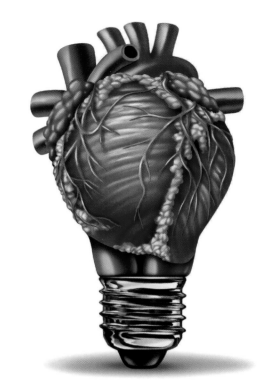

The circulatory system of the body includes the heart, lungs, arteries, veins, capillaries, coronary vessels and blood. This system facilitates the to and fro movement of nutrients, gases, blood as well as hormones.

When you are unwell, your doctor some times advices a blood test. What does this blood removed from your body look like? It doesn't look like water; it gets separated into a layer of pale liquid plasma and a solid layer of blood cells.

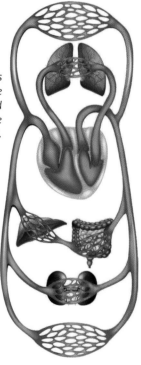

The blue vessels indicate impure blood and red vessels indicate pure blood.

Constitution of blood

Blood constitutes 55 per cent plasma and 45 per cent blood cells.

Different types of blood cells are produced in the bone marrow of human beings by a process known as haematopoiesis.

Plasma: The plasma is a liquid containing water, proteins, glucose and nutrients. It performs the function of transportation.

Red blood cells (RBCs): Red blood cells possess the red pigment haemoglobin, which carries oxygen.

White blood cells (WBCs): White blood cells help in fighting against infections.

Platelets: Platelets help in clot formation, thus preventing bleeding.

Inhaling oxygen.

Blood circulation

Blood circulates in the body through arteries, veins and capillaries. The heart acts as a pump and makes the blood flow through the blood vessels. There are two types of circulation that simultaneously occur in the body. One is the systemic circulation by which organs, tissues and cells get a supply of oxygen-rich blood by the vessels coming from the left ventricle of the heart. Another is the pulmonary circulation by which oxygen inhaled by the lungs enters blood and carbon dioxide is released.

WBCs and RBCs

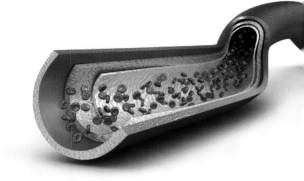

The blood is the most important connective tissue in the human body. It consists of a pale liquid part, the plasma and many blood cells.

Red blood cells

Red blood cells, also called as erythrocytes, are non-nucleated, biconcave disc-shaped cells. RBC is the most abundant cell in the blood and makes up to 40 per cent of the total blood's volume.

Have you ever wondered why blood is always red in colour not white or yellow? This is because of the presence of a protein called haemoglobin. Haemoglobin is a respiratory pigment, mainly composed of iron, which binds with either oxygen or carbon dioxide and helps in their transportation.

These cells are produced inside the bone marrow with the help of the hormone erythropoietin. After seven days of their production, mature RBCs enter into the bloodstream. As these cells are non-nucleated, they give more space to the haemoglobin and facilitate their easy movement across small blood vessels. This property, besides giving them flexibility, decreases their lifespan to 120 days.

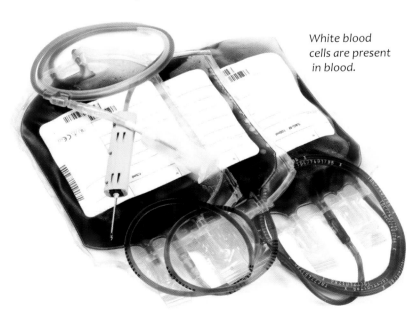

White blood cells are present in blood.

Functions

1. Transportation of oxygen and carbon dioxide
2. Maintenance of homeostasis

White blood cells

White blood cells, also known as leukocytes, are irregularly shaped, nucleated cells with a short life span of about three–four days. They constitute only one per cent of the blood.

Based on the presence or absence of cytoplasmic granules, they are classified into two groups: granulocytes and agranulocytes. Neutrophils, eosinophils and basophils are granulocytes and lymphocytes and monocytes are agranulocytes.

Functions

1. They are our bodyguards as they fight infections. They produce a special protein called antibodies for fighting various foreign elements.

2. They develop the immunity of our body.

Besides these cells, platelets are also present in the blood that help in the coagulation of blood.

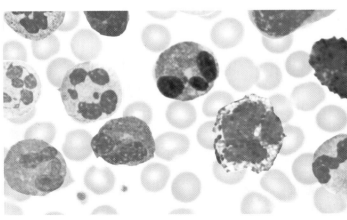

White blood cells.

Respiration

We know that we cannot stay even for a minute with our nose and mouth closed. We need to breathe. It is a process that goes on without our control.

Respiration is the process of taking in oxygen and giving out carbon dioxide into the environment. This can be confused with breathing; however, breathing involves only inhaling and exhaling, and respiration is the process where the gaseous exchange occurs in the cells of the body. The food we eat gives us energy only when it is oxidised, which is achieved by the process of respiration.

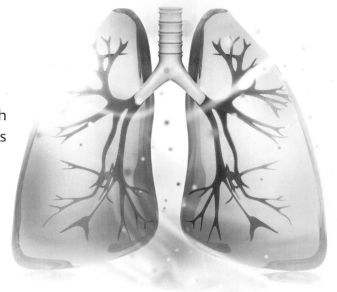

Organ system

The organs involved in respiration are nose, trachea, bronchi, bronchioles, lungs and diaphragm.

Process of respiration

Lungs are one of the largest organs of the body. In the human body, there are two lungs present in the chest cavity. The gases are exchanged in the alveoli air sacs present in the lungs passively by the process of diffusion. Diaphragm, a membrane-like structure, creates space for the air coming in and pushes the air out of the lungs by its expansions and contractions. Different types of muscles like pectoral muscles, external intercostal muscles and accessory muscles aid in the process of respiration. Nostrils have small hair that act as a filter and remove the dust and dirt from the air that is breathed in.

Factors affecting respiration

The main factors affecting respiration are temperature, carbon dioxide, light, oxygen, extinction point, water, respiratory substrates, stimulation, climacteric fruits, inhibitors and protoplasmic factors.

When the surface volume ratio is high, the respiration is efficient. As the human body has a large volume, ventilation is required, which affects the process of respiration. The transport pigment called the haemoglobin also plays an important role in the process of respiration.

For example, when your body is doing a heavy workout, blood is pumped faster and hence the rate of respiration also increases.

A man inhaling fresh air through his nose.

Digestion

The digestive system is one of the vital organ systems of our body. It is surprising how digestion actually occurs within the body and how we get energy from food. Food is the essential source of a body to obtain energy, vitamins and minerals. Digestion is the process that changes food into a simpler form, which our cells can absorb.

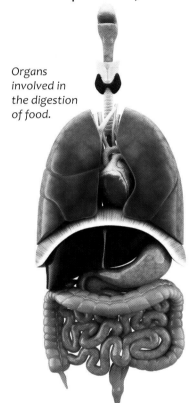

Organs involved in the digestion of food.

Organ system

Different organs involved in the digestive system are teeth, oesophagus, pancreas, stomach, gall bladder, liver, small intestine, large intestine and anus.

The entire passage through which the food journeys, from the mouth to the anus, is called the gastrointestinal tract. It is a 20 to 30-feet-long tube.

Passage of food

Our body prepares itself for the incoming food as soon as we think of eating any food or just smell it. The different steps that food goes through to get digested are as below:

Mastication or chewing: The whole process of digestion starts from the mouth, where the teeth crush and chew food. This process is called the mastication of food. The saliva from the salivary glands mixes with food, forming a semi-liquid mass called bolus. The starch digests at this stage.

Swallowing: This bolus then passes through the oesophagus. In this stage, no digestion occurs and food passes through this pipe by peristalsis movement into the stomach.

Stomach: As food comes to the stomach, it gets mixed with gastric juice, which is mainly composed of pepsin and hydrochloric acid. At this stage, protein digestion occurs.

Small intestine: The food leaving the stomach is called chyme. Chyme enters the duodenum, the first part of the small intestine and mixes with the digestive enzymes coming from the pancreas and liver. At this stage, the remaining digestion occurs.

Large intestine: The food then enters the cecum, colon and rectum. Water and minerals are re-absorbed by the colon, and the waste material goes out of the body through the rectum and a small opening called the anus. The process of removal of waste products is called defecation. The alimentary canal prevents the back flow of food at every stage.

Reproductive System

In the human body, the reproductive system causes the birth of a new young one or offspring. It is one of the most important systems in the human body. Different organisms living on this Earth have unique capacities of reproduction.

Types of reproduction

Asexual reproduction: Some organisms can give birth to their offspring on their own. Fission, budding, fragmentation and formation of rhizomes, and stolons are the mechanisms of asexual reproduction.

Sexual reproduction: Organisms that have two different sexes can reproduce sexually and give birth to their offspring. As a result of mating, male and female produce their offspring.

Organs involved in reproduction

Male sex organs: The testes, epididymis, seminal vesicles and prostate are male reproductive organs.

Female sex organs: The vagina, uterus, ovaries and fallopian tubes are female reproductive organs.

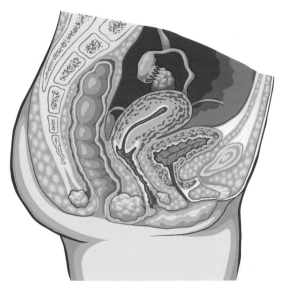

Lateral view of the female reproductive system.

Functions of the reproductive system

- To produce sperm and ovule
- To transport and sustain these cells
- To nurture immature offspring
- To produce hormones necessary for the production of cells, maintaining pregnancy and delivering the baby

A pregnant woman in her third trimester.

Body Repair

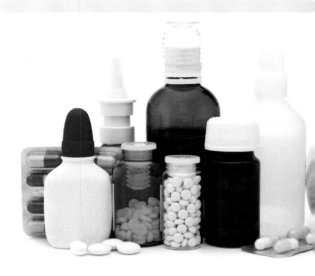

The human body is an intricate structure with different organs working harmoniously together. At any given point, different biological processes occur, like the circulatory, digestive and central nervous systems. If the working of any of these systems gets affected, it affects the whole body. Through their life, a person suffers from at least one infection and that can extend up to dozens.

The human body is vulnerable to many diseases.

Different disorders and diseases

Diseases can vary in both severity and diversity, and can affect any part of the body. With the growth in industrialisation and agriculture, the prevailing diseases have multiplied and increased to a great number.

Skin can get infected by bacterial, viral or fungal infections. The nervous system can encounter infections, injury, tumours and degenerative conditions. Structural defects and heart muscle constrictions are cardiovascular diseases. Cancer, tumour, arthritis, anaemia, diabetes and many more diseases have now become very common.

Ancient treatments

In ancient times, limited treatments were available. The doctors had no other choice but to cut limbs off if they got infected. If a person was wounded, the only treatment available was to remove all the tissues and pus from that area, and the process could be quite painful.

Modern treatment

With the advancement of science and medicine, antibiotic, anti-inflammatory, antiviral and anti-fungal medicines were discovered. These are capable of not only treating the diseases but also relieving human beings of pain.

In the modern world, not only can infected body parts like the heart, liver, lung and kidney be replaced, but even the blood of the entire body can be replaced with new, fresh blood. A handicapped person can get an artificial limb attached.

Currently, cosmetic surgery is utilised by many people to alter their physical appearance. Human beings can also undergo sex change with medical surgery.

Naturopathy

Naturopathy is the treatment of a disease by natural means. This field has also made great advancement in recent years. This treatment has the advantage of nil side effects.

Nutrition in Plants

One of the most important and basic things required by all living organisms is food. The components of food are proteins, minerals, carbohydrates, vitamins and fats. For all living things, all of these components are very significant. All plants and animals require food for their growth and energy.

Photosynthesis

The mode of nutrition used by plants is known as photosynthesis. Plants make food for themselves with the help of chlorophyll; the items required by plants to make food are sunlight, water and carbon dioxide. Roots absorb water. Leaves take in carbon dioxide from the air and absorb sunlight with the help of chlorophyll in the leaves. After the process is completed by leaves, they produce carbohydrates and oxygen. Carbohydrates are stored in the leaves as starch and oxygen is released into the atmosphere through the stomata.

Rafflesia or the corpse flower.

Modes of nutrition in plants

Substances of chemical nature that provide nourishment to living organism are known as nutrients. Plants are the only organisms on the planet that can make their own food.

Autotrophic nutrition: The word "auto" means "self" and "trophos" means nourishment. Some plants are called autotrophs because they can make their own food. Plants that convert carbon dioxide, water and nutrients into food with the help of photosynthesis are known as autotrophs, and this mode of nutrition is called autotrophic nutrition. For example, your normal rose bush creates its own food.

Heterotrophic nutrition: The word "heterotrophic" is a combination of two words; "hetero" meaning others and "trophos" meaning nourishment. Certain plants are incapable of conducting photosynthesis, and they latch onto other plants and organisms for their nutrition. These plants are called heterotrophic plants and this mode of nutrition is called heterotrophic nutrition. Heterotrophic nutrition occurs in two types of plants: parasitic and saprophytic.

Mistletoe is a parasitic plant as it attaches itself to the stem of a healthy plant for nutrition. Mushrooms are saprophytic plants as they feed on dead and decaying plants for nourishment.

Process of photosynthesis.

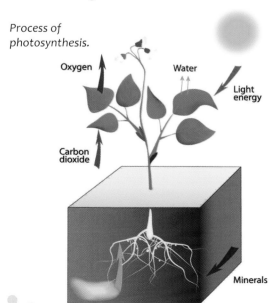

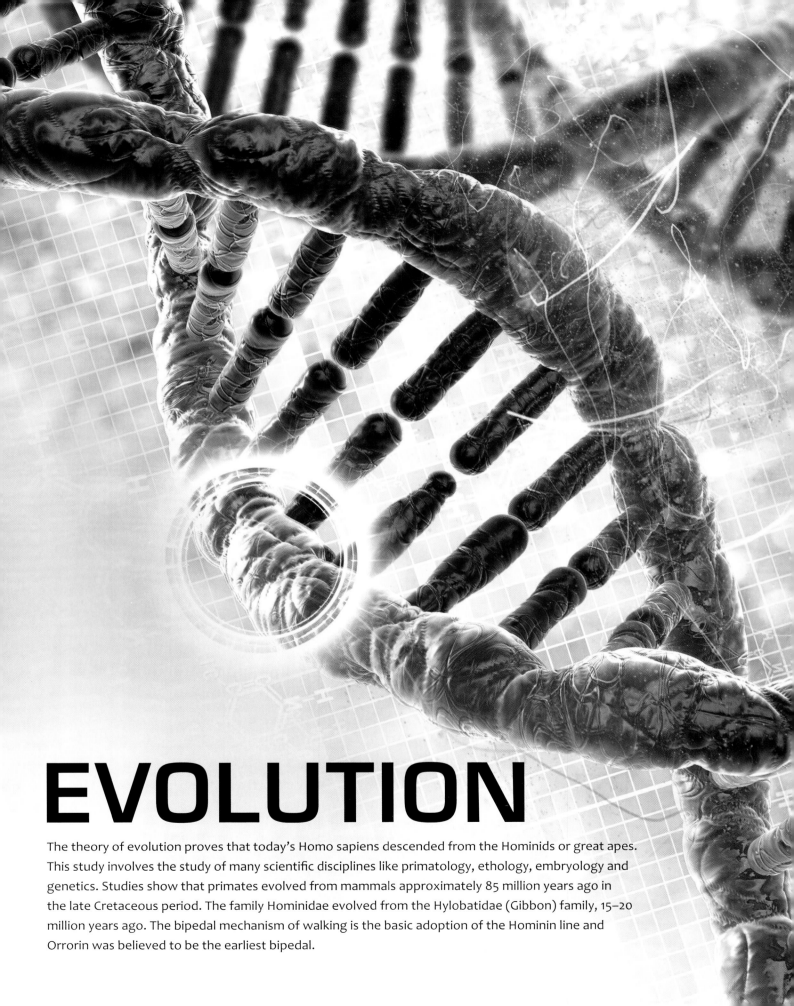

EVOLUTION

The theory of evolution proves that today's Homo sapiens descended from the Hominids or great apes. This study involves the study of many scientific disciplines like primatology, ethology, embryology and genetics. Studies show that primates evolved from mammals approximately 85 million years ago in the late Cretaceous period. The family Hominidae evolved from the Hylobatidae (Gibbon) family, 15–20 million years ago. The bipedal mechanism of walking is the basic adoption of the Hominin line and Orrorin was believed to be the earliest bipedal.

Evolution of Birds

The evolution of birds began in the Jurassic period, the earliest birds being the torpedo dinosaurs named Paraves. Birds belong to the class Aves. Archaeopteryx lithographica was the earliest known bird. Aves are considered to be the descendants of the ancestors of a specific modern bird species, like the house sparrow or an Archaeopteryx or some species close to the Neornithes.

Evolution of birds from dinosaurs

Even after so many years of research and study, the debate regarding the relationship between the dinosaur, Archaeopteryx and modern birds still continues. Evolution, as we know, is a process that takes years. However, bird species are presently approaching the point of extinction faster than any other species. The extinction of a species shows the permanent loss of a range of genes. As birds are considered to be evolved from theropod dinosaurs, some of their properties seem to have changed in the process. There is no evidence that the animals were evolving into birds, but various complex steps helped in this.

For example, Compsognathus was the first species to have feathers. Short, hair-like feathers developed, which provided them insulation and protection. It is not proved why they were of different colour and sizes.

Evolution of wings

Another point of study is the change in the digits of dinosaurs. The first theropod dinosaurs had hands with small digits and one long digit. Many scientists showed that this would lead to the evolution of birds. Slowly, these digits were lost through the species. The wrist bones, underlying the first and second digits became semi-circular, which allowed the hand to rotate sideways. This allowed the birds' wing joints to move in a way that could create a thrust for flight. In spite of this, birds classification and phylogenetic studies are still undeveloped and require a lot of research.

The house sparrow could have the same ancestors as all the aves.

Archaeopteryx lithographica.

3D rendering of a dinosaur with developed wings and joints.

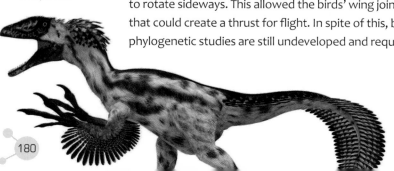

Model of Tarbosaurus Tyrannosaurid Theropod Dinosaur with hands at a theme park.

Mechanism of Evolution

There are many mechanisms according to scientists that showed how a completely new species evolved from the existing one. This occurred by changes in the genes through generations. The methods by which the changes occurred are natural selection, biased mutation, genetic drift, genetic hitchhiking and gene flow.

Genetic hichhiking

The genes that are present close to chromosomes are difficult to be separated; thus, they are wholly inherited as a combination. If one of the genes is dominant, then the other gene gets profited and becomes prominent in the population. This process is called genetic hichhiking.

Natural selection

It is the process in which only the organisms that are more fit for the environment survive and others don't. This is the main principle of the process of natural selection. An organism produces more number of progeny than the number that survives and only organisms with genes that are more fit for the environment survive.

Genetic drift

It is the process by which, in the absence of selective forces, the frequency of a particular gene either increases or decreases. This can result in the evolution of a completely new species.

Gene flow

It is the exchange of genes between two populations or species.

Biased mutation

This is the main criteria for the selection of genes by nature. Consider two genes, A and B, having the same fitness for the environment, but mutation prefers gene A more than gene B. Then, more and more organisms with gene A are produced. Naturally, the population with gene A will increase.

Long neck of a giraffe developed through adaptation.

Variation

An individual organism's physical appearance gets affected by both its genes and the effect of the surroundings. Changes in the physical appearance of organisms are caused due to differences in their genes. Variation occurs when a new allele substitutes an old one. Natural selection can be the cause of evolution if the offspring have a lot of genetic variation.

Inheritance

Before Mendel gave us the laws of genetics, inheritance was understood to be the main process. But if blending inheritance would have been true, genetic variance and natural selection would have to be completely discarded. The Hardy–Weinberg principle showed how variation occurred in a population. Selection, mutation, migration and genetic drift were the processes that cause variations in genes.

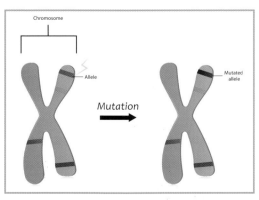

The process of mutation leading to changes in genes.

Variations in genes

Variation means mutations in genetic materials, reshuffling of genes and genetic migration between populations. Although there was a constant introduction of new variation by mutation and gene flow, the genetic structure of a species was identical in all individuals of a species. A little difference in the genetic structure could amount for a great change in the physical appearance of the species. For example, the human genes defer from chimpanzee genes by only 5 per cent!

Similarly, cat genes are different from human genes by only 10 per cent. The genes are present within every cell of the human body. Even the slightest change in genetic matter can rewrite the entire structure of the living being.

Food Chain

A food chain is the order of transfer of matter and energy in the form of food from one organism to another. Food chains intertwine locally into a food web because most organisms consume more than one type of animal or plant. Plants that convert solar energy to food by photosynthesis are the primary source of food.

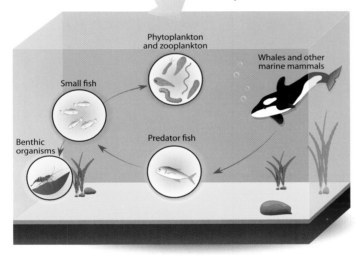

Solar energy

Marine food web.

Phytoplankton and zooplankton

Whales and other marine mammals

Small fish

Benthic organisms

Predator fish

Tiger attacks a deer that eats plants.

A real life food chain

Consider a grassland. There are various insects that live in it. One of them is a grasshopper that feeds on it. However, this grasshopper is then hunted by rats. Now, rats become prey for reptiles like snakes. So, snakes hunt the rats. Snakes are in turn hunted by predator birds like eagles. The food chain begins from grass and ends at the eagle. If the eagle were to die, it would be fed upon by the microorganisms in the soil, converting it into food for the plants. That is how the loop is closed.

Energy loss

As energy is lost at each step in the form of heat, chains do not normally encompass more than four or five tropic levels. People can increase the total food supply by removing one step in the food chain. Instead of consuming animals that eat plants, people eat plants directly. As the food chain is made shorter, the total amount of energy available to the final consumers is increased.

Food chain types

In a predator chain, a plant-eating animal is eaten by a flesh-eating animal. In a parasite chain, a smaller organism consumes a part of a larger host and may itself play host to even smaller organisms. In a saprophytic chain, microorganisms live on dead, organic matter.

Human Evolution

Human evolution is the process by which human beings developed on Earth from the now extinct primates. Zoologically speaking, humans are Homo sapiens, a culture-bearing, upright-walking species that live on the ground and first evolved in Africa between 100,000 and 200,000 years ago. We are now the only living members of what many zoologists refer to as the human tribe Hominini. However, there were many before us.

Historical evidence

The extensive process of change by which humans originated from ape-like ancestors is called human evolution. Scientific evidence shows that the physical and behavioural traits shared by all people originated from ape-like ancestors and evolved over a period of approximately six million years.

In addition, we and our predecessors have always shared Earth with other ape-like primates, from the modern-day gorilla to the long-extinct Dryopithecus. The extinct hominins are related to us and so are we and the apes (both living and extinct). This fact is accepted by anthropologists and biologists everywhere.

The skull of a Dryopithecus ancient ape.

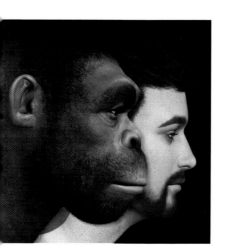

Current day humans and our predecessors have always shared Earth with other ape-like primates.

Charles Darwin

The exact nature of our evolutionary relationships has been the subject of debate and investigation since the great British naturalist Charles Darwin published his monumental books *On the Origin of Species* (1859) and *The Descent of Man* (1871).

Darwin never claimed, as some of his Victorian contemporaries insisted he had, that "man descended from the apes", and modern scientists would view such a statement as a useless simplification—just as they would dismiss any popular notions that a certain extinct species is the "missing link" between man and the apes.

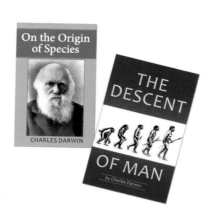

Charles Darwin's theory on the evolution of man.

The missing link

There is theoretically, however, a common ancestor between us and the apes that existed millions of years ago. This ancestral species does not constitute a "missing link" along a lineage but rather a node for divergence into separate lineages. This ancient primate has not been identified and may never be known with certainty, because fossil relationships are unclear even within the human lineage, which is more recent. In fact, the human "family tree" may be better described as a "family bush", within which it is impossible to connect a full chronological series of species, leading to Homo sapiens that experts can agree upon.

Creative representation of the prehistoric man.

Excavations and finds

Ancient human fossils and archeological remains give many vital clues about our evolution. These fossil remains include bones, tools and other evidences (such as footprints, evidence of hearths or butchery marks on animal bones). Ideally, the remains are buried and preserved naturally. They are usually found either on the surface due to exposure by rain, rivers and wind erosion or by digging the ground. Scientists learn about the physical appearance of the earlier humans and how it changed by studying fossilised bones. We can understand how these predecessors moved around, held tools and how the size of their brains changed over a long time by examining the bone size, shape and markings left on the bones by their muscles. We can understand how early humans made and used tools, and lived in their environments by studying archeological evidence. This helps us draw parallels to us as well as other species.

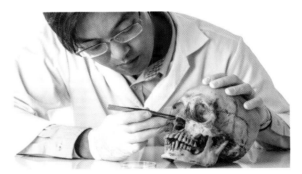

Scientist studying human fossil.

Extinction of Species

The causes of extinction were prehistorically dominated by natural Earth processes such as geological transformation of Earth's crust and major climatic oscillations, as well as species interactions. However, since the ascent of the modern man during the Holocene, the causes of extinction have been dominated by the activities of humans.

The Woolly Mammoth is an extinct species of elephant.

Extinct species

Thylacine, also known as the Tasmanian tiger, became extinct in 1936 as it was hunted to protect the sheep and small farm animals.

Quaggas became extinct in 1883 due to being hunted indiscriminately for their meat and leather.

Dodo birds became extinct around the 1670s. They were known to have been hunted by sailors on a large scale as they were so easy to catch. Also, the pets of these sailors had developed a taste for Dodo eggs.

Passenger Pigeons went extinct as recently as 1914. They were also hunted on a large scale for their meat.

FUN FACT

Sabre-toothed tiger evolved into the modern tiger by the process of migration.

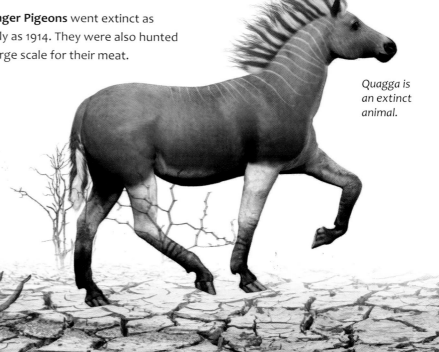

Quagga is an extinct animal.

Causes of extinction

Darwin was the first to fully articulate the concepts of speciation and extinction as applied to natural succession, although he never used the terms evolution or extinction (1859). The primary cause of human-induced extinctions is simply the human overpopulation of planet Earth. The most important causal anthropogenic activities are habitat destruction, overexploitation, pollution and the introduction of alien species to an environment. Habitat destruction elements include conversion to agricultural land, deforestation, overgrazing and urbanisation. Within these activities, the process of habitat fragmentation is sometimes the hidden cause of major biodiversity loss. Overexploitation consists of intensive mineral and other geological resource extraction, overharvesting of wild flora and fauna (mainly for food), hunting or fishing, threatened fauna and killing of threatened fauna on a large scale for herbal or cultural extracts.

As per scientists, long lasting natural calamities are the major cause for extinction.

Extinct Dodo bird.

Natural mass extinction

Mass extinctions are periodic elevations in the extinction rate above the background level. Such extinctions are caused due to catastrophes. Approximately, over 95 per cent of all extinctions have occurred as background events with the rest consisting of catastrophic events. These events were geologically rapid, occurred worldwide, had a large number of species going extinct at the same time period and spread across all the world's ecosystems. The five major extinction events that have been recognised as the big 5 are as follows:

• The Ordovician event that happened 438 million years ago, when 100 families went extinct.

• The Devonian event, 360 million years ago, when 30 per cent of the families went extinct.

• The end Permian, 245 million years ago, the biggest extinction of all time when over 50 per cent of all families were lost.

• The late Triassic event when 35 per cent of the families died.

• The Cretaceous Tertiary (K-T) event, 65 million years ago, which ended the reign of the dinosaurs.

Human-driven extinction

The impact of pollution includes the build-up of toxic atmospheric substances, discharge of water pollutants into water reserves, chemical contamination of soils and noise pollution.

Introduction of alien species is usually an unintended activity where seeds, stowaway fauna aboard ships and other viably reproducing biota are transported by humans to a new environment that has insufficient resident predators (or predators unfamiliar with and therefore naive to the new prey) to control the invading taxon or exotic predators. Here, the native fauna are often unable to recognise the invading organism as a threat and end up getting destroyed in large numbers.

DNA

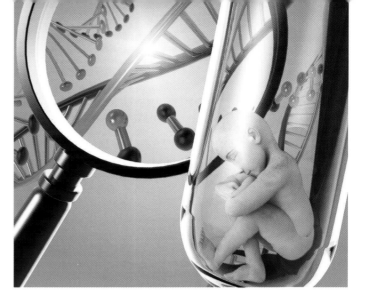

DNA is the abbreviation for deoxyribonucleic acid. It is the hereditary material of all living organisms. You can identify organisms on the basis of their DNA. DNA can be called the biological storage of information. It is a long, linear, double-helical structured polymer found in the nucleus of a cell associated with the transmission of genetic information.

Analysing DNA samples.

Discovery of DNA

The quest for the discovery of DNA began in the early 1950s. English molecular biologists Francis Crick and American molecular biologists James Watson were the two men who got the Nobel Prize in 1953 for the discovery of three-dimensional, double helical structure of DNA. However, the contribution of Swiss biologist Friedrich Miescher, English chemist Rosalind Franklin, American biochemist Linus Pauling and Kiwi molecular biologist Maurice Wilkins should not be forgotten.

DNA location

Nucleus of the eukaryotic cell.

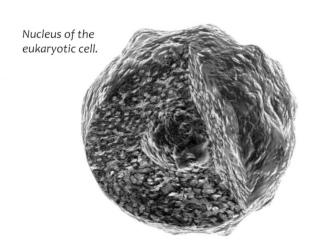

DNA is found in different locations in different types of cells. In eukaryotes, DNA is present inside a cell in the nucleus. As the cell is very small and organisms have many DNA molecules per cell, each DNA molecule must be tightly packaged. This packaged form of DNA is called a chromosome. During DNA replication, it unwinds so that it can be copied. DNA found in the cell's nucleus is known as nuclear DNA. An organism's complete set of nuclear DNA is called its genome. Besides the DNA located in the nucleus, humans and other complex organisms have a small amount of DNA called mitochondria in their cell structure. Mitochondria generates the energy that the cell requires to function properly.

FUN FACT

If the DNA of a single individual was unwound and linked together, it would go all the way to the Sun and back, three hundred times!

Classification

Nucleic acid – There are two types of nucleic acids found in living organisms RNA and DNA.

Nucleobase classification – The nucleobases are of two types. The first type is purines, adenine and guanine, and the second type is pyrimidines, cytosine and thymine. The arrangement of the two nucleotides provides the information for building and maintaining an organism's identity. This is called a base pair.

Grooves – The double helix forms spaces or grooves of unequal sizes between the strands, which provides a binding site for the proteins.

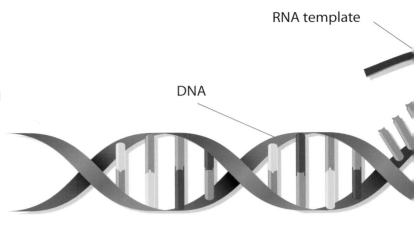

RNA template

DNA

DNA composition

DNA consists of two polynucleotide chains coiled together. Each of the nucleotide is composed of a nitrogen-containing nucleobase with monosaccharide sugar called deoxyribose and a phosphate group. Nucleobases can be adenine (A), guanine (G), cytosine (C) or thymine (T). The structure of DNA is like a ladder with the base pairs as the ladder's rungs and the sugar and phosphate molecules as the vertical sidepieces. An important property of DNA is that it can replicate.

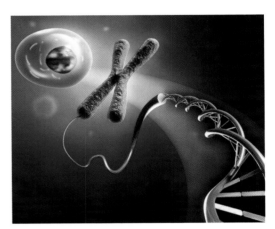

Formation of an animal cell from DNA.

What is the DNA double helix?

The term "double helix" describes the DNA's winding, that is, its two-stranded chemical structure. This shape can be best described as a twisted ladder. The shape gives DNA the power to pass along biological instructions with great precision. From a chemical standpoint, the DNA's double helix's sides of the ladder has strands of alternating sugar and phosphate groups. These strands run in opposite directions. Each "rung" of the ladder is composed of two nitrogen bases paired together by hydrogen bonds. Because of the highly specific nature of this type of chemical pairing, base A always pairs with base T and base C always pairs with base G. DNA's unique structure enables the molecules to copy itself during cell division.

Scientist studying DNA Helix.

Know Your Gene

The gene is a basic physical and functional unit of heredity that is transferred from an organism to its offspring and gives specific characteristics to the offspring. The word gene is taken from the Greek word genesis meaning "birth" or genos meaning "origin". The gene is a locatable region of genomic sequence, which is associated with regulatory regions, transcribed regions and other functional, sequence regions.

Women   *Men*

Female and male chromosomes.

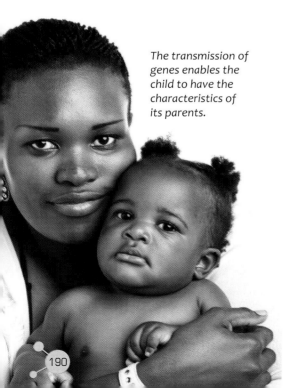

The transmission of genes enables the child to have the characteristics of its parents.

Discovery of genes

Gregor Mendel worked from 1857 to 1864 on edible pea plants and found the evidence of a hereditary material. It was rediscovered by European scientists Hugo de Vries, Carl Correns and Erich von Tschermak. Charles Darwin gave the term gemmule for the unit of inheritance and that later came to be known as chromosome, coined by German biologist Wilhelm Hofmeister. The word gene was coined by Danish botanist Wilhelm Johannsen.

Function of gene

All organisms have genes related to their traits, from the eye colour to the many biochemical processes of life. The expression of genes encoded in DNA begins by the process of transcription of the gene into a messenger RNA. Genes also possess codons, which serve as words in the genetic language. Then, by the process of slicing and translation, a protein forms. The genes are translated from mRNA to protein. Genes act as instructions to make the molecules called proteins.

Gene expression

The process of producing a molecule of either RNA or protein that is biologically functional is called gene expression and the molecule that is produced at the end is called a gene product.

Genetic code

Genetic code is the rule by which the information in a gene is translated into a specific protein. The gene is a distinct arrangement of nucleotides, which determines the order of the monomers in a polypeptide. In human beings, most of the genes remain the same but less than one per cent are different because of which each person possesses his/her unique physical identity.

Mung bean is genetically modified.

Mutation

If we were to observe the natural places around us, we will find an enormous number of various beetles in different places. How can so many different organisms evolve having nearly, but not completely, the same genetic makeup? The answer is mutation. When a change takes place in the nucleotide in the genome of an organism, a sequence occurs. This is called mutation.

Few examples of different types of mutation of fruits and vegetables.

Exotic mutation in a pineapple making it look different from others.

Kiwi in apple is a modification concept.

Unusual mutation of carrot.

What is a mutation?

As nucleotides are the building blocks of DNA, their mutations cause changes in the phenotype of the organism. Mutations are also called errors in the genes. The frequency of the mutation is very low, around one in a hundred million bases. DNA polymerase plays an important role in carrying out mutations. There are some chemicals and also UV radiation that can cause mutations and are called as mutagenic substances.

Types of mutations

Mutations can be classified on the basis of how much effect can they have on the structure, function, fitness or protein sequence, or on the basis of its inheritance ability. The main types of mutations are given below.

1. **Point mutations**
   It is the smallest mutation in which change occurs in only a base pair.
2. **Nonsynonymous mutations**.
   It is the mutation in which an amino acid sequence changes, thus forming a new protein.
3. **Synonymous mutations**.
   It is the mutation in which the change only occurs in the sequence that hold the code for the amino acids.

Genetic disorder in a sheep caused by mutation.

Effects of mutations

Mutation, however, is a very powerful tool as even a small mutation produces a large change in the phenotype. But if we consider the evolutionary aspect, it proves that a large number of mutations produce small effects. The mutations can be beneficial, harmful or neutral depending upon the context and location.

The Birth of a New Species

The term species is always being argued about. In biological terms, we can say that species is a group of organisms that interbreed and are reproductively separated from other organisms. Speciation is the word used for the process by which a completely new species evolves. In nature, the process of speciation occurs by four ways: allopatric, peripatric, parametric and sympatric.

Speciation

Speciation is the event of a lineage splitting that produces two or more separate species. It is usually difficult to estimate when speciation has occurred because it is a gradual process. If speciation has to occur, members of an ancestral species must be separated from each other. Thus, separating organisms into two populations results in two separate gene pools. These gene pools can be isolated through geographical or biological methods. Moreover, altered reproductive methods can isolate two populations of the same organisms.

Allopatric

This occurs when two populations of the same species separate geographically from one other. They adapt differently according to their environments. They face different mutations and genetic drifts, and become completely different species unable to reproduce with one other.

Peripatric

In this type of process of speciation, a small group of organisms gets separated from the rest of the population and slowly evolves into a different species than the main population, because of the genetic drift.

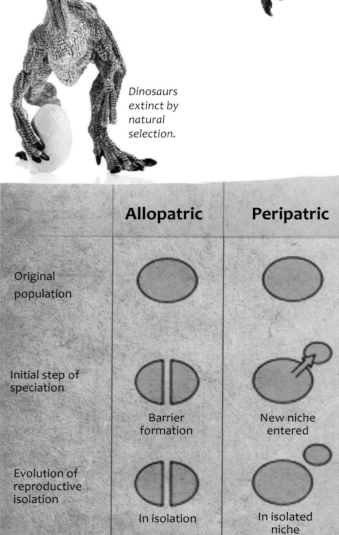

Dinosaurs extinct by natural selection.

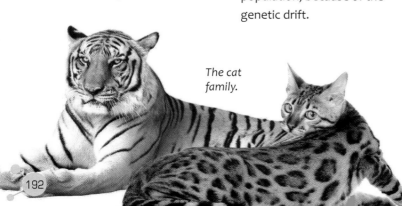

The cat family.

	Allopatric	Peripatric
Original population		
Initial step of speciation	Barrier formation	New niche entered
Evolution of reproductive isolation	In isolation	In isolated niche
New distinct species after equilibration of new ranges		

Dates that grow on the island are the Cretan species of date palm. This is an example of speciation by geographical isolation.

The tick surviving on the body of a dog comes close to cospeciation except that the dog's body doesn't provide an environment long enough for the ticks to evolve.

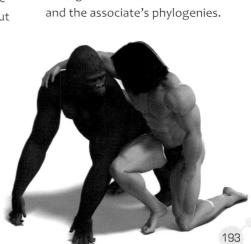

Parapatric

In this type of process, there is no geographical barrier between the two species, but natural selection is the dominant factor, which causes only a particular type of species to survive and even if two species interbreed, their offspring is unable to survive.

Sympatric

This is a process in which two or more types of species evolve from the same ancestor without any geographical barrier an both types of species are ab to survive.

With so much progress in science, there are ways by v we can induce speciation by animal husbandry, agricultu using laboratory experimen

Cospeciation

Cospeciation is the process where one population speciates in response with another and is a result of the associate's dependence on its host for its survival. In 1913, Fahrenholz termed cospeciation, however, in almost all instances, except those cases where the host is pathologically dependent on its associate, this principle is rarely, strictly adhered to. Deviations to the interpretation of Fahrenholz's rule are demonstrated by topological incongruence between the host and the associate's phylogenies.

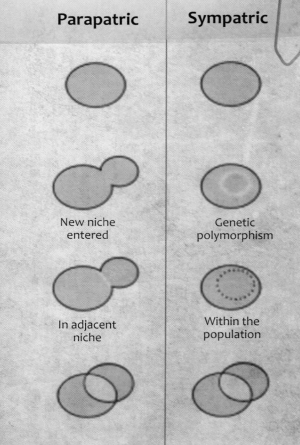

Parapatric	Sympatric
New niche entered	Genetic polymorphism
In adjacent niche	Within the population

Genetics

The study of genetics includes variations, mutations, hereditary traits, genes and their structure, functioning, behaviour and distribution, and some other related topics. Epigenetics and population genetics are the subfields of genetics. Gregor Mendel, popularly known as the "father of genetics", studied genetics in the nineteenth century on pea plants.

What is genetics?

In genetics, we study genes and genetic code. Genes are the structures by which physical traits and characteristics are inherited.

In the human body, there are about 20,000 genes. A genetic code or a genome is somebody's genetic information. The presence of a particular type of gene is generally expressed with their function, which is transmitted to the offspring in the form of a particular sequence of amino acids. In common language, we can understand genetics as a science of the inheritance of different traits from the parents to their offspring. A baby with brunette parents will have black hair colour and a baby with blonde parents will have blonde hair. The shape of the nose and colour of the iris of a young one are likely to match their parent's. Thus, these are some of the many traits, which are inherited across generations.

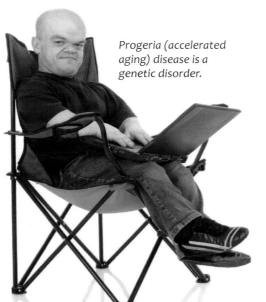

Progeria (accelerated aging) disease is a genetic disorder.

Genetic disorders

Diseases like colour blindness are hereditary and also known as genetic disorders. The types of genetic disorders are single-gene, autosomal dominant and recessive, X-linked dominant and recessive, Y-linked and mitochondrial. Colour blindness is a sex-linked disease. Colour blindness is the inability to differentiate between colours. This disease is mostly dominant in males. Females tend to be the carriers of this disease.

Genetics as a cure

Genetic research is the study of DNA and genes. These studies are used for the identification of genes or other factors, which are responsible for producing diseases. If we can find out the cause of a disease, it becomes easier to find a cure for it and also find ways to control the spread of that specific disease. Nearly, every disease we know today has some genes responsible for its occurrence. Some diseases have small and others have a large genetic contribution. The development of modern scientific research is in progress and in search of cures of diseases to enable us to lead a better life.

Advancements in genetics

There are many studies being carried out for more elaboration on the structure and organisation of genetic makeup, the regulation of gene expression and the study of variations and changes in genetic composition. Researches are occurring to elaborate fundamental biological problems using systems ranging from model organisms to the human body itself. Organisms chosen for experiments are those having short generations and hence, genetic manipulation becomes easy. For example, gut bacteria Escherichia coli, the plant Arabidopsis thaliana and baker's yeast (Saccharomyces cerevisiae) etc., are used for genetic manipulations. DNA manipulation is also currently possible in laboratories. Restriction enzymes are used for cutting DNA at a particular sequence and producing the required fragments of DNA. DNA fragments, by visualising through gel electrophoresis, can be separated. This is a vast field, where the possibility of many more researches still exists.

UK scientists are seeking permission to genetically modify the human embryo.

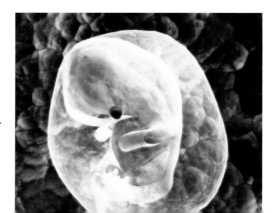

Human Genome Project

The Human Genome Project (HGP) was one of the greatest feats of exploration in history. An international research effort was made to sequence and map all genes – together known as the genome – of the members of our species, Homo sapiens. Completed in April 2003, it gave us the ability to read nature's complete genetic blueprint for building a human being.

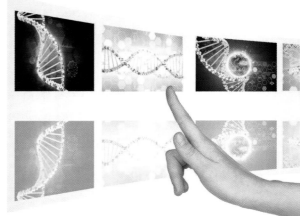

The advantage

The hereditary material of all the multi-cellular organisms is the famous double helix of DNA, which contains all of our genes. DNA, in turn, is made up of four chemical bases, pairs of which form the "rungs" of twisted, ladder-shaped DNA molecules. All genes are made up of stretches of these four bases, arranged in different ways and in different lengths. HGP researchers have deciphered the human genome in three major ways: first, determining the order, or "sequence", of all bases in our genome's DNA; second, making maps that show the locations of genes for major sections of all our chromosomes; and lastly, producing linkage maps – complex versions of the type originated in early Drosophila research, through which inherited traits (such as those for genetic disease) can be tracked over generations.

DNA helix.

Revelations

The HGP has revealed that there are probably, approximately, 20,500 human genes. The completed human sequence can now identify their locations. This ultimate product of the HGP has given the world a resource of detailed information regarding the structure, organisation and function of the complete set of human genes. This information can be thought of as the basic set of inheritable "instructions" for the development and function of a human being.

Publication

The International Human Genome Sequencing Consortium published the first draft of the human genome in the Nature journal in February 2001 with the sequence of the entire genome's three billion base pairs about 90 per cent complete. A startling finding of this first draft was that the number of human genes appeared to be significantly fewer than previously estimated, which ranged from 50,000 genes to as many as 140,000. The full sequence was completed and published in April 2003.

Inheritance

Inheritance means the transfer of traits from parents to their offspring. Mendel studied inheritance and its theories became the core of classical genetics. Mendel worked on pea plants and performed hybridisation on them and his results became famous as Mendel's law of inheritance.

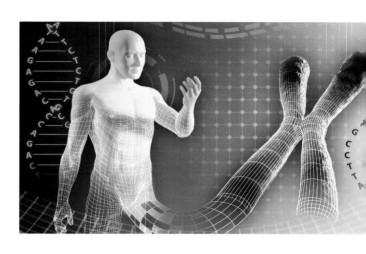

Inheritance of parents' characters - two different strands, one from each parent.

Mendel's contribution

Previously, all researchers were of the view that these theories applied only under certain circumstances, but it was later proved wrong. Mendel studied garden pea plants, which he planted in the backyard of the church. He then described the law of segregation, law of dominance and law of independent assortment. These three constituted Mendel's law of inheritance. He took two plants, one with white flowers and the other with purple flowers. In the first generation, he found that the offspring had purple flowers and in the next F2 generation, the ratio of purple to white flowers was 3:1.

The laws

The plant with BB genes will bear purple flowers. Those with Bb genes will also bear purple flowers. Only the one with bb genes will bear white flowers. This is based on the principle of dominance. As the dominant gene B, which is for the dominant coloured flower (purple) becomes heterozygous with the recessive gene b which is for the recessive coloured flower (white), the chance of getting a plant with white flowers is one in four. This is the law of dominance. During gamete formation, the two types of genes of parents become separated. The sperm or egg carries either B or b gene only. During fertilisation, the two genes combine to form a pair of genes in their offspring. This is the law of segregation. The law of independent assortment is that the two genes can segregate independently during the formation of gamete.

The child has traits of both its parents.

FUN FACT

From Mendel's laws, we know that it is possible for a couple with dark eyes to give birth to a light-eyed child. However, the chances of this happening are very less.

Cloning

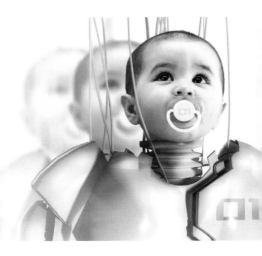

The process of creating a genetically identical copy of a cell or an organism is called cloning. Cloning happens all the time in nature. Prokaryotic organisms, such as bacteria and yeasts, create genetically identical duplicates of themselves using binary fission or budding. Eukaryotic organisms such as humans have cells that undergo mitosis. For example, the skin cells and the cells lining the gastrointestinal tract are clones.

Identical cells.

FUN FACT

In the 1880s, German Scientist Hans Driesch cloned the first animal ever. Using an embryo cell, he cloned a sea urchin.

Process of cloning

In biomedical research, cloning is broadly defined to mean the duplication of any kind of biological material for scientific study, such as a piece of DNA or an individual cell. For example, segments of DNA are replicated exponentially by a process known as polymerase chain reaction (PCR), a technique that is used widely in basic biological research. The type of cloning that is the focus of much ethical controversy involves the generation of cloned embryos, particularly those of humans. These are genetically identical to the organisms from which they are derived and could subsequently be used for research, therapeutic or reproductive purposes.

A computer generated image representing cloning.

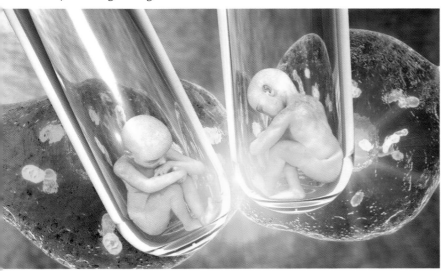

Cloning achievements

Reproductive cloning was originally conducted by artificial "twinning", or embryo splitting, which was first performed on a salamander embryo in the early 1900s by German embryologist Hans Spemann. Later, Spemann, who was awarded the Nobel Prize for Physiology or Medicine (1935) for his research on embryonic development, theorised another cloning procedure known as the nuclear transfer. This procedure was performed in 1952 by American scientists Robert W. Briggs and Thomas J. King, who used DNA from embryonic cells of the frog Rana pipiens to generate cloned tadpoles. In 1958, British biologist John Bertrand Gurdon successfully performed nuclear transfer using DNA from adult intestinal cells of the African clawed frogs (Xenopus laevis). Gurdon was awarded a share of the 2012 Nobel Prize in Physiology or Medicine for this breakthrough.

Twinning

ECOLOGY

The word ecology was coined by German zoologist Ernst Haeckel, who applied the term ökologie to the "relation of the animal both to its organic as well as its inorganic environment". The word comes from the Greek word oikos, meaning "household", "home" or "place to live". Thus, ecology deals with the organism and its environment. The concept of environment includes both the organisms themselves and their physical surroundings. It involves the relationships between the individuals within a population and between the individuals of different populations. These interactions between the individuals, populations, and organisms and their environment form the ecological systems or ecosystems. Ecology can thus be defined as the study of the relationships that exist between all living things and their environment. Scientists who study ecology are called ecologists.

Biosphere

In the term biosphere, bio means life and sphere means surrounding. Scientists use the term sphere for describing various parts of Earth where life exists, such as atmosphere, lithosphere, hydrosphere, geosphere, anthrosphere and cryosphere. All these spheres, together, constitute the biosphere. The layer of gases around Earth is called atmosphere. Lithosphere is the solid surface layer of Earth and hydrosphere is the layer of water that makes our planet look blue.

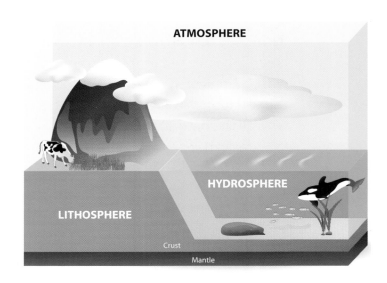

The hierarchy of biological organisation as can be seen in our biosphere.

What is the extent of the biosphere?

Biosphere is the global-ecological system, which is the home of all living organisms along with their surrounding environment. From the depth of the oceans to the highest mountains, every place where life is possible comes under the biosphere. Even the microorganisms that we find deep underground and the birds that fly very high and look like a dot to us, come under the biosphere. After so much progress in science, it is still not possible to define the boundaries of our biosphere.

Effect of non-living factors on living organisms and vice versa

The evolution of life can be studied from non-living matter itself. That is why they remain correlated to a great extent, influencing each other. All the living organisms on Earth are very closely related to their surroundings; they get adapted to their surroundings for their survival. As many natural factors affect our life, like rotation, revolution and the tilt of Earth's axis, even minuscule changes in the weather and air can change our climate. Biologically and chemically, too, Earth undergoes change continuously.

Biodiversity

In 1968, American biologist Raymond F. Dasmann gave the term, biodiversity to the world. Biodiversity or biological diversity is the variation in the life found on Earth along with all the natural processes. Biodiversity includes variations in a gene, ecosystem and species.

Why is it important?

You would have heard or read somewhere that tigers are in danger and the number of tigers is decreasing very fast. The government is taking steps to save this species. Do you know why these measures are important? What will happen if there are no tigers left? Being the carnivorous and dangerous animals that they are, you might want to get rid of them, but they should not disappear as every species is important for life on Earth.

As we know, there is a great bonding between living organisms and their surrounding environment; they both depend on each other. By the destruction of any species, the food chain gets disturbed. This affects the ecosystems and, simultaneously, the life of human beings as well.

Distribution of species

We cannot find the same type and number of species everywhere. They are unequally distributed, depending on various factors like altitude, temperature, type of soil, physical features and the other species found in the area. The highest biodiversity is found in the areas of rainforests.

Human, the main culprit

During the early life of human beings, the number of species living on Earth was very large. But as human beings made progress, the number of species decreased steeply. Because of human beings, there have been great changes in climate, seasons, atmospheric gases, water and land. These changes, in turn, affect the habitats and behaviours of different species, and cause their extinction.

SILENCE PLEASE !

RESPECT THE ORANGUTANS

Hydrologic Cycle

Our Earth is known as the "blue planet". Do you know why? Because three-fourth of the planet is covered by water. But we cannot see so much water around us as its distribution is not uniform. We also cannot find all of the water in liquid state.

What is the water cycle?

You know how on heating, water evaporates and changes into water vapour. Similarly, when you keep ice outside the freezer, it melts quickly into water. So water goes from one state to another with the change of temperature. This occurs in nature too. Here, water continuously moves from one state to another and from one resource to another.

The journey of water, when it circulates from land to sky and back again, is called the water cycle or hydrologic cycle. The water cycle can explain the existence and movement of water on Earth.

Water moves through all four areas of Earth: atmosphere, lithosphere, hydrosphere and biosphere. In this process, it is stored in the atmosphere, oceans, lakes, rivers, soils, glaciers, snowfields and groundwater.

The whole cycle involves various steps and interactions with the physical processes in this journey.

Role of the water cycle

As you would have heard, the human population is growing at a very fast pace. Just think how much water each individual consumes in a day and how much of it goes down the drains.

Water cycle is the process that circulates water throughout the globe, and makes it clean and available to us. Rain water is known to be the purest of all forms of water on Earth.

Water cycle is always related to the transfer of energy, so it is responsible for temperature changes.

There are many other roles played by the water cycle, like sedimentation and erosion, which help in shaping geological features.

Many ecosystems depend on the water cycle for their existence. The flow of water and ice transports many materials across the world.

A symbolic representation of how pollution in cities is affecting ice at the poles.

Percolation

Global water distribution

Over 96 per cent of our world's total water supply is saline. Furthermore, of the total freshwater, over 68 per cent is in the form of ice and glaciers. Another 30 per cent of freshwater is present in the ground. Thus, fresh surface-water sources, such as rivers and lakes only comprise approximately 1/150ᵗʰ of one per cent of the total water.

This is why it becomes necessary for us to save water. The rate at which we are using water is very high as compared to the rate at which the water cycle takes place. Hence, it becomes important that we use water very carefully and save as much of it as possible, every day.

A visual representation of how water travels through our environment to create the life encouraging water cycle.

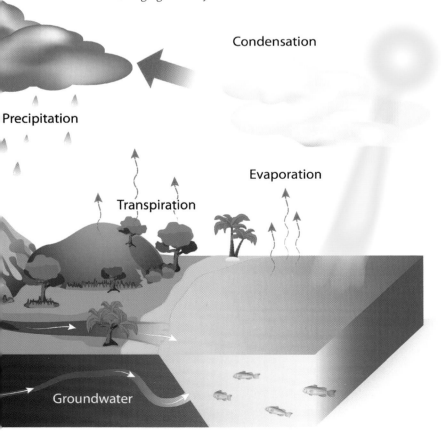

Various processes of water cycle

Evaporation

The Sun, which is the source of heat and light, drives the process of the water cycle. Water from resources like seas, lakes, oceans and land gets evaporated by absorbing heat. Evaporation is the process of conversion of water into water vapour. Plants also lose water by the process of transpiration, which keeps them cool. This is like plants sweating. This water vapour in the atmosphere moves, but is not visible to us. Water vapour, due to its low density as compared to other gases, reaches a great height.

Condensation

This is the process by which the clouds that we see in the sky are formed. As the water vapour rises up, it encounters low temperature, and condenses into water droplets, forming clouds.

Precipitation

Air currents move the clouds from one place to another, making them collide, fuse, grow and fall out on Earth's surface as precipitation, as they become too heavy for the air to keep hold of. In cooler regions, water falls down as snow and we enjoy snowfall.

Collection

The rainwater then either goes into the oceans, rivers or it may fall on land. When it falls on land it increases the levels of groundwater, which is used by plants, animals and human beings for drinking and many other purposes. Some of the water goes deep underground to form aquifers. Aquifers hold fresh water for a very long period of time.

Runoffs

Water moves across the land as runoffs. These include both surface and channel runoffs. Water also evaporates back to the atmosphere or can be extracted for human consumption.

Ecosystem

In the rainy season, you would have seen many plants growing around your home. For your study, take any one that has not been disturbed for many days and observe the different types of organisms and insects in it. There are some non-living factors that support their growth, like sunlight, water, temperature, pressure, nutrients and turbulence in the place. This plant is a simple example of an ecosystem.

Definition

Ecosystem is the term used for the community of living organisms that live, stay, feed, reproduce and interact in the same area or environment. An ecosystem is always accompanied by the energy flow and cycling of elements between the biotic and abiotic components present in it. An ecosystem can be as small as a plant and as large as a desert or ocean.

An ecosystem can be described as the study of the flow of energy and materials through organisms and their environment.

Classification

There are different types of ecosystems as climate varies from place to place. Broadly, ecosystems are classified into two categories: the aquatic ecosystem and terrestrial ecosystem.

Aquatic ecosystem includes marine and freshwater ecosystems while terrestrial ecosystem largely depends upon the type of dominant vegetation. It is further divided into categories like forest, littoral, riparian, urban and desert. The term biome is used for the vegetation types, such as tropical rain forest, grassland and tundra.

Each component is essential

Do you understand why everything is interconnected? To understand, perform a small test. If you obstruct the sunlight reaching the plant that you observed, all living organisms will diminish slowly as every plant depends on sunlight and each organism feeding on the plant depends on them for their life. Thus, each and every part of an ecosystem works together in a balanced system.

FUN FACT

The smallest, oldest surviving ecosystem in the world is a garden in a bottle, planted by David Latimer in 1960, which was last watered in the year 1972 before it was tightly sealed.

Oxygen

Water

Light energy

Carbon dioxide

Minerals

Process of photosynthesis by which plants convert sunlight into energy.

What is the process of ecosystem?

While studying an ecosystem, attention is mainly focussed on the functional aspects of the system. The functional aspects include the amount of energy produced by the process of photosynthesis, that is, by a biotic component and how this energy flows through other organisms via the food chain.

The whole process can be understood as energy enters the biological system in the form of light energy and changes into organic molecules via photosynthesis and respiration, and is further converted into heat energy that is used by organisms for various activities.

The nutrients also continuously get recycled in an ecosystem. It goes from one organism to another and also gets decomposed. Elements, such as carbon, nitrogen and phosphorus enter the life cycle and, sooner or later, due to excretion and decomposition, get mixed with abiotic components, completing the cycle.

Threat to ecosystems

An ecosystem can be considered healthy if each and every species living in it is not being damaged by human interaction, natural disasters or climatic changes. Fire, storms, floods and volcanic eruptions are some of the natural disasters faced by various ecosystems. An ecosystem can be regarded as healthy and sustainable when all the elements are in balance, and all the species reproduce and contribute in increasing the biodiversity.

An image representing the objects that smoke affects.

Ecosystem

Aquatic Ecosystem

Terrestrial Ecosystem

Littoral

Forest

Fresh water

Marine

Riparian

Urban and desert

Aquatic Ecosystem

Aquatic ecosystem is the ecosystem that is present in the water bodies on our planet. There are complex and intricate interactions between organisms and their environment. All organisms live, feed, reproduce and exchange matter and energy inside water bodies. The water may be fully saline, brackish or fresh. Marine habitats range from coasts and continent shelves to the deep sea. A great biodiversity is found because of variations in temperature, pressure, salinity, wind, wave action, tides, currents, light and substrate.

The coral reef is an example of a marine ecosystem.

Types of aquatic ecosystem

Aquatic ecosystem is classified into two categories: freshwater ecosystem and marine ecosystem. These two types of ecosystems are extremely diverse in structure. The physical constraints and opportunities are quite separated. Of the 70 per cent water on our planet, only one per cent of water constitutes fresh water and most of it is frozen in the polar ice caps.

In the marine ecosystem, sodium, chlorine and other dissolved materials constitute 85 per cent of the total composition. Life is believed to have evolved in saltwater as many phyla of animals live here.

Freshwater ecosystems are also very diverse in nature. Lakes, ponds, rivers, streams and wetlands with a good range of depth and flow rates come under this category. They are classified under lentic, lotic and wetlands. Of the world's known fish species, 41 per cent are found in the freshwater ecosystem.

A place where the river meets the ocean is called an estuary; it is usually shallow and very productive in nature.

Fresh water ecosystem.

View of an estuary.

Life in water

Animals like planktons, crayfish, snails, worms, frogs, turtles, insects and fishes are found in the freshwater ecosystem. Plants found in this region are water lilies, duckweed, cattail, bulrush, stoneware and bladderwort. Its biome varies dramatically from small trickling streams to wide rivers.

About 80 per cent of the solar energy reaching the ocean is absorbed in the first 10 m. Most deep-sea organisms are nourished by organic matter fixed by photosynthesis near the surface. There are entire biological communities on the seafloor that are nourished by chemosynthesis on the ocean floor and not by photosynthesis at the surface.

The Hawaiian green sea turtle of the aquatic ecosystem.

FUN FACT

The deep ocean displays the blue colour of pure water often called a "biological desert" as the open ocean is an area nearly devoid of life.

Importance

The aquatic ecosystem is very important for life on Earth. Can you imagine how our lives depend on aquatic organisms? Just take into account how often you need water from the time that you wake up till the time that you go to bed every day. If we use water so extensively, from where will we get pure water for drinking? Though we have studied that Earth is 70 per cent water, not all water is fit for drinking. Therefore, it is a limited resource, which is purified by aquatic organisms.

Let's get back to the fact that the aquatic ecosystem purifies water, recharges ground water and recycles nutrients that are used by human beings. Moreover, they can attenuate floods. Freshwater ecosystems are a good source of water for human beings as the water is used for many purposes like drinking, producing electricity and transportation.

A major portion of oxygen demanded by the human population is met by algae and other plants of the oceans.

The largest electric power producing facility in the USA is the Grand Coulee Dam on the Columbia River (freshwater ecosystem).

Marine Ecosystem

We know that there is over 70 per cent water on Earth's surface. Therefore, the marine ecosystem is the largest ecosystem in the whole planet. Oceans and seas constitute 97 per cent of the total water content.

A horseshoe crab lives in a salt marsh.

What is a marine ecosystem?

Though we have five main oceans, the marine ecosystem can further be divided into many smaller ecosystems depending on the types of species found in them. These include salt marshes, intertidal estuaries, lagoons, mangroves, coral reefs, deep sea, sea floor, rocky shores, submarine canyons, seamounts, chemosynthetic ecosystems, open slopes, deep basins and many more.

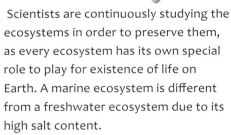

Why study it?

Scientists are continuously studying the ecosystems in order to preserve them, as every ecosystem has its own special role to play for existence of life on Earth. A marine ecosystem is different from a freshwater ecosystem due to its high salt content.

The marine ecosystem is very important as it affects terrestrial climate greatly. Wind circulation, rainy season, weather of coastal regions and current production are all under the control of the oceans' movements.

Life at sea

Presently, one million species of the ocean are identified, but scientists say that there are approximately nine million species that still need to be identified and classified.

In response to the various conditions available in the ocean, different types of animals and plants live here. It includes many plants, such as the phytoplanktons and algae like kelp. Many fishes like shark, swordfish, clown fish, eel and seahorse are found here. Among the mammals living in the sea are blue whales, walruses and otters. Octopus, cuttlefish, oysters, snail and slugs are the types of molluscs living in the ocean.

Organisms living in the ocean can also be classified, depending upon their eating habits, as producer, herbivorous, carnivorous and scavengers.

Ocean light zones

When we peep into a well or a deep tank, we can barely see anything. Imagine shining a light on the water surface. There will still be complete darkness at the deepest bottom of the tank and no light can reach it. Similarly, the deep areas in oceans are much deeper than the height of Mount Everest at some places. The ocean is divided into three zones based on the amount of light that penetrates it. Sunlit or euphotic zone is the uppermost layer of the sea or ocean where light can shine through and 90 per cent of the organisms exist here.

Twilight or disphotic zone is the middle zone getting extremely minuscule light. Organisms producing their own light by bioluminescence exist here.

Midnight or aphotic zone is the deepest part of the ocean. In this zone, it is always too cold and dark, just like a freezer, but it can be lit. Only a few animals can live here, mainly those who can survive by getting energy from the cracks.

Maximum light penetrates to the uppermost layer of the sea.

Man and sea biome

A large biodiversity is found in the marine ecosystem and it is considered as having great resistance towards invasive species and other changes that cause the depletion of various species. However, human beings are causing disturbance in the marine ecosystem. Some fishing practices like bottom trawling, disposal of oil and other wastes, over fishing, growing demand for seafood and coastal developments are all causing damage to this sea biome.

FUN FACT

The Great Barrier Reef off the coast of Queensland, Australia, is the world's largest coral reef. It is made up of 2100 individual reefs and 800 fringing reefs, and is the only living organism that's visible from space.

Freshwater Ecosystem

The term "freshwater" itself clarifies the condition of the water being fresh, having less salinity and good for consumption. Lakes, ponds, rivers, streams, springs, estuaries and wetlands are included in the freshwater ecosystem. From the total of 70 per cent water on Earth, only one per cent is available as fresh water and another two per cent is in a frozen state on the polar caps.

Comparison of biodiversity

Biodiversity in oceans depends upon light and nutrients from the coastland. As we go deeper and farther from the coast, the biodiversity will go on decreasing. However, in case of lakes and ponds, as they are comparatively smaller and shallower than oceans, light can penetrate deeper. In winter, due to their stagnant water, they often freeze, creating an anaerobic condition inside the water.

Biodiversity is more when the depth of the ocean is less.

Classification

This ecosystem is classified into two groups. One is a free flowing lotic ecosystem and the other is a lentic ecosystem with still water.

Ponds and lakes come under the lentic category. The temperature of lakes changes over time. Based on the type of biotic community, four zones are found in lakes. These are littoral, limnetic, euphotic and benthic.

Streams and rivers constitute the lotic ecosystem. Light, temperature, flow and chemistry are factors affecting the biome in this ecosystem in which water is more oxygenated due to the flow.

Waterfall is a free flowing lotic ecosystem.

FUN FACT

Do you know which is the largest freshwater lake (in terms of volume) on Earth? It is Lake Baikal in central Asia.

Freshwater biome

Depending upon the size of the ecosystem, the number of organisms differ but the basic structure remains the same.

As we know, the base of any food chain in any ecosystem is occupied by the plants producing food by photosynthesis. In a freshwater ecosystem, different types of plants, mosses and algae are found. In flowing water, they have a special capacity to attach to the place instead of being carried away. In sources where water is stagnant, water lilies, algae and duckweed can be seen in floating state.

A variety of fishes, birds, insects, amphibians and crustaceans are found here. In estuaries, many clams, shrimps and fishes are found.

A turtle in still water.

Role of freshwater ecosystems

Freshwater ecosystems act as natural filters, reducing pollution, controlling floods and providing food and habitat for aquatic organisms. They are very important for energy production, transportation and recreation.

We get water for drinking from freshwater resources only. Of the total fish species that we enjoy in our food, 40 per cent exist within freshwater itself.

Threats on freshwater ecosystem

As human beings work progressively daily for making their life easier and safer, they are neglecting the conservation of the ecosystem. As ecosystems are very essential for each organism's survival, we should strive to preserve them.

Overuse, dams, pollution, diversion and non-native species are among the threats faced by freshwater ecosystems. Acidification, eutrophication and pesticide contamination are the major chemical stresses faced by them. Also, global warming is the cause of floods and drought faced by all organisms and human beings.

The global extinction rate of freshwater species is four to six times higher than the marine or terrestrial ecosystems.

How can we prevent this from happening to the ecosystem? Each and every individual can take some steps for preserving this. We love to visit clean parks with many fishes and birds near it and it is possible to observe them only by keeping them clean and by conserving water.

Forest Ecosystem

What comes to your mind when you come across the word "forest"? You tend to form a picture in your mind of different wild animals, birds and insects living in a dense cluster of trees. Thirty eight per cent of Earth's surface is covered with these forests. In different types of climates, forests with different variety of flora and fauna are present.

Definition

"Forest ecosystem" is the term used for biotic and abiotic components and their interactions with each other, and with the environment in the forest.

Informally, we can say that different species of animals, birds, insects, microorganisms, trees, herbs and shrubs living together and exchanging energy is called a forest. Abiotic components include the surrounding air, climate, soil, water, organic wastes, rocks, pebbles and so on.

Types of forest ecosystems

Though forest ecosystems are too diverse to study, they are classified into three groups based on their location on Earth.

1. **Rainforests**

   The forests found in the tropic region near the equator are rainforests.

2. **Temperate forests**

   These are located between the regions of taiga and the rainforests. Because of their location, these forests have a moderate temperature and four distinct seasons occur here. The soil of these forests is very fertile because of a good amount of rain.

3. **Taiga**

   These are located in the northern hemisphere.

Biodiversity

Adaptation is the main phenomena to determine which type of species can be found in a particular ecosystem. For example, we can find pine and fir trees in the colder regions but not in the hotter regions. Different types of adaptations, such as shape and size of the leaves, depth of the root and fur or hair on the body of the organisms are found.

Thus, by knowing the climatic conditions, we can assume which type of species will be able to survive in a particular ecosystem. Furthermore, the complexity of the forest will indicate the biodiversity found in it.

Types of flora and fauna

To understand the biodiversity found in forests, it is necessary to divide the forest into layers.

Canopy

The topmost layer is the layer of tall trees called the "canopy". These trees provide shade to the entire forest, filtering sunlight, other radiations and rain. In this way, they protect the lower layer of trees and organisms. They also have deep roots so that they can face challenges from the environment like wind, storm, lightning and meet their water requirements.

The animals found in this layer are birds, tree frogs, snakes, lizards and hard-bodied insects.

The Understory

This is the layer of the forest that has trees, which are not yet fully grown or haven't reached their maximum height. The layer of canopy not only protects them from direct sunlight and rain, but also causes them to grow at a slower rate.

Because of their thinner foliage, the biodiversity of animals found here is quite great. Birds, butterflies, caterpillars, frogs and tree mammals like varieties of squirrels, raccoons and monkeys are found here.

The shrub layer

This is the layer of forest covered by shrubs, which are short woody plants. Different types of spiders, insects, birds, snakes and lizards live here.

The olive shrub.

Forest floor

The floor of the forest where mosses and a variety of flowers grow always remains covered with humus, making it more fertile. Hornets, butterflies, birds, worms, slugs, snails, centipedes, millipedes and many microorganisms get nourished here.

A wide range of vertebrates, non-vertebrates and microorganisms are found in the land of forests, which continue the food chain.

Role of forest ecosystem

The forest ecosystem plays a vital role for the survival of life on Earth. It cleans the air, regulates the water cycle, prevents drought and flood, gives wood and many other food products, prevents air and noise pollution, regulates the cycle of nitrogen, magnesium, phosphorus and calcium, and makes the soil fertile.

FUN FACT

The boreal forest, or the sub-polar taiga, is a vast tract of unbroken forests found in the northern hemisphere between the tundra and the taiga. These forests of evergreens are frozen for almost nine months in a year.

Trees protected by the canopy come under the understory.

The tallest tree is the canopy.

Desert Ecosystem

If we ever visit a desert, we would be surprised to know that it is also a type of ecosystem. One-fifth of Earth's surface is covered by deserts. Although the number of plants and animals living here is quite low, it is still a vital biome to study. More than one billion people live on the land of the desert. These are the areas that receive less than 10 inches of rain per year.

Deserts are extremely cold during the nights and extremely hot during the days.

Definition

"To desert" means "to abandon". The deserts are the arid, dry regions on Earth having animals, plants and microorganisms adapted to these harsh conditions.

At least one desert is present on each of the continents except Europe and Antarctica. The Sahara desert in northern Africa is the largest desert on Earth.

Types of deserts

We mostly know of deserts which are hot and dry, but some cold deserts also exist on Earth. These are the deserts of Antarctica and Greenland, where vegetation is very rare, like in the hot deserts.

FUN FACT

The Sahara Desert, the longest desert in the world, is located in northern Africa, spanning across 12 different countries.

Components of ecosystem

Organisms can remain alive in this harsh and dry environment with adaptations only. These areas don't receive rains frequently and when it rains, organisms adapt to make use of these infrequent short periods of great abundant rainfall.

Abiotic components include latitude, longitude, soil and climate.

Biotic components comprise these classifications:

Producers

Plants like cacti, creosote bush, sagebrush, rice grass and salt bush are found in deserts. These have adaptations as follows:

1. They can store and find water with roots scattered at a shallow level to absorb little rainfall.
2. They have broad leaves with a waxy coating.
3. Thorns and deadly poisons are present on the body of the plant.

Consumers

Locusts, yucca, darkling beetles, ants and arachnids are some insects living in deserts. Among reptiles, rattle snakes, lizards and frilled lizards are adapted to this life. Gila woodpeckers, roadrunners and galahs are among the birds living here. Some mammals like hamsters, rats, kangaroos, horses, foxes and lions live in this ecosystem. Camel, the ship of the desert, is the most important mammal found in this ecosystem.

Decomposers

Some bacteria and fungi are found here.

Cactus is an example of a producer.

Camels are the consumers.

Role of the desert ecosystem

They are brilliant locations to farm solar energy. You would have witnessed a lot of windmills in these areas. They play a role in tourism and recreation. Unlike other ecosystems, human beings are not depleting desert land, but increasing them.

Primary characteristics of the deserts

Low rainfall and more evaporation are the main features of deserts. These are clear lands and we can see for miles with the naked eye.

The Sun shines brightly during the day, causing sand to warm up to a 100 °C at some places with very low humidity. The exact opposite is true for the nights.

Clouds don't visit these deserts. Can you imagine a sky without clouds? Clouds form a covering or a blanket which can decrease the amount of the sun rays entering Earth's surface. As there are no clouds, no water bodies and not even vegetation that can absorb the heat, the days become too hot and the nights become too cold.

The soil is very dry and low in organic nutrients but rich in minerals. Not all deserts have only sand; some have rocks, pebbles or red sand mixed with it.

Man saving himself from the scorching heat of the desert.

Problems Faced by Earth

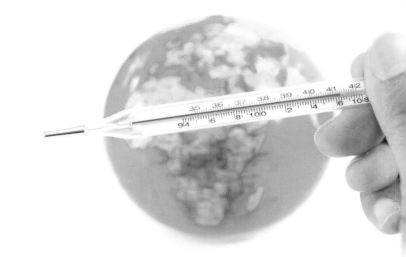

Whenever we want to take a beautiful picture, we stand near a beautiful flower or a flowering plant. We feel relaxed when we are on a nature walk. We try to maintain a garden in our house.

Why does everyone love to be in the lap of nature instead of being in a concrete building? It is because Earth is really the mother of life. The different ecosystems living in it have their own beauty. However, we have currently distanced ourselves from nature and, as a result, nature too has turned its back on us.

Earth Day

A graphical representation of our future if we continue polluting the environment.

FUN FACT

The UN Intergovernmental Panel on Climate Change (IPCC) is established for fighting climate change problems.

What are the problems faced by Earth?

On 22nd April, we celebrate Earth day. Why is there a need to celebrate this day? It is to alert and educate people regarding the necessity of conserving nature and taking up the habit of recycling waste materials.

There are enormous problems that Mother Earth is facing today. Among them, the major problems are extinction of species, global water crisis, global warming, energy or oil consumption, deforestation, desertation, air pollution, overflowing landfills, mining, population explosion, ocean currents, erosion, climate change, clearing land for agriculture, introduction of invasive species and many more.

What should we do?

Recycling of materials, preserving water, conserving power and planting trees are some of the ways by which everyone can contribute to saving our Earth.

Issues Earth faces

Some of the major problems that have blown up to monstrous proportions are:

1. Population explosion

Our present growth rate is over 75,000,000 people per year. In the near future, there will be a rising need for everything: house, food, clothes, jobs, etc. For meeting the demands of an increasing population, we will have to clear more lands for agriculture, dig more mines, establish more industries, clear more forests and use more chemicals for increasing the productivity of agriculture and industries. We will use a higher amount of natural resources and pollute the environment more. Scientists are assuming that after a few centuries, if the population explosion is not controlled, we will end up striving for our basic needs.

Overpopulation

2. Pollution

Human beings are consuming and polluting too much. There are different types of pollution: air, water, noise and soil pollution. We are progressing at a fast rate but we must also take into consideration the implications that it has on our environment. What will happen if the air we breathe is not pure or the water we drink is not safe?

All natural resources are limited. The main problem is how we access them, our manner and efficiency.

We are polluting the atmosphere by eliminating our gaseous wastes in it. This is responsible for the rise in temperature across the globe and global warming. We are diminishing and polluting our own freshwater resources as well by releasing our wastes, chemicals, etc., in them.

Heavy smoke from industries leads to polluted air.

3. Global warming

Our pollution has created a hole in the ozone layer, whose job is to protect us from harmful radiations of the Sun. We have damaged our protective layer, because of which we are facing many skin problems, cancer, etc. It is also affecting plants and animals.

4. Climate change

In May 2015, Nepal faced a massive earthquake, causing a lot of casualties. In 2010, China saw floods and a heat wave struck Russia. The reason is that our planet is getting warmer day by day. We are releasing gases like carbon dioxide in the atmosphere, which are responsible for this warming. We are facing hot summers, cold winters and rains in any season of the year. This is only the beginning of climatic repercussions.

Global warming and climate change leads to melting glaciers that in turn affects the habitat of the living organisms that balance the Earth.

5. Mining

We dig Earth to obtain iron, copper, nickel, diamond, granite, etc. As a result of mining, we are disturbing ecosystems by releasing poisonous wastes in water, cutting plants and destroying the habitats of animals.

Mining destroys land and soil, and imbalances the ecosystem.

Water Pollution

Water pollution is the contamination of water bodies like rivers, lakes and ponds by chemicals, radioactive substances, pathogens, microbes, etc., causing modifications in the physical, chemical and biological properties of water. The main cause of water pollution is dumping untreated wastes in the rivers and lakes. It is difficult to imagine it but if you throw even a single empty bottle of sunscreen or plastic bag into the river, you become a contributor in the increasing water pollution.

Causes of water pollution

For an ideal society, clean and plentiful water is a necessity, but our activities and development are constantly hurting this natural resource. The major causes of water pollution are:

1. Sewage waste
This includes human wastes from paper to plastic and whatever we flush out into septic tanks. In some places, these are linked to the water sources and are polluting them. Sometimes, during rain, the sewer line overflows and pollutes waterbodies.

2. Agricultural waste
Fertilisers, pesticides and insecticides used by farmers can get into water through runoff. Animal waste pollutes lakes and streams when it gets washed away into them.

3. Industrial waste
Industrial waste drains into rivers introducing lead, cadmium, mercury and polychlorinated biphenyls in it. Poisonous gases released in the air mix with the rain and reach waterbodies.

4. Radioactive waste
Nuclear power plants, industries, medical and scientific centres release radioactive waste into water and have long-lasting effects on humans.

5. Plastic
Plastic is used in our daily life. It is non-toxic and non-degradable, and remains in water for hundreds of years. It harms fishes and affects the ecosystem.

Measures of controlling pollution

Awareness – People should be made aware of water pollution, its effects and control measures.

Wastewater treatment plants – More treatment plants with greater filtering capacities should be established to properly treat water.

The laws – The government should enforce strict laws for controlling pollution.

Check runoff – Runoffs from mines and quarries should be regularly checked to prevent them from connecting to water sources.

By applying some practices at an individual level, for example, by using environment friendly products, reducing the use of pesticides and insecticides, knowing what to throw in the drains and toilet pots, we can control water pollution.

Polluted Yamuna river near Taj Mahal in Agra, India.

Air Pollution

Air pollution is the contamination of air, which changes the physical, chemical and biological characteristics of the atmosphere. It affects all other ecosystems on Earth. Industrial chimneys, people smoking in public places, cars running without pollution check are some factors causing air pollution.

Main sources of air pollution

Coal was the source of air pollution in olden days but is rarely used now. Some sources of pollution are:

1. **Fossil fuel burning** – About 96 per cent of sulphur dioxide is released in the atmosphere by burning coal and petroleum products, and from power plants and industries. Vehicles release carbon monoxide and nitrogen oxides into the air, which we end up breathing. Even traditional biomass plants cause pollution.

2. **Ammonia** – Today, to enhance productivity, a lot of fertilisers, pesticides and insecticides are used in agriculture that release ammonia in the atmosphere. Ammonia is the most hazardous gas found in the atmosphere.

3. **Industries** – Many pollutants like carbon monoxide, hydrocarbons, organic compounds and harmful chemicals are released by different manufacturing industries and petroleum refineries.

4. **Mining** – Most of the workers and people living in the areas near mining places suffer from many respiratory diseases because of harmful gases, dust and dirt.

5. **Household** – Main household pollutants are particulate matter, new paint, cooking smoke and tobacco fumes formed by smoking.

Effects of air pollution

Do you know about the great London Smog that occurred in 1952? It was the result of air pollution covering the whole city with a blanket of smog with no air to breathe and no visibility.

Global warming, introduction of greenhouse gases in the atmosphere and a hole in the ozone layer are the major effects of air pollution.

Acid rain is also a monster generated from air pollution. It can have an adverse impact on all living organisms coming in its contact.

Pollution also affects wildlife in their migration and adaptations. It also causes eutrophication in water sources.

Air pollution causes mortality rates to increase significantly. It causes respiratory infections, heart diseases, chronic obstructive pulmonary disease like emphysema and chronic bronchitis, strokes, lung cancer, asthma and also affects the central nervous system.

Children are more susceptible to respiratory diseases because of the presence of soft tissues in their respiratory organs.

What can be done to control air pollution?

Some steps can be useful towards controlling air pollution individually. These are the use of public transport, conserving energy, developing a habit of recycling, using energy efficient devices, etc.

Although the government has taken steps and formulated laws for controlling air pollution, it should be made stricter to make people obey them. The Clean Air Act is also a step towards creating and maintaining a healthy community.

Pollution over a city.

Other Types of Pollution

Pollution is the contamination of the natural environment with foreign substances or naturally occurring contaminants. Pollution affects the whole ecosystem: the air we breathe, the water we drink or the land on which we build our homes.

We are familiar with a few types of pollution, such as air and water pollution. Let's look at the different types of pollution that have different causes and consequences.

Oil spill near the beach.

Artificial lights have various side effects.

Types of pollution

Some forms of pollution that Earth is facing are:

Soil pollution

If we visit a construction site of any house or a place where the land is burrowed deeply, we will observe that the soil there contains a lot of plastic materials, some polythene bags and a lot of garbage. This condition is termed as soil pollution.

It happens because people litter without thinking how it would affect the environment. If we throw an empty packet or bottle or litter on the roadside, then we, too, are contributing to soil pollution.

Household dumping and littering, sewage spills, oil spills, radiation spills, industrial wastes and extensive use of chemicals in agriculture, like pesticides, insecticides and fertilisers, to increase productivity are some of the sources of soil pollution. Mining of different substances completely changes the soil quality in that area and affects the ecosystem gravely.

Soil erosion, shortage of food, water pollution and desertification are some of the consequences of soil pollution.

Light pollution

When we excessively use artificial lights on the roads, highways and at home all night, it is termed as light pollution. It affects the sleep cycle and is responsible for hormonal changes in the bodies of organisms.

Noise pollution

People generally use loudspeakers when they are celebrating or have a personal occasion. Even on the road, we can hear a lot of horns and other loud sounds.

NOISE POLLUTION

All these noises not only affect the hearing ability of human beings but also of the animals living nearby. If a newborn is exposed to such loud sounds, there is a high possibility that it may have an adverse effect on its delicate ears.

You would be surprised to know that the presence of trees can absorb most of the sound. This can be one more reason to encourage tree plantation.

Thermal pollution

Around the world, the summers are becoming hotter as compared to a decade ago. This is because we are making Earth hotter and hotter, day by day due to our activities.

Thermal pollution occurs when excess heat is released into the air or water during any process and has long-term effects. Many of the power plants and industries use cold water from lakes and rivers to lower the temperature of the plant parts. This water is then released back to the lakes and rivers. This activity kills many fishes and plants living there, disturbing the whole ecosystem.

There are many more reasons for thermal pollution, like building of more cemented floors and releasing heat trapping particulates in the air. Also, the trees and water sources which can absorb heat are diminishing very rapidly from the scenario.

Radioactive pollution

It is a rare type of pollution but extremely deadly as well. It occurs due to accidents of nuclear power plants or leakages. Improper disposal of the radioactive wastes is also one of the reasons behind this pollution.

The severity of this type of pollution can be estimated by considering the case of World War II, when USA attacked Hiroshima and Nagasaki with nuclear bombs, killing millions of people and infecting those who were left alive, along with their future generations, with deadly diseases.

Measures for controlling pollution

Pollution, in all its types, has an adverse effect on the environment. Thus, it is necessary to take steps for its control. Many countries worldwide have encouraged their legislations for the enforcement of laws to control such types of pollution.

But as good citizens, we too can help in this initiative by some practices like recycling, reusing, waste minimisation, checking our vehicles regularly for pollution, not littering anywhere, etc. Thus, we are the ones who can make our Earth clean and green.

Recording heat generated at the chimney with infrared thermal cameras.

Nuclear bomb attacks had severe side effects on cities.

FUN FACT

Delhi in India is the most polluted city on the planet in terms of air pollution.

Approximately, 80 per cent of waste in India is dumped in the river Ganga.

River Ganga in Varanasi.

Population Explosion

Population explosion is a major obstacle in the progress of any developing country. The term "population explosion" is used to indicate the rapid growth rate of human beings in a short period in an area. This gives rise to many other problems like shortage of food, place, jobs and every natural resource on Earth.

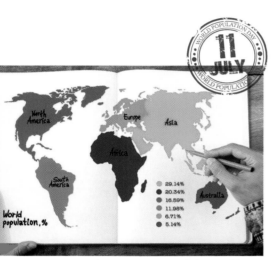

A colour coded map of the world denoting the densely and the sparsely populated continents.

The population density of Sao Paulo, Brazil is 9000 people per sq km.

World population explosion

According to the records, in 2013, the total world population was 7.2 billion. It has jumped drastically in a few hundred years. It is the estimation of the United Nation Population Fund that the population of the world would be around 10 billion by 2025.

The approximate ratio of three births over one death is found in countries worldwide. Among them, the more developed countries have effective population control as compared to less developed countries.

Consequences of population explosion

1. Increase in different types of pollution
2. Unemployment
3. Lack of proper food and nutrition
4. Poverty
5. Housing problem
6. Lack of proper education facilities
7. Faster depletion of natural resources
8. Increase in competition in every step of life of an individual

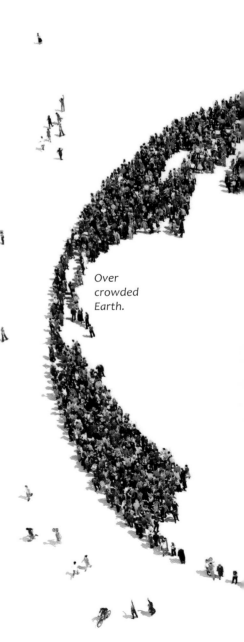

Over crowded Earth.

Reasons of population explosion

There is a progressive advancement in the field of science, daily. We are stressing more on hygiene, sanitation, nutrition and proper growth requirements. All these factors increase the birth rate and decrease the death rate, giving a longer life to human beings. This is the reason for overpopulation.

Birth rate

Previously, people would plan bigger families because most children died before reaching the age of 5 or 6. When the industrial revolution happened, there was an unbelievable advancement in the fields of science and technology, and many medicines, vaccines and treatments were discovered, which increased the survival rate of the infants.

Poverty

It is also one of the reasons for the increasing birth rate. People produce more children for having more earning hands in the family. Also, people under the poverty line have no means to get contraception.

Cultural norms

Backward thinking people keep believing in their cultural belief and prefer a boy child to a girl child, and as a result, keep conceiving till a boy is born, increasing the size of their family.

In some religions, abortions are frowned upon while others are against contraception. People who have blind faith refuse to use contraception in spite of it being available.

Death rate

Overpopulation can affect the economic growth of a country very seriously. But, it cannot stop advancement in the field of science. Humans have won over many deadly diseases and discovered various treatments. This has decreased the death rate from 12.5 in 1981 to 8.7 in 1999.

Immigration

Immigration decreases the chances of job opportunities and education in developed countries. Progress in the fields of transport, industries and agriculture has played an important role in overpopulation too.

Controlling measures

There are many birth control measures available in the market, and the government is making them popular and inspiring people to use them. As it is not possible to increase the death rate, we can only control the birth rate.

Adopting will also help in the education of impoverished children rather than adding to the population.

Immigration

Climate Change

We see that from time to time, it rains even when it is not monsoon. This change in seasonal pattern is very strange and is the result of disturbance in the whole ecosystem of Earth. This term is called climate change.

What is climate? What are the factors affecting climate?

Climate is the weather condition of a place, which stays the same for a long period of time. It doesn't stay the same forever and also changes from place to place. It depends on various factors like the amount of sunlight received by Earth, proximity to oceans and altitude, plate tectonics, volcanic eruptions and biotic processes. If the factors influencing climate are imbalanced, it will result in a change of climate.

Extremely hot summers are an example of climate change. Most countries reach a temperature of 46 °C or above. The reason can be that either too much heat is entering Earth or not enough amount of heat is going out. As climate change is a global problem, we need a remedy that can be implemented at a global level.

Climate change can be caused by either "internal" or "external" mechanisms. Whether the mechanism is internal or external, the resulting response of the climate system might be fast, slow or a combination.

Over 100 people participated in the global warming attention march in New York City.

FUN FACT

The amount of carbon dioxide being released into the atmosphere today is the highest than it has ever been in the last 650,000 years!

Earth is turning into a fireball

Sun is the primary source of heat for Earth. Radiations emitted from the Sun are absorbed by Earth's land, oceans and plants, and this makes the planet hotter. The amount of radiations absorbed by Earth always vary depending upon its position relative to the Sun. During the night, the light absorbed is radiated back to space. The land can radiate more heat as compared to water sources and vegetation. This is the reason why deserts are colder at night.

In the lower atmosphere, there is a layer of gases like carbon dioxide, methane and nitrous oxide, which together constitute the greenhouse gases. These gases have the capacity of holding heat. Thus, they prevent Earth from becoming a ball of frozen ice at night. This is the natural phenomenon for maintaining a moderate temperature through the day and night, making survival of life possible on Earth. However, current changes in the system have altered this mechanism.

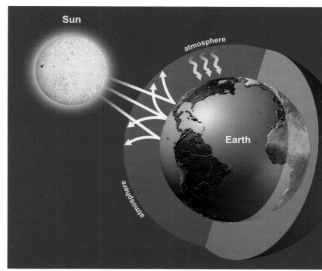

The greenhouse effect.

Disturbance of the natural phenomena

We are increasing the quantity of greenhouse gases to a very high level. We are burning fossil fuels, such as coal, petroleum products and oil, cutting down trees and clearing land. This is all increasing carbon content in the atmosphere.

If we observe, from 1900 to present date, the atmospheric concentration of carbon dioxide has increased from 300 ppm to 400 ppm (part per million). The carbon content level has increased to the extent that our planet has become engulfed in a thick, heat-trapping blanket.

Our planet is becoming warmer day by day. Over the past century, the average global temperature has gone up by almost 1 °C, which is also known as global warming.

Adverse results of climate change

This high temperature of Earth is melting glaciers and increasing sea levels, chances and severity of storms, floods, wildfires and heat waves.

Earth's average temperature is expected to rise by as much as 4 °C over the next.

Effect of high temperature on the habitat of living organisms in polar regions.

Causes of Climate Change

Climate is the long-term weather condition of a place. Climate change is the change in temperature, precipitation, winds and other factors for a prolonged time. Although climate has been dynamic since millions of years, it has come under scrutiny since the last few years. This is due to the speed of climate change and its effect on human beings and other species.

Climate change affecting the world

Scientists are continuously studying the reasons for climate change to find solutions for it.

Scientists of NASA have even researched whether we should blame the Sun for this climate change or not. However, they found that we should not, because the Sun plays no role in this climate change.

Global warming is a change that occurred much faster than any other climate change. Since the late nineteenth century, global temperature has gone up by 0.85 °C.

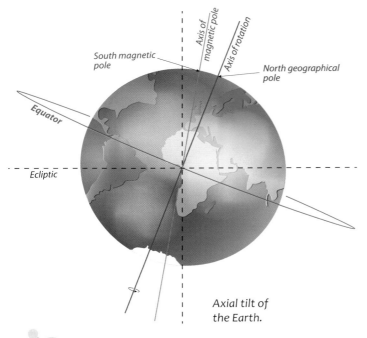

Axial tilt of the Earth.

Causes of climate change

Continental drift – Scientists have collected fossils of plants and animals from various continents and have discovered that

Before   **After**

approximately 200 million years ago, all continents were a part of a large land mass. Subsequently, they got separated and moved apart forming different continents with variations in climates. Scientists believe that this drift has not stopped and continues to take place even today.

Volcanoes – Though volcanic activities are episodic, studies have shown that the large volume of gases released by volcanic eruptions can stay for long in the atmosphere and influence the climate.

Earth's tilt – Earth's tilt is responsible for the various seasons of land. An increase in the tilt will lead to an increase in the severity of the season. As we know, Earth revolves around the Sun in an orbit. Its axis of revolution is not fixed, but there is always some gradual change in the direction of the axis. This change in axis can be a reason for climate change.

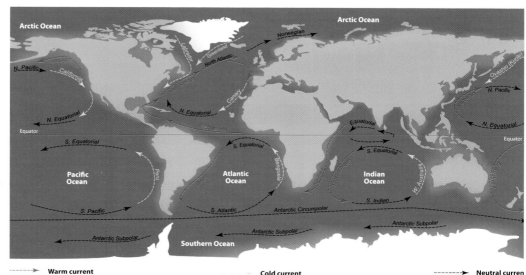

The flow of ocean currents.

----▶ Warm current   ——▶ Cold current   ------▶ Neutral curren

Ocean currents –

Oceans covering three-fourth of Earth's surface can absorb double the amount of heat as compared to land. Ocean currents can transfer heat across the planet. These currents are responsible for climate changes in many parts of the world.

2. **Human or anthropogenic causes**

Earth is the only planet in the solar system on which life exists. There are many factors that support the survival of life. The greenhouse effect is one of them. It is a blanket of gases in the lower atmosphere, preventing Earth from extreme temperatures and maintaining it at a constant value.

Greenhouse gases are water vapour, carbon dioxide, methane, nitrous oxide and chlorofluorocarbons. The quantity of these gases has increased due to various human activities. The primary source of carbon dioxide, which is the main culprit, is burning fossil fuels like coal, oil and natural gas. Cutting down trees and clearing land for agriculture and building purposes have removed forests, which have the capacity of absorbing carbon dioxide to a great extent. As the concentration of these gases is increasing, they are absorbing more heat and making the surface warm. Carbon dioxide is responsible for 64 per cent of global warming.

3. **Short-lived climate factors**

These are responsible for an important amount of climate change from anthropogenic substances. Some of these have a climate warming effect "positive climate forcers", while others have a cooling effect "negative climate forcers".

Some negative climate forcers are sulphate aerosols, which wash away with rain and exert a cooling effect.

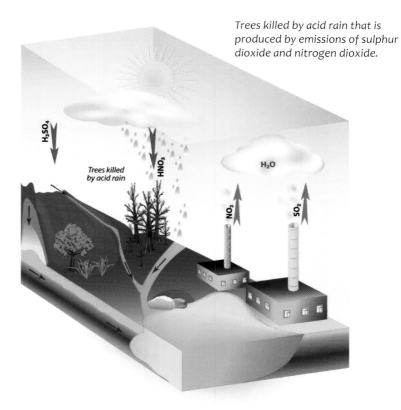

Trees killed by acid rain that is produced by emissions of sulphur dioxide and nitrogen dioxide.

FUN FACT

Nitrogen oxides have 300 times more heat-trapping capacity than carbon dioxide.

Methane, a cause of climatic change, is generated in the intestines of herbivorous animals.

Consequences of Climate Change

Have you noticed the extremely high temperatures that we are facing these summers? This is happening in almost all the countries. Scientists have declared that by around 2050, many species will lose their lives because of this rise in temperature. In the twentieth century, we are facing a 17.2 °C rise in temperature. It has caused serious changes in the environment that will affect our lives in the long run.

Consequences

Human beings have brought about permanent alterations to our planet's geological, biological and ecological systems.

Type of weather

Every weather we experience is becoming more extreme. We are experiencing more hot days and fewer cold days. Some tropical regions receive extreme precipitation. The frequency, length and intensity of heat waves striking the surface of Earth have greatly increased. Increased temperature means increased evaporation of water; this acts as a fuel for storms and hurricanes. Chances of flooding, wildfires and drought conditions have gone up.

Increase in sea level.

Cryosphere

The cryosphere is the part of land that is permanently covered with snow and ice. There have been observations that the ice on the Arctic sea has decreased greatly, alpine glaciers are melting and the ice cover of the Northern parts is greatly reducing. This molten ice, upon mixing in oceans, makes them hotter.

FUN FACT

The occurrence of climate change-related incidents have increased four fold between 1980 and 2010.

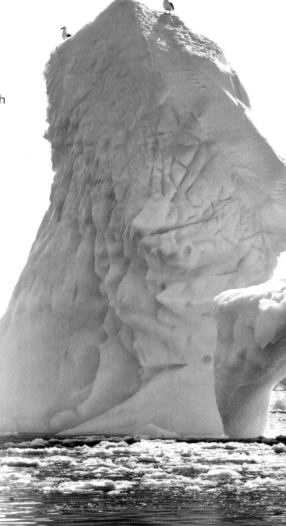

Oceans

Carbon dioxide, the gas that is most responsible for climatic change, is absorbed in large quantities by oceans. It causes the acidification of ocean water. Approximately 90 per cent of the heat released in the atmosphere is absorbed by oceans, which makes them hotter and causes them to expand.

Food supply and food security

A major concern is to find new sources of food, in case of uncertain rainfalls or fluctuating weather conditions. Farmers also face unexpected attacks of weeds, diseases and pests. This is the reason that the cost of the food grains is increasing day by day. Transportation is also affected by hot weather and flooding that causes scarcity of many commodities.

Soil cracked with weed that resulted in barren land.

Health

Smog is greatly increased because of hot climatic conditions. It causes the spread of asthma among other health issues. Many diseases like cancer are spreading because of the harmful rays of the Sun. The extension of wildfires causes the degradation of the quality of air. Fresh water is affected by the rise in temperature supporting the production of different pathogens. Health is greatly influenced by climatic change because of the decreasing quality of food, air and water. The agriculture industry and economy have also been affected.

Water resources

Water resources have been affected to a great extent. Many aquatic species have reached the edge of extinction due to climatic changes. Flood and droughts are common and also affect the forest ecosystem.

Dead fish due to floods.

Migration and conflict

In the future, there will be a conflict for the basic needs and tendency of all living organisms, including human beings, to migrate in search of a better place. The coasts will be wetter, the mid-continental areas will be drier and the sea level will rise unexpectedly.

Species extinction

There are many ecosystems that are at a risk of collapsing due to the change in weather. Coral reefs in the oceans, which are sensitive towards small changes, are deteriorating. As ice melts on the Polar regions, animals like polar bears and walruses are starving for food. The number of endangered species is increasing day by day.

Wild animals migrating for better living conditions.

Global Warming

Global warming and climate change are two terms that are very closely related to each other. Climatic change is the change in the climate of a particular place, whereas global warming is the increase in the temperature of Earth's surface.

What is global warming?

Global warming is the rise in temperature of the whole surface of Earth, including oceans, land area and the lower layers of the atmosphere. Global warming is the reason for the changes in Earth's climate.

The debate regarding the existence of global warming is continuously going on. Scientists have proven by many facts that the temperature of Earth has risen approximately 0.4–0.8 in the past 100 years. A major part of the heat absorbed by Earth goes into oceans, which causes the ice on the Polar regions to melt. This has created confusion among scientists when they attempt measuring global warming.

Gases and water vapour rise into the atmosphere and trap all the heat released by the Sun.

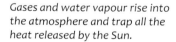

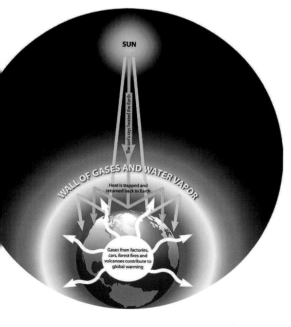

Greenhouse effect and greenhouse gases

The lower layer of the atmosphere that is getting warmer is an extremely thin layer. Many greenhouse gases are found in this layer that possess the capacity to capture heat. Thus, these gases ultimately warm the surface of Earth. This process of absorption and emission of heat by the gases is called the greenhouse effect.

Carbon dioxide, CFCs, ozone, methane, nitrous oxides and water vapour are commonly considered to be greenhouse gases. A balanced amount of these gases prevents our planet from becoming too hot or too cold. Water vapour is a naturally occurring greenhouse gas, which balances its quantity on its own.

In recent years, many human activities have contributed to increasing the quantity of these gases tremendously. These are burning fossil fuels, coal, petroleum, oil, deforestation, and increasing use of land for agriculture and building purposes.

The percentage of carbon dioxide has increased approximately 100 ppm in just a few years. CO_2 is the gas that can remain in the atmosphere for a very long period of time and have adverse effects on the atmosphere.

Effects

Recent studies have shown that drought, climate changes and earthquakes are also the result of global warming. There are many impacts of global warming on our environment as listed below:

1. Rising level of oceans
2. Changes in rainfall quantity and pattern
3. Occurrence of events like flooding, droughts and hurricanes
4. Melting of the glaciers and ice at the poles
5. Extinction of species
6. Widespread of endemic diseases
7. Damage to the ocean ecosystem causing the coral reefs and planktons to vanish
8. Acidification of the ocean water

Global warming can result in changes in the ecosystems, causing some species to move farther north and evolve and multiply, while others won't be able to move and might become extinct. This will upset the balance of nature and cause repercussions beyond comprehension.

The effect of global warming on the water bodies of Earth.

Solutions

Carbon sequestration, mitigation and adaptations can be looked at as possible solutions.

Mitigation

These are the combinations of activities for reducing the emission of greenhouse gases and formation of carbon sinks. Energy conservation, increasing energy efficiency and use of low-carbon energy technologies like renewable energy, nuclear energy and carbon capture can prevent global warming. There are basic things that can be done at home. Turning off the fans, lights and all the electronics in the house when not in use could contribute to the environment. Unplug electronics that can be unplugged. Avoid the use of air conditioners and deodorants that have CFC in them as they contribute to global warming.

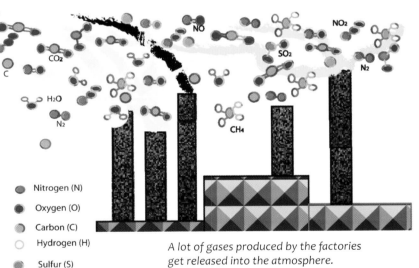

Nitrogen (N)
Oxygen (O)
Carbon (C)
Hydrogen (H)
Sulfur (S)

A lot of gases produced by the factories get released into the atmosphere.

Carbon sequestration

Carbon sequestration is the technique of capturing carbon by different ways like increasing plankton growth in the oceans or draining the released carbon dioxide into oil wells. This method has not yet been implemented.

FUN FACT

Due to global warming, the Montana Glacier National Park has only 25 glaciers instead of 150 that existed in the year 1910.

Arresting Global Warming

If we study the seriousness of global warming, it can be very daunting. There is no single solution to it but by carrying out a few steps, we can control global warming. Every individual can play a role in controlling this problem.

Stopping the emission of greenhouse gases today will not immediately bring down the temperature; however, it would definitely make a difference in the long-term.

Solutions

Reduction in emissions

IPCC has declared that we have to reduce the emissions of greenhouse gases by 50–80 per cent to attain the required harmless concentration. As an individual, we can do this on a personal level, as well as encourage the government to take some steps in this direction.

The gases released from industries, vehicles and power plants should be analysed properly before being released into the air. In addition, the vehicles used should be properly maintained and inflated. Air travel contributes more to global warming than any other means of transport, so travel less by air.

Stop deforestation and promote plantation

We can control up to 20 per cent of the emissions from reaching the atmosphere by stopping deforestation. As forests can absorb large quantity of emissions, they act as natural sequesters. Growing more and more plants, recycling paper, buying used furniture and goods, using improved agricultural practices, and forest management are some practices that we should adapt compulsorily. We should not waste paper and make use of cloth instead of paper tissues. These practices can take care of a major chunk of the existing emissions.

Promote plantation.

Boosting energy efficiency

Energy is primarily used in power generation and for heating and cooling spaces. With some adjustments in our way of living, we can control the emission of many pounds of carbon dioxide into the atmosphere.

Some of these ways are:

- Use CFLs or LEDs lighting
- Use thermostats
- Electrical appliances with more energy stars should be purchased
- Regularly clean the filters in air conditioners and furnaces, and defrost the freezer.
- Electrical appliances should not be left on standby mode.
- Refrigerators and freezers should not be kept near furnaces, dishwashers or boilers as they end up consuming more power.

FUN FACT

The Arctic, which is already the fastest warming part of the planet, will see temperatures rise by 1.1 °F per decade by 2040.

Mass bike ride in Thailand to reduce fuel consumption and global warming.

Recycled products.

- Replace air conditioners, fridges and furnaces that have been used for more than 4–5 years with new ones as they consume more power and give out more emissions after a certain period of time.
- The house should be properly insulated for maintaining the temperature and to lessen the burden on the heater and the cooler.
- Avoid using hot water for washing clothes and utensils.
- Use sunlight to dry clothes instead of using dryer every time.

Green transportation; public transport

Drive less and walk more. Plan car pooling or use public transport for travelling instead of using your own vehicle. Electric, smart cars and cars that run on vegetable oil or some other renewable source of energy. Their use should be encouraged. Use a bicycle instead of a car; it is not only healthy for the body but also for the environment. Additionally, you will save money on fuel.

Use of renewable sources of energy

We can use solar energy for cooking, heating and power supply. Currently, energy can be produced by the Sun, wind and burning biomass. The shift towards the use of renewable sources of energy can save money and reduce the emission of harmful gases too.

Conserve water

It requires a lot of power to draw water to the tanks and purify it. So, by conserving water, we can save energy as well.

Adaptation of zero carbon or low carbon technologies

With the advancement in science, many technologies using zero or very less carbon have come into existence. They should be used more frequently.

Eat more local food

Eat natural food instead of processed and packed foods. Eat vegetables and fruits that are grown in your locality instead of imported ones as a lot of fuel gets used in the production, packaging and transportation of food that is grown far away from you.

Reduce, reuse and recycle

We should not buy things unnecessarily and if needed, buy eco-friendly products. Always try to reuse your resources instead of buying new products with the same function. Recycle paper, bottles, glass, steel, aluminium foils, etc.

Spread awareness

The information provided to people for controlling global warming is often misleading. They should be properly guided as to how and what measures should be adapted to control global warming. Be a part of a global warming community and make yourself aware of many facts and solutions related to it.

Be prepared for the impacts

There are some consequences of global warming that are inevitable, like the sea level rising, extreme temperatures, growing wildfires and severe heat waves. Thus, we should be prepared for them. By adapting some simple changes in our daily life, we can reduce our carbon footprint and can give our future generation a better planet.

BEING PART OF THE PROBLEM

Endangered Species

We all know that our planet has many ecosystems, which are closely correlated and interconnected. Wildlife is also one of them. A great biodiversity is found among animals on Earth, but due to gradually changing conditions like climate changes, diseases, hunting by human beings and habitat loss, many animal species are now either extinct or on the edge of extinction.

What are endangered species?

International Union for Conservation of Nature (IUCN) has classified animals into various categories like extinct, critically endangered, endangered and not threatened species. Endangered species are those that are under threat of extinction. These are species that have had a higher mortality rate than birth rate over a long period of time. According to records in 2012, 3079 animals were marked under red list of this endangered species.

This list shows the level of danger that the species is facing. They are either disappearing fast from the scene or very sparsely populated. The rate of extinction of species by humans is far greater than that occurred naturally. Palaeontologists suggest that about a third of amphibians, a quarter of mammals and every one out of eight birds are under the category of endangered species.

Animals that are endangered

The list of endangered species is very long; from king tiger to the giant clam. Given below are a few names:

- Panda
- Greater horseshoe bat
- Siberian tiger
- Loggerhead turtle
- White tailed eagle
- Mandarin duck
- Mountain gorilla
- Jackass penguin
- Arcadian redfish

- Bluefin tuna
- European eel
- Goliath grouper
- Whale shark
- Indian elephant
- Indian rhino
- Bengal tiger
- Indian lion
- Gaur
- Lion tailed macaque
- Tibetan antelope
- African elephant
- African wild dog
- Aye-aye

- Arabian oryx
- Bactrian camel
- Aleutian Canada goose
- Bison
- Boa constrictor
- Bobcat
- Black-footed ferret
- Chinese giant salamander
- Polar bears
- Dodo bird
- Ivory-billed woodpecker

Reason for the long list of endangered species

Over-hunting and over-fishing

These are some practices that create problems for a species to thrive. Animals are often hunted for food, medicine, leather products and providing a safe environment to other domestic animals and people.

Loss of habitat

Humans are rapidly clearing forests for meeting the demand of wood products. There is a growing need of land for agriculture, housing, transport and many other purposes. In this process, we deprive animals of their natural home.

Invasive species

Introduction of a new species to an area, either intentionally or accidentally, can damage the whole ecosystem or make the native species endangered. This happens due to additional competition for food, shelter and reproduction for which the native species are not adapted.

Climate change

Due to global warming, there are drought, flooding, rise in sea level, melting of glaciers, storms, ocean acidification and extreme temperatures. The animal body cannot quickly adapt to these adverse conditions and they end up losing their lives. Polar bears that live on the poles of the Earth are diminishing fast, because of the rapid melting of the ice.

Pollution

We are polluting the environment on a very large scale by making air, water and soil unfit and unhealthy to use. Pollution has snowballed into such a huge issue that it kills not only animals but human beings as well.

There are industries that do not follow the safety procedures and dump their waste into the flowing rivers. This not only destroys the aquatic life of that water body but also poisons the animals and the humans that drink from it.

Garbage, plastics, oil spills, introduction of heavy metals and chemicals, and many other human activities have harmed the species to the great extent.

FUN FACT

The logo of WWF is a giant panda; the animal, which is on top of the list of endangered species.

The destruction of Panama Mangroves are threatening the lives of sloths.

Steps for conservation of species

Habitat preservation

An optimum approach is to stop deforestation and preserve the natural habitat of animals. More national parks, sanctuaries and marine protected areas should be developed.

Restoration of habitats

Sometimes, restoration of the degraded habitats is possible by maintaining the land and environment, removal of invasive species and the reintroduction of the native species.

Captive breeding

This is the process of providing breeding environment to animals in fully controlled and restricted settings. For example, many types of snakes, like Boa Constrictors, are bred in captivity.

Anti-poaching measures and laws

The government should make laws and apply strict punishment for the hunting of endangered species or selling any item that is made from the skin, bones and teeth of these endangered animals.

Government initiative to save Rhino in Nepal.

Remove fragmentation barriers

We should watch closely for the barriers that we make by building roads, farms and cities through the forests. These activities create hurdles in the lives of the animals.

Control pollution

By stopping pollution and global warming, the nature can once again become a safe haven for animals. That can save this ecosystem.

A plant grown in a controlled, artificial environment.

Waste and Recycling

With the onset of industrialisation and urban growth, big dumps of waste have covered a large area of land. Waste is all the things that we throw away. This not only affects hygiene but also harms the lives of animals, birds and trees found in that area.

At present, the government has become active in this area and has opened many buy-back centres, drop-off centres and curbside collection units.

Birds flocking over a landfill.

Methods of Waste Disposal

Landfill
Landfills are the most popularly used method of waste disposal that focus on burying the waste in the land. There is a process used that eliminates the odours and the dangers of the waste before it is placed into the ground.

Incineration/Combustion
Incineration or combustion is another disposal method in which municipal solid wastes are burned at high temperatures. This converts them into residue and gaseous products. It can reduce the volume of solid waste to 20–30 per cent of its original volume, along with the space they take up and the stress they put on the landfills.

Recycling
Recycling is the process of transforming waste material into new products to prevent the consumption of fresh materials.

Why recycle?

Just imagine, if you do not sweep your house for one week and make a mess, how will your house look? There will be dust, dirt, flies, cockroaches and germs everywhere. The same is the case with our Earth. So, what can be done to make it clean? There are ways like waste management and recycling for the removal of wastes and decreasing landfills.

Plastic bottles can be easily recycled into new plastic products.

What to recycle?

Many things that we throw in the dustbin are recyclable like cans, newspapers, boxes, cardboard, plastic bottles, envelopes, glass bottles, jars and clothes. Different types of wastes are treated differently and recycled into consumable products.

Reduce, reuse and recycle

There are three Rs – reduce, reuse and recycle, which can help in waste management.

To reduce means to consume less or not more than necessary. This can be done, for example, by using a cloth towel instead of tissue papers, using cloth bags instead of polythene bags while shopping and by avoiding use of plastic plates and spoons. This way you can reduce the use of non-recyclable or non-environment friendly items.

To reuse means to make a habit of reusing old items. We can reuse things like old furniture, packages, boxes in creative ways or give them to the needy.

Recycling is the process of taking old discarded materials and making new products from them. This way we can reduce the amount of energy and raw materials used in the production of fresh material. We can also control pollution at a personal level by reducing waste.

Recycle: a way to a clean and green Earth

By recycling various things in our everyday life, we can help make the world better. We can reduce soil, air and water pollution. We can also reduce the amount of carbon dioxide released due to garbage burning and conserve natural resources. Following are a few ways of recycling:

Reuse plastic bags
Reuse your plastic shopping bags for future groceries or as a garbage bag.

Buy rechargeable batteries
Batteries are filled with toxic materials, so go green by buying batteries that you can recharge.

Electronics and the Earth
If your laptop or phones have stopped working and you plan to discard them, drop them at the electronics recycling depot.

Compost
All biodegradable food-related garbage like egg shells and banana peels can get decomposed and add to the quality of the soil. Invest in a compost or plan to build one with help from your neighbours.

Sheets and clothing
Donate your old sheets and clothing to thrift stores or animal shelters to be used as bedding and cleaning materials.

Spending green
Support eco-friendly companies by buying products made from recycled material.

Get crafty
You can reuse jars, tubs and paper to make artistic craft work. You can use newspapers, old jars, tin cans and plastic containers to make collages or bags. You could use old pop bottles and empty jars as planters for flowers and herbs for your garden.

Recycle paper and daily items
The best way to recycle is to do it every day in your home. Sort newspapers and magazines, plastic containers and bottles and assorted paper while recycling, and urge your friends and family to do the same.

Nuclear Waste

After nuclear fuel is used in a reactor, the remnants are referred to as nuclear waste. It appears similar to fuel that is loaded into the reactor. After a nuclear reaction, many uranium atoms split into various isotopes of almost all of the transition metals on the periodic table of elements. This waste is hazardously radioactive and remains in that state for several years.

An atomic bomb is essentially a nuclear reaction that creates a lot of nuclear waste.

How dangerous is nuclear waste?

When nuclear waste is released from the reactor, it is so lethal that by standing unshielded within a few meters of it, a person could receive a lethal radioactive dose within a few seconds and would die of acute radiation sickness. A few radioactive isotopes in the mix of spent fuel are gaseous and need to be carefully contained so that they do not escape to the environment and cause radiation damage to living things. Practically, nuclear waste is never unshielded but is kept underwater for a few years until its radiation decays to levels that can be shielded by concrete in large storage casks.

Recycling nuclear waste

Nuclear energy should be created in an eco-friendly way.

As over 90 per cent of nuclear waste is uranium, it contains 90 per cent usable fuel! This can be chemically processed and placed in advanced fast reactors to close the fuel cycle, which has much less nuclear waste and much more energy extracted from the raw ore. Plutonium and the minor actinides are the longest living nuclides in nuclear waste and can be used as fuel. If these materials are recycled and burnt in fuel, nuclear waste would only remain radioactive for a few hundred years, which would drastically reduce storage concerns. In general, nuclear waste remains radioactive for a few hundred thousand years.

Nuclear waste explained

Nuclear waste needs to be treated and contained.

Many of the isotopes in the nuclear wastes are very radioactive for a very long time before they decay and become stable. The radioactivity results in the waste continuing to emit heat long after it has been removed from the reactor.

SCIENTISTS

Humans have progressed immensely over the last centuries. This has been accomplished by the great contributions of some people in the field of science. These great scientists have made amazing inventions and discoveries that transformed our lives. Galileo made outstanding discoveries in the fields of physics and astronomy. Charles Darwin illustrated the theory of evolution. Archimedes was responsible for laying the foundation of calculus. Thomas Edison created 1093 inventions, including light, power, battery, telegraph and mining. Sir Isaac Newton discovered the laws of motion, studied sound and invented the telescope.

How Scientists Work?

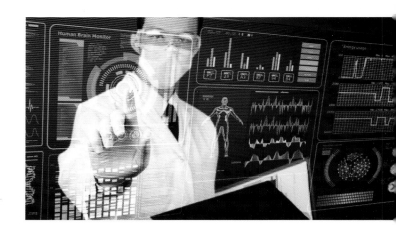

A scientist is a person who has expertise in one or more areas of science. He/She is a person who engages in a systematic study to acquire knowledge and to prove an idea. They figure out patterns and rules to explain their working. A scientist does his/her work through a systematic, scientific method.

Characteristics of scientific method

It is an extremely difficult and time-consuming method. A properly conducted research can take up to 2 to 5 years for its completion. Some steps can require a lot of repetitive investigations. Researches can be called for modifications or questions can be raised by the scientific community. This method is unpredictable and dynamic.

Scientific conclusions are always reversible.

A scientist carrying out a chemical experiment.

Steps of scientific method

1. **Questioning** – The basis of scientific researches is questioning. What, how, where and when always intrigues a scientist.

2. **Forming a hypothesis** – It is based on the knowledge obtained while raising a question after thoroughly studying the existing researches.

3. **Predictions** – The logical consequences are determined for the hypothesis.

4. **Experiment** – Taking one of the predictions and through a series of experiments, scientists try to find whether their hypothesis is true and fits in the real world or not.

5. **Recording of observations** – The observations are recorded and compared to previous researches. If the results don't support the hypothesis, then there is a need for new hypothesis. And if they do but are not too strong, then there is a need of more testing and experimentation.

6. **Conclusion** – The results drawn are communicated to the public with the help of published articles in journals, presentations at conferences, universities and in social media.

Each step of the scientific method is always under the process of modification and constant reviewing.

The scientific method is not as simple as a recipe, but requires intelligence, imagination and creativity.

What do Scientists do?

From a light bulb to mobile and laptops, everything that we use in our daily life is a result of scientific inventions. The basis of all the scientific inventions is asking a question. If there is no curiosity to know and understand new things there will be no inventions. Scientists are the most curious people because they always want to know more and try to find the answers to their questions.

A scientist studying microorganisms under a microscope.

How do they work?

When a question arises in a scientist's mind, they start doing experiments and gaining more information about the reasoning behind it. The moment they gain success and find the result, a new invention is born or discovery is made. Scientists do their work in a well-systematic and organised manner. We call it a scientific method. This is the method which includes steps from the birth of a question, working towards and answer to the creation or discovery of a new invention.

Outreach of researches

The communication of researches is also very important to make it beneficial to the humankind. There are many ways of communicating researches like publishing them in journals, presenting them in conferences, universities and by using social media networks. The life on Earth has revolutionised only because of the advent of science and technology.

Steps involved

Observation is an important step leading to an invention. Microscopes, telescopes, various machines and tools are used for observation. Scientists usually make different classes of observations. They use different tools like thermometer, weighing balance and spectrophotometer for finding out heat, mass, distance, time, volume, radiations and many other measurable parameters.

Weight balance machine.

A spectrophotometer.

Famous Physicists

There have been a large number of world-renowned physicists who have made many useful contributions to the field of physics. Some of the popular ones are mentioned below.

Galileo Galilei

Galileo (1564–1642) was an Italian mathematician, physicist, astronomer, engineer and philosopher who played a key role in the scientific revolution during the time of the Renaissance. He discovered the telescopic confirmation of the phases of Venus and discovered four large satellites of the Jupiter and analysed sunspots. His work in applied science has been noteworthy with his invention of the thermometer. His contributions for the betterment of the working of telescope and compass is incredible.

Galileo thermometer.

FUN FACT

Albert Einstein's favourite scientist was Galilei Galileo.

As a child, Einstein was very slow at learning and learnt to speak very late.

Sir Isaac Newton

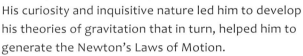

Isaac Newton (1642–1727), was an English scientist, mathematician and physicist. He proposed many path breaking theories at the age of 23 years.

His curiosity and inquisitive nature led him to develop his theories of gravitation that in turn, helped him to generate the Newton's Laws of Motion.

The famous principles by Sir Isaac Newton have been instrumental in formulating the laws of motion and the universal knowledge of gravitation as a force. He is also well-known for his invention of the reflecting telescope and developing a theory of the colour based spectrum of a prism. Sir Isaac Newton has been a renowned and key figure in the scientific revolution over the years. His foundation theories of classical mechanics, creditable role in the development of calculus and various contributions to the field of optics have been noteworthy.

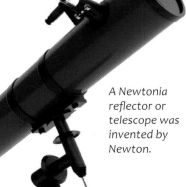

A Newtonia reflector or telescope was invented by Newton.

Nikola Tesla

In any list of famous scientists, especially physicists, the one name that should never be forgotten is that of Nikola Tesla. Nikola Tesla was an American-Serbian futurist, physicist, mechanical engineer, electrical engineer and inventor who was born in Smiljan, which is located in the modern-day Croatia. He was responsible for designing the modern day alternating current (AC) electricity supply system. Due to his work, he gained the reputation of being a "mad scientist" in popular culture. He dropped out of Graz University of Technology and worked part-time for George Washington who patented and licensed his AC induction transformer and motor technology. He also worked on high-frequency and high-voltage power experiments in New York and was responsible for the early possibilities and invention of wireless communication. He died on 7th January, 1943 due to coronary thrombosis.

A magnifying transmitter or Wardenclyffe tower was invented by Nikola Tesla.

Albert Einstein

Albert Einstein (1879–1955), the man known for his theories and wonderful denominations in the world of Physics, was a German theoretical physicist. Albert Einstein was also a great philosopher of science.

Einstein is known best for developing the theory of relativity, one of his two viable pillars in modern physics and also for his equivalence formula of mass-energy that is, $E = mc^2$, the very equation that is famous in the world of science.

He was awarded the Nobel Prize in Physics in the year 1921 for his contributions to theoretical physics and also for his discovery of the law of the photoelectric effect that later became pivotal for quantum theory.

The solar panel is an invention based on Einstein's mass-energy theory.

Niels Bohr

Niels Henrik David Bohr was a Danish physicist, who was born on 7th October, 1885. He made a large number of significant contributions in comprehending the atomic structure and quantum theory, and received the Nobel Prize in the year 1922 for his work in this field. He developed the Bohr Atomic Model in which he stated that the energy levels of electrons are specific and electrons revolve around the atomic nucleus in stable orbits, but they can jump from one energy orbit/level to another. He provided the principle of complementarity that stated items can be distinctly examined in regards to contradictory properties, for example, streams/waves of particles. He also founded the Institute of Theoretical Physics, which is currently known as the Niels Bohr Institute and is located at the University of Copenhagen.

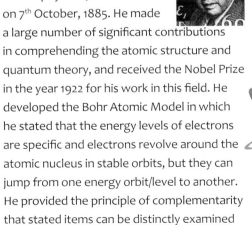

The atomic model was designed by Bohr.

C.V. Raman

Sir Chandrasekhara Venkata Raman (1888–1970) was born in the former Madras province in India. He was a physicist, who did path-breaking work in the field of light scattering. His work earned him several accolades and a Nobel Prize for Physics in 1930.

There is a phenomenon itself that has been given his name that is, The Raman scattering. This is an occurrence where when light traverses a transparent material the deflected light's wavelength gets affected.

For his research and contributions to the world of science he was felicitated with the Bharat Ratna in 1954, the highest civilian award in India.

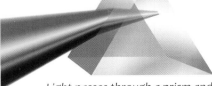

Light passes through a prism and breaks into rainbow colours due to change in wavelength.

Famous Chemists

The field of science that deals with the composition, properties, structure and alteration of matter is known as chemistry. The scientists who study chemistry are known as chemists. A few world renowned chemists are given below.

John Dalton

John Dalton was an English chemist, meteorologist and physicist, who was best known for his work in modern atomic theory. Dalton was a lecturer and was interested in meteorology. He would spend time learning how to use meteorological instruments and taking periodic readings. In his famous atomic theory, he stated that tiny particles called atoms form elements. Different elements have atoms of different sizes and mass. He believed that atoms were unique, as they couldn't be created, divided or destroyed by chemical process. Atoms of identical elements are always identical. He proved that atoms of different elements could be identified by their atomic number. Atoms of different elements combine to form compounds. Compounds are unique, having a specific relative number of atoms. Dalton's theory was the first important step towards modern atomic theory.

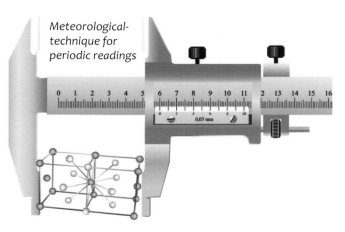

Meteorological-technique for periodic readings

Sir Humphry Davy

One of the great chemist and inventor, Sir Humphry Davy is known for his innovations in the field of chemistry, especially the discovery of various alkali and alkaline earth metals. He also assisted in comprehending the attributes of chlorine and iodine and invented the Davy lamp, which helped miners to work in the mines even with the presence of flammable gases. In the year 1807, he worked with electrochemical decomposition by isolating pure sodium, magnesium, calcium, barium and potassium molecules. During his research, he accidentally discovered cool flames, which were low temperature flames that worked with a mixture of fuel and air that chemically produced immensely weak flames. He also found that chlorine was an element and gave it its name. Moreover, he put forward a system that can be utilised to calculate the ratios of various chemical combinations. He discovered the very first electric light by connecting two wires to a single battery and then affixing a strip of charcoal on the two wire ends. This charged the charcoal strip and made it glow. Thus, the very first arc lamp was discovered.

The miners safety-lamp was invented by Humphry Davy.

Michael Faraday

One of the greatest scientists and chemists of the nineteenth century was Michael Faraday. He helped convert electricity into an attribute that can be easily utilised. Some of the significant discoveries, which were made by him, comprise electromagnetic induction, electrolysis and diamagnetism. He made significant contributions to the field of electrochemistry and electromagnetism. He is known for the Faraday Constant, the Faraday Cage, the Faraday Effect, Faraday's Law of Induction and various other significant contributions to the field of physics and chemistry.

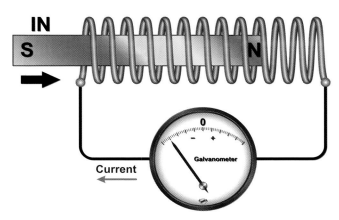

Electromagnetic induction
was invented by Faraday.

George Washington Carver

George Carver is known for his calm nature, his innovation in the field of crop management and agriculture. He faced many hardships during his lifetime. He faced slavery, racial abuse and the loss of his family. He was also rejected from various colleges. In spite of all his hardships, he produced several innovations in the field of chemistry and agriculture. In the 1930s, he became a leader in the field of chemurgy that was quite an advanced area in the field of chemistry. This field focussed on the utilisation of various agricultural products for manufacturing and industrial purposes.

Crop management and agriculture advanced
due to Carver's studies.

Marie Curie

Famous Polish chemists, Marie Curie and her husband Pierre Curie, were early researchers in radioactivity. In 1891, Marie went to Paris and joined Sorbonne University to study physics and mathematics, where she met Pierre Curie. They got married in 1895. Pierre Curie was the professor of the school of physics and chemistry. Marie and Pierre worked together exploring radioactivity, based on the work conducted by the physicists Henri becquerel and Roentgen. In 1898, the Curies discovered the elements polonium and radium. She was presented with her first Nobel Prize in 1903 for physics along with Pierre and Henri becquerel, for research in the area of radioactivity. Pierre Curie died in the year 1906, after which Marie took over the task Pierre was conducting, making her the first lady to teach in Sorbonne.

She was committed to continue the work she and Pierre Curie started together. In 1911, Marie was presented with her second Nobel Prize for her discovery and isolation of radium and its compounds. In addition, she proved that radium can successfully cure certain illnesses. Till date, her discovery plays an important role in the treatment of cancer. She has also introduced the use of X-ray technology and radium in medicine.

The X-ray is a technology
based on Madame
Curie's research.

FUN FACT

John Dalton was colour-blind. This did not stop him from learning about it and researching it. This is why colour-blindness is also referred to as Daltonism.

Famous Biologists

The natural science, which is connected with the examination of life and living organisms, including the study of their taxonomy, distribution, evolution, growth, function and structure is known as biology. The field of biology is quite vast and several biologists have made significant contributions to it. However, the six most famous biologists who made significant contributions are mentioned below.

Antonie van Leeuwenhoek

Antonie van Leeuwenhoek is famously known as the first microbiologist because he was the first to observe bacteria underneath a microscope. Leeuwenhoek nurtured his interest in lens-making while working at his shop. His interest in microscopes combined with his knowledge of glass processing, resulted in a very important and technical discovery in the field of science. He placed the middle part of a small rod of lime soda glass into a very hot flame and then pulled the hot glass apart to create two long strands of glass. Then, he reinserted the end of one strand in the flame to create a small glass sphere of high quality. He discovered that the smallest lenses rendered the highest magnifications and these spheres soon became lenses for his microscopes. It is believed that Leeuwenhoek built over 200 microscopes that had various magnifications but only a few of them survived.

Edward Jenner

The "Father of Immunology", Edward Anthony Jenner was an English scientist who is known for the discovery of the world's first vaccine – the smallpox vaccine. He also explained the brood parasitism of the cuckoo. After various successful tests, in the year 1798, he published his research on the book entitled *An Inquiry into the Causes and plus the Effects of Variolae Vaccine or Cow–pox*. His idea of vaccination was mocked by his fellow doctors; however, it was later found that vaccinations actually work and by the 1800s, a large number of doctors were utilising vaccines to cure patients.

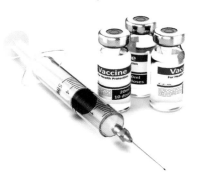

A vaccine is used not only to cure a disease but also to protect a person from acquiring it.

Robert Brown

Robert Brown, a famous botanist from Scotland, was a pioneer in the field of microscopy. He was one of the first biologist who explained the cell nucleus and discovered the Brownian motion. He also made significant contributions to the field of paleo-botany, which is the study of prehistoric plant life.

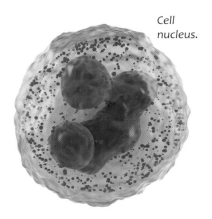

Cell nucleus.

Charles Darwin

The first name that should come up while discussing the field of biology is that of Charles Darwin. Not much can be said about his early life except for the fact that he was a British scientist who was born on 12th February, 1809 in Shrewsbury, United Kingdom.

He supported the theory of Evolution and his writings introduced the idea of evolution into mainstream science. He collected various scientific evidences, which supported his theory of Natural Selection.

He wrote the books *The Voyage of the Beagle* and *On the Origin of Species*, both of which are quite significant in the field of biology.

Louis Pasteur

The present day concept of vaccination against various diseases was first put forward by the French microbiologist and chemist, Louis Pasteur. He is particularly known for his significant advances in prevention and causes of diseases, and his innovations have helped save countless lives. He diminished the death rate of the puerperal fever and developed the first vaccines for anthrax and rabies. His medical innovation provided the backing for the germ theory of disease and its application. Additionally, he is known for pasteurisation, the process that is utilised to treat wine and milk, so that they are not contaminated by bacteria. He is popularly known as the "Father of Microbiology". On top of his contributions to microbiology, he also Contributed to the field of chemistry, his most important work was on the molecular foundation of the asymmetry of various racemisation and crystals. He was also responsible for putting forward the ideals of Optical Isomers. He died in France on 28th September, 1895.

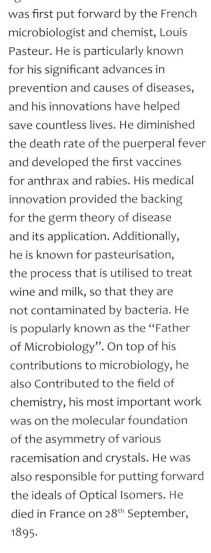

Pasteurised milk is created by a process invented by Pasteur.

Gregor Mendel

Gregor Johann Mendel was a Moravian scientist renowned for creating the science of genetics. Mendel performed hereditary experiments by statistically analysing the experiments of breeding. His studies coupled with his vast knowledge of natural sciences were what guided him through the experiments. He chose to use pure variety pea plants that had been cultivated in a controlled atmosphere. Mendel crossbred several seeds and collected the results based on the seven most evident variations and seeds. He inferred that tall plants created both long and short offspring while short plants only created short offspring. He concluded that the tallness of the plant was its dominant trait while that of shortness was a recessive trait. These results were not influenced by whether the plant was female or male.

The first heredity law, which is the law of segregation, is based on Mendel's observations on the breeding of plants. It states that genes exist in pairs and the paired gene becomes divided when the cell is divided. Each paired gene is present in both halves of the egg or sperm.

Mendel formulated his law by studying the hybrid of green and yellow peas.

Famous Ecologists

Compared to physics, chemistry or biology, ecology is a relatively new field of science. It is the field of science that is related to the scientific examination and analysis of the interactions between various organisms and their environment. Even though the field is new, there have been several ecologists who have made significant contributions towards it. A few of them are given below.

Leonty Ramensky

Leonty Grigoryevich Ramensky was a Russian plant ecologist who formulated several important ideas that were unnoticed in the West. He graduated from the Petrograd University in 1916 and obtained a Ph.D. in biology in 1935. He worked at the Research Institute of the Voronezh government and from 1928 at the State Grassland Institute. Ramensky was a proponent of the perspective that biotic communities comprise species behaving individualistically. This was in strong contrast to the prevailing view of communities as super-organisms. Thus, he was marginalised within the Russian scientific community and was only posthumously rehabilitated by Russian ecologists. Subsequently, the significance of his ideas were appreciated by the ecologists in the West.

Emma Lucy Braun

One of the prominent and foremost expert in the field of ecology, Emma Lucy Braun was born on 19th April, 1889. She earned her degree from the University of Cincinnati. Ecologist and biologist, Emma Braun is considered to be one of the most well-known experts on the eastern United States forests. She has written more than 180 articles on ecology that have been published in over 20 journals. Her research was mainly focussed on the vascular and deciduous forests. She was the first woman President of the Ecological Society of America. Her research included the comparison of the present day flora in a specific region to the flora of the same region a century ago. Furthermore, she received the Mary Soper Pope Medal in botany and is considered to be one of the 50 most outstanding botanists. She also fought for the conservation of natural areas and set up various natural reserves.

The study of ecology also happens in the controlled environment of a lab.

John Thomas Curtis

He is very well-known for his everlasting contribution towards creating numerical procedures in the field of ecology. John Thomas Curtis was born in Wisconsin on 20th September, 1913. With the assistance of fellow ecologist J. Roger Bray, he created the procedure of polar ordination (famously known as the Bray–Curtis Ordination) along with the in-built measurement of distance that is known as the Bray–Curtis Dissimilarity. He has also authored several seminal papers on the analysis of ecological gradients and was awarded the Guggenheim Fellowships twice – in 1942 and 1956. He and 39 of his Ph.D. students authored the book known as *The Vegetation of Wisconsin – An Ordination of Plant Communities*. This book is one of the significant contribution to the domain of plant ecology and has led to the establishment of the Wisconsin School of North American Plant Ecology.

Curtis compared the ecological systems of two places that were geographically apart.

Howard Thomas Odum

Howard Thomas, an American ecologist, is known for his work on the ecosystem ecology and for his provocative proposals for additional laws of thermodynamics. Odum studied many fields associated with ecology, systems and energetics. He analysed ecosystems worldwide and pioneered the study of several areas, some of which are now distinct fields of research. He made significant researches on the subjects of ecological modelling, ecological engineering, ecological economics, estuarine ecology, tropical ecosystems ecology and general systems theory. He also wrote on radiation ecology, systems ecology, unified science and the microcosm. He was one of the first to talk about the use of ecosystems for life-support function in space travel.

Odum studied the effects of the law of thermodynamics on ecological systems.

James Brown

James Hemphill Brown was born on 25th September, 1942 and is currently an American biologist and ecologist. His research and work mainly focussed on two aspects of ecology – one is the community ecology and population of harvester ants and rodents. The other field of his research was the large-scale questions associated with the body size distribution and abundance, and geographical animal ranges.

This research prompted the creation of macro-ecology. The term was coined by him in a research/thesis paper that was submitted by him and Brian Maurer together.

The subject of James Brown's research was harvester ants.

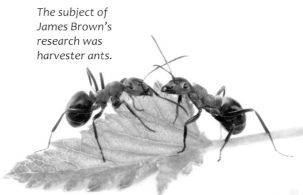

Index